TEACHING CHILDREN WITH HIGH-LEVEL AUTISM

Teaching Children with High-Level Autism combines the perspectives of families and children with disabilities and frames these personal experiences in the context of evidence-based practice, providing pre- and in-service teachers and professionals with vital information on how they can help children with high-level autism reach their full potential. Many children with high-level autism are capable of regulating their behaviors given the right interventions, and this cutting edge text explores multiple methods for helping such children succeed academically, socially, and behaviorally. The book:

- draws from interviews with twenty families who have middle- and high-school-aged children with high functioning autism or Aspergers syndrome;
- presents a synthesis of the most cutting edge research in the field;
- provides practical advice for educating children with high-level autism;
- is authored by two special education professors who are also both the parents of children with disabilities.

Teaching Children with High-Level Autism is essential reading for anyone who works or plans to work with children on the upper range of the autism spectrum.

Pamela LePage is a Professor in special education at San Francisco State University. She is also the parent of a 15-year-old child with autism, and is one of the founders of the Autism Social Connection, a grassroots community-based program that provides integrated socialization programs for children and adults with autism and their families and friends.

Susan Courey is an Associate Professor in special education at San Francisco State University. She is also the parent of a child with Tourette syndrome and a child with Attention Deficit Disorder and a learning disability in mathematics.

TEACHING CHILDREN WITH HIGH-LEVEL AUTISM

Evidence from Families

BY PAMELA LEPAGE AND SUSAN COUREY

Routledge
Taylor & Francis Group
NEW YORK AND LONDON

First published 2014
by Routledge
711 Third Avenue, New York, NY 10017

and by Routledge
2 Park Square, Milton Park, Abingdon, Oxon OX14 4RN

Routledge is an imprint of the Taylor & Francis Group, an informa business

Library of Congress Cataloguing-in-Publication Data

LePage, Pamela, 1962–
Teaching children with high-level autism : evidence from families / Pamela LePage, Susan Courey.
pages cm
Includes bibliographical references and index.
1. Autistic children—Education. 2. Autistic children—Education—Standards. 3. Autism in children. 4. Autistic children—Care. 5. Parents of autistic children. I. Title.
LC4717.L46 2013
371.9—dc23
2013013429

ISBN: 978-0-415-63082-5 (hbk)
ISBN: 978-0-415-63083-2 (pbk)
ISBN: 978-0-203-76235-6 (ebk)

Typeset in Minion
by Apex CoVantage, LLC

Printed and bound in Great Britain by TJ International Ltd, Padstow, Cornwall

Contents

Chapter One
Introduction

Many years before Susan Courey and I began writing this book, we started serving together on the board of an agency that provided socialization services for high-functioning children on the autism spectrum. Since that time Dr. Courey and I have enjoyed working with this agency, developing autism workshops for school districts, and teaching at San Francisco State University. We talked about the possibility of writing a book because it was clear to us that even acknowledged experts in the field of autism perpetuated misconceptions about how children with high-functioning autism learned, developed, and socialized. But it was when I met Mason and his mother that my idea for writing a book with Dr. Courey changed for me from a nice idea to an important goal.

When I first met Mason, I was scheduled to go to his family's house to conduct an interview because his mother wanted to find a socialization program that he would enjoy and would help him make friends. Mason was in his room when Iarrived, so I was able to spend some time talking to his mother. Donna was easy to talk to, and she was eager to talk about her son. As a seventh grader with autism, Mason had trouble making friends. Autism is a neurological disorder that is defined by people having trouble in the areas of socialization, communication, and imagination. The one and only common characteristic among all children, however, is socialization. Mason's mother was determined to get him involved with a program that would help him make friends, even if she had to spend her savings because this program was expensive. She warned me, however, that her son had no intention of attending any program and she hoped that I could talk him into it.

After my chat with Donna, I went into Mason's room because he didn't want to come out. He was behind his computer, and he didn't look up when I walked in. I could tell he was already angry and ready for an argument. The first thing he said to me was, "I don't want anything to do with that autism stuff! I am not like those other kids!"

I answered back, "How many kids with autism do you know?"

He said that he had met a few kids and that he definitely wasn't like them. I told him that I knew some kids with Asperger's and high-level autism and maybe he hadn't met the right kids. I told him kids with autism were all very different but some were like him. Mason was obviously smart; he had been surfing the Web before I entered his room and reading various sites to get answers to his questions. He already knew quite a bit about socialization and what he was "supposed to be doing." His speech was clear and concise, and he knew what he wanted, or, more specifically, what he didn't want. He was angry, but he knew how to control his anger. I did not have the impression that at any minute he might start yelling or throwing something. I could also tell that although he was resistant, he was not recalcitrant. I was sure that he would try out this program if I told him what he needed to hear. As frustrated as he was, he knew that he needed help making friends.

He told me straight out that he refused to go to any program where there were "therapists" in the building. As far as he was concerned, he never wanted to see another therapist in his life. At this age, many children are tired of feeling as though they need to be "fixed." I told him there would be no therapists in the building.

He responded that he did not want to go into any group where some adult was going to tell him what to do or how to act. He didn't want to have another "class" on the weekend, because he hated school.

I told him I had the perfect program for him, a program that brought teens with high-level autism together to make films, where the teacher is considered a "facilitator," and the idea is for the teenagers to make their own decisions and to be independent. It took me a while but by the time I left I had convinced him to try the program by reassuring him that he could always quit if he did not like it.

The first few weeks Mason was in the program he was quiet. He didn't interact much with the other teens. But he did not quit. It took him a couple of months to warm up, but soon he was participating like all the other kids and having fun. Over time, I saw him transform from a very angry teen to one who laughed and talked and acted silly with his peers. He really liked the teachers, and he fit in with the other kids.

In turn, his mother made friends with the other mothers and started feeling more supported. She brought one of Mason's friends from his school to the program and created opportunities for her son to interact with other children outside the program by inviting kids over to her house.

Today, Mason still struggles academically in school, but not as much as before, and he has friends, both at the socialization program and at school. At age 16, he is no longer the angry teen I first met. In his first year in the program he went from failing a number of his classes to getting mostly Bs on his last report card. Also, Mason was diagnosed with autism when he was 10 years old, so the idea that all children on the spectrum need to have early intervention before a child attends kindergarten to turn their lives around is just not true for all children with autism spectrum disorders (ASD). Although it is important to have early intervention whenever possible, teachers and therapists at all stages can have a dramatic effect on the lives of children with autism. Children with high-level autism have an amazing capacity to improve when they get support, but they can also decline or stagnate when they do not get the supports they need. That is why it is important for teachers to know how to work with these children.

What Is This Book About?

This book is about how teachers can help children with high-level autism reach their full potential. Like many parents, teachers of children with autism often wonder: How can I help this student succeed in school alongside typically developing peers? What supports are available to help them function to their fullest abilities? What can I do to help this student become a happy, independent adult? These questions are difficult to answer, even regarding children who may be classified with high-functioning autism. At certain times, children with autism can come across as extremely intelligent, talented, or brave, and at other times they can seem immature, naive, or inexplicably irritating. Sometimes a child with autism can seem incredibly insightful and yet continue to put his or her pants on backwards. Occasionally these children become victims of bullies, and sometimes it is the other way around when children with ASD shout out angry words that come across as mean and unfiltered. It is difficult for teachers to determine what their autistic students need, and it is even more difficult for their typically developing peers to understand these children as they struggle to navigate the social world themselves.

In this book, we work to unravel the mystery of high-level autism for teachers, discussing what we know about children on the spectrum, describing the types of educational research that will help teachers to develop instruction, and providing suggestions for managing behavior. Although we talk about educating children at all ages in this book, we focus a bit more on older children, from about fourth grade through high school, because in the research world many people have already focused on young children. We also emphasize children's strengths rather than on how teachers can remediate their deficits. For example, many children with high-functioning autism can focus deeply for long periods of time, have well-defined interests, and have great memories for facts associated with their interests. In the world of technology, children who can focus for long periods of time have an advantage over those who cannot. Children who have passionate interests are actually lucky compared to those who have no passions. These strengths alone can move children forward if teachers are able to use them to their advantage.

We are not only authors, we are special education professors, teachers, and parents of children with special needs, and our experiences have led us to believe strongly that any child can grow up to live a happy and productive adult life depending on how he or she is treated and educated. The first author is a parent of a 15-year-old child with autism, and the second is a parent of two children with disabilities, one with learning disabilities (LD) and attention deficit disorder (ADD) and the other with Tourette's syndrome. Together, we share our stories and explain how our own experiences have helped to shape our professional work and community involvement. We know the types of questions teachers have about autistic children in their classes, not only from our professional experiences as special education professors and our personal experiences with our children and parent support groups, but also because we have been special and general education teachers ourselves. We will offer both our professional and personal views, and we will focus on evidence-based practices. We believe that *all* children should be treated with dignity and respect and educated to the best of our ability.

Although difficult, many typically developing children can overcome barriers from the outside, such as lack of financial support, lack of information, or traumatic family experiences (LePage, 1997; Levine & Nidiffer, 1995). For children with special needs, significant barriers imposed on them from the outside world will almost always result with adults on the spectrum who are not only unhappy, but who will have trouble living and working independently (Henniger & Taylor, 2013). These children need adults to help them through the system so they can develop as self-advocates, able to articulate what they need and eventually educate others about how they perceive the world around them.

In the first part of the book, we provide basic information about autism, focusing on questions that teachers want answered. We not only talk about what we know about autism and Asperger's, we also discuss topics that many people are curious about, such as, "Are children with ASD really more likely to have a parent who is an engineer?" or "Are there more children with autism born to wealthy, educated parents?" and "What characteristics do children with autism share?"

In the second section, we present and discuss various interventions that are now available for children with autism, what teachers should watch out for as they use these interventions, how they have been used in the past, and when and why they are considered evidence based.

In the third section, we share ideas regarding how teachers can help children with autism to reach their full potential. We talk about early childhood through high school and how teachers can help children as they move through different stages of development at different ages. We also present the complexities of some of the interventions used at different ages and explain how some of them are much more difficult to implement than one might imagine, and why.

In the final section of the book, we discuss various teaching strategies, including those that help children in all areas and in all grades. We also talk about the complexities of working with parents. Finally, we discuss educational placements, and how parents choose the best setting for their child.

Teaching Children With High-Level Autism: A New Population

Among our motivations to write this book is our belief that much of the information about children with high-level autism is often incomplete or inaccurate. The population of children we write about in this book can be considered a new population of children, and a new population of children living with autism.

In the 1990s, autism seemed to appear out of nowhere. Prior to the 1990s, only 1 in 10,000 children were born with autism; in the 1990s it became 1 in 166 children. Today in the United States that number has grown to 1 in 50 children who have been diagnosed with autism (Blumberg et al., 2013). This number represents an average between boys and girls, because boys are born with autism at a ratio of 5 to 1 compared to girls. Some of this increase in prevalence can be attributed to better diagnostic measures and access to professionals, but diagnosis alone does not account for the dramatic increase, and researchers are examining genetic and environmental factors that may help to explain it. Even if there were more children born with high-level autism before the spike in the 1990s who were not diagnosed accurately, these adults did not receive any of the services they needed as children, so they did not grow up in the same way as the children today. And, even for those children who were diagnosed properly in the past, they also did not receive access to the resources they needed because in the past professionals did not understand this population. Very little research has been conducted on the development or the potential of high-level children with autism compared to children with more severe autism. It would seem that those who were high on the spectrum must have gone through general education with few supports, and those just a bit lower on the spectrum must have been placed in special education with children who had more challenges.

In addition, we still don't know the reason for the huge spike in the number of babies being born with autism since the 1980s and 1990s. Whatever is causing the rate of autism to climb may also be changing the population. Thus, the population of children with autism that is now in school and college may not be the same as the adults with autism who were born before the 1980s and 1990s.

Most books about teaching children with autism lump all children with autism together, even though children higher on the spectrum are very different from those lower on the spectrum. When higher functioning children on the spectrum are combined with children who have classic autism (children who are more challenged), it is difficult to identify the best strategies for both groups. In the past, most instructional practices were developed for children with classic autism and were later modified to suit the needs of children higher on the spectrum. This might be a place to start, but these populations are so different that it would be like developing strategies for children with Down syndrome and then modifying them for children with learning disabilities—two groups with very different needs.

One of the reasons why this lumping of disparate groups was done in the past was because when children with autism were diagnosed at a very young age it was unclear what their level of functioning would be when they got older (i.e., low, moderate, or high). In addition, young children with high- and low-level autism are more similar than older children with high- and low-level autism. Nobody can predict what abilities children will develop over time. Just because a child cannot talk at age 2 does not mean that he or she will not talk by age 3. Just because a child has repetitive behaviors that seem out of control when he is 4 does not mean he won't be able to regulate those behaviors by the time he is 8. We do not know the potential of children with autism. This is true for typically developing children as well. However, children with autism have an even greater degree of variability in their abilities because autism is a spectrum disorder, representing a range of symptoms from very mild to severe or even profound.

Unlike their counterparts in the past, many of these children are born with high-functioning autism, which has also been called Asperger's or pervasive developmental disorders not otherwise specified (PDD-NOS). Today, more than 20 years after the spike in autism, we are watching as these children graduate from high school and enter college or try to find jobs. Some are doing well with simple accommodations and assistance, whereas others are joining the ranks of the unemployed and require a host of disability services, including independent living programs and work programs, as well as socialization, recreation, and mental health services.

Scientists, therapists, physicians, and parents are beginning to realize that overcoming autism-related challenges is not something that can only be addressed through early intervention via therapy in preschool and kindergarten. Autism is a condition that families must spend years addressing in order to prepare their children for adulthood.

Thus, as children with autism grow up it is very important to help them better understand the social world and to learn to regulate (when they choose) their autistic behaviors so they can make decisions about who they want to be when they are adults, rather than having those decisions imposed on them by their autism.

The Change in Diagnostic Criteria

The definition of autism has always been controversial because autism is defined by symptoms of a disorder, and the symptoms of autism do not follow a precise or identical pattern across every child with autism. In fact, most experts would agree that no child or adult with autism is the same. None of them display all the characteristics of autism, and each characteristic manifests itself in different ways in different children. We have never seen a more diverse group of children or adults, and we have never seen two children with autism who are exactly the same.

When a child is first diagnosed with autism, parents want to provide that child with as much support and "treatment" as possible in hopes that their child will move beyond the autism or at least develop a more mild form of autism, as opposed to a more "severe" form of autism. In the *Diagnostic and Statistical Manual of Mental Disorders*, 4th edition (*DSM-IV*) (American Psychiatric Association, 2000) experts claimed that there were three types of autism: Asperger's, classic autism, and PDD-NOS. The *DSM-IV* also included childhood disintegrative disorder (CDD) and Rett Syndrome.

In the upcoming 5th edition of the *DSM* (*DSM-5*), the first four categories—Asperger's, autism, PDD, and CDD—are now under the umbrella of "autism," (American Psychiatric Association, 2013). Rett Syndrome can be diagnosed with a genetic test, so it has been eliminated from the autism category in part because autism is a disorder that is diagnosed solely on symptoms. In this book we still talk about Asperger's and PDD-NOS because the participants in the research study that sets the stage for this book were diagnosed in the 1990s. As a result, many of them were diagnosed with Asperger's or PDD-NOS, and so this is how they identify themselves.

The change in the definition of autism in the *DSM-5* has fueled a controversy (Wing, Gould, & Gillberg, 2011). One reason for this is because some parents think this new definition might replace a more precise description of their children's symptoms, and many adults with Asperger's consider the Asperger's label part of their identity. Frequently when people hear the word "autism" they immediately think of the more severely challenged child, and not a high-functioning child. As a result, parents fear that the new broadened *DSM-5* categories will make the autism diagnosis even more vague than it was before and that higher-level children might even lose their diagnosis and have more trouble receiving the supports they need. However, children with Asperger's and PDD-NOS have in the past had trouble getting funding for services because their disability wasn't considered severe enough to warrant services. So for others the change will be welcomed. Since everyone will be diagnosed with autism it might be easier to get support.

Finally, in the new *DSM-5* social communication disorder (SCD) has been added as a new category (outside the autism spectrum) to provide diagnostic coverage to children who present with only social communication problems and do not display the repetitive and stereotyped behaviors (Ozonoff, 2012). As a result, children who have pragmatic language problems and social problems will probably start receiving a diagnosis of SCD rather than autism. This should cut down dramatically on the number of children diagnosed with autism.

This demonstrates how the fields of education and medicine are not exact sciences, but rather, like other fields of study, participate in the ongoing construction of knowledge, offering particular frameworks for how we see the world. They do not offer "truth," but informed theory, which can change at any time with empirical evidence. In the next *Diagnostic and Statistical Manual of Mental Disorders,* definitions will likely shift again. That is why it is important for teachers to always question what is known about autism, particularly as they test educational theories to create a toolbox of strategies that can meet the differing needs of children on the autism spectrum.

Interviewing Families

For the study that forms the basis of this book, we interviewed parents of children with autism and their children. There has been limited research exploring the experiences of parents and children from these families. We thought it was important to not only hear from parents, but also to get the perspective of adolescents. We collected personal stories through individual in-depth interviews, and we asked the parents to fill out a demographic questionnaire. All interviews were collected in person at a location chosen by the parent. The parents' tapes usually lasted between 60–90 minutes and the teenagers' tapes lasted about 30 minutes. All tapes were transcribed verbatim and each quote was coded and organized into themes. Throughout the book, we will not only use stories from the lives of real families, but we will present research and talk about how the families' stories add to a new and emerging body of knowledge about high-level autism.

We also collated research about ASD, both to inform our study and to provide our readers with up-to-date information about these conditions. Ultimately, we provide recommendations for teaching so that teachers can help children with autism reach their full potential.

We also talk about other adults and children on the spectrum who have written personal stories and essays, such as the article *Kiss My Asperger's: Turning the Tables of Knowledge,* by David Connor (2011), who argues that children with autism may come across as socially odd, but only because we are familiar with (and therefore accepting of) the strangeness of our current social customs and habits.

We hope that our book motivates teachers to start talking to parents of children with autism and also to the children themselves. Parents and kids have a lot to say, and everyone wants to be heard. This in and of itself is a great first step to improving classroom teaching. Whether it is worried parents, concerned but confounded school psychologists, teachers from both segregated and inclusive classrooms, curious children and adolescents, or college counselors needing information, we can all learn through the personal accounts of people with Asperger's about how they interpret the world and manage their daily lives.

Conclusion

In writing this book, we not only focus on how teachers can help children with autism change by developing social skills, but we also talk about how teachers can help typically developing peers change, as well as other adults, making the school a more welcoming place for children with autism. For children with autism to thrive, they need to feel safe, accepted, and valued in the classroom. Some of their behaviors may be unusual, and some may even be unacceptable, but in either case these children will need time and space to change themselves throughout their childhood. If their parents (or preschool teachers) could simply tell them to "stop flapping" (for example) and that was all it took, we wouldn't have a problem. But these children cannot change overnight. Typically developing children need to learn to accept children on the spectrum and to give them time to change as they grow up. Similarly, the only way for children with autism to change is for others to allow them a safe path of exploration to better understand who they are, what "typical" means, and who they want to be in the future.

However, that doesn't mean that typically developing children need to simply stand back and be accepting, for example, if a child with autism is rude. And, a child with autism should not necessarily accept the "typical" way either. It is our belief that both groups of children have a role in changing the social dysfunction of each other's cultures. Unless people think that a place where hierarchical bullying is common, where children grow up too fast, where difference is barely tolerated, and where competition is so severe that our children are terrified of failure is a good place to grow up, then our "typical culture" also needs to change. Very few children with neurological disorders have ever had the chance to speak for themselves. In this book, we give these children, and their parents, the opportunity to share their experiences and voice their opinions about what educational opportunities will best help them reach their full potential.

References

American Psychiatric Association. (2000). *Diagnostic and statistical manual of mental disorders* (4th ed.). Arlington, VA: American Psychiatric Publishing.

American Psychiatric Association. (2013). *Diagnostic and statistical manual of mental disorders* (5th ed.). Arlington, VA: American Psychiatric Publishing.

Blumberg, S. J., Bramlett, M. D., Kogan, M. D., Schieve, L. A., Jones, J. R., & Lu, M. C. (2013). Changes in prevalence of parent-reported Autism Spectrum Disorder in school-aged U.S. children: 2007 to 2011–2012. *National Health Statistics Reports Number 65* (pp. 1–11). Hyattsville, MD: National Center for Health Statistics.

Conner, D. J., (2013) Kiss My Aspergers: Turning the Tables of Knowledge: International Journal of Inclusive Education, 17,(2), 111–129.

Henniger, N. A., & Taylor, J. L., (2013). Outcomes in adults with autism spectrum disorders: a historical perspective. Autism. 17(1) 103–116.

LePage, P. (1997). *From disadvantaged girls to successful women: Education and women's resiliency.* Westport CT: Praeger.

Levine, A., & Nidiffer, J. (1995). *Beating the odds: How the poor get to college.* San Francisco, CA: Jossey-Bass.

Ozonoff, S. (2012). DSM-5 and Autism Spectrum Disorders—Two decades of perspectives from the editorial. *Journal of Child Psychology and Psychiatry*, *53*(9), 4–6.

Wing, L., Gould, J., & Gillberg, C. (2011). Autism spectrum disorders in the *DSM-5*: Better or worse than the *DSM-IV*? *Developmental Disabilities*, *32*, 768–773.

Chapter Two
Autism Basics, Prevalence and Causes

What Is Autism?

Autism is sometimes referred to as a condition rather than a developmental disorder or disability by adults with Asperger's or high-functioning autism, in part because they believe that the term autism refers to a set of differences in the way people think and perceive their social context rather than a set of deficits. The medical community views autism as a neurological disorder. Needless to say, there is a lot of confusion surrounding the definition of autism, especially because in the past it was almost always associated with severe intellectual impairments. Today in the United States a majority of children with autism (58%) are born with mild impairments, 34% with moderate impairments, and only 6.9% with severe impairments (Blumberg et al., 2013). The terms high-functioning and high-level autism are often used interchangeably, but we choose to use the term high-level autism to refer to the children we talk about in this book for two reasons. First, it is the term the teenagers used most often when they described themselves. Rarely did the children use the term high functioning. Second, this seemed a simple way to define where these children fell along the autism spectrum (high on the spectrum), as opposed to describing their level of functioning, which to us seemed like a judgment call. Many people in our society don't have autism and still don't function well.

Although we focus on children with high-level autism, in this book we strongly believe that all children who experience challenges from autism are part of the same community, and whether children can be described as low, middle, or high on the spectrum is nebulous at best and impossible to measure. We believe, however, that different groups included under the broad autism category would still benefit if educators focused more narrowly on the specific needs of various populations of children who have autism whenever possible.

One difference between a child with high-level autism and classic autism is whether either child has cognitive impairments and the severity of those impairments or intellectual disabilities and also other skills that might hinder their ability to live or work independently in our society. Children with high-level autism usually have cognitive abilities that are comparable to or greater than those of their typical peers. These children still might have auditory processing problems similar to children with learning disabilities. Although those processing problems do not translate into intellectual disabilities, they nonetheless represent learning challenges that many children with autism must overcome to be successful.

As was mentioned in Chapter 1, in the newest version of the diagnostic manual (*DSM-5*) autism has become an umbrella term used to describe the entire spectrum of autism symptoms. According to the APA's Autism Workgroup, these changes signal how symptoms of the disorders represent a continuum from mild to severe, rather than being distinct disorders (Ozonoff, 2012).

Rett Syndrome has been eliminated from the autism category altogether, because scientists now know the genetic basis of that disorder. In addition, SCD has been added as a new category (outside the autism spectrum) to provide diagnostic coverage to children who present with only social-communication problems and who do not display the repetitive and stereotyped behaviors of ASD (Ozonoff, 2012).

However, in this book we talk about PDD-NOS and Asperger's as well as classic autism as they have been described in the *DSM-IV* because this is the way the children of the families who participated in the study for this book were diagnosed and came to understand their condition. In the *DSM-IV*, ASD was broken into five subgroups. In the following sections we provide brief definitions and characteristics of these subgroups.

Classic Autism

Children with *classic autism* have severe challenges, including impaired social interactions and communication and repetitive or stereotyped behavior. Children with classic autism may have problems talking and relating to people and may be hypersensitive to their environment. Certain sounds, colors, and textures may upset them. Some cling to schedules, such as eating the same foods or watching the same shows every day at the same time. Changes in routine can upset them. Many people with classic autism also have intellectual disabilities. Leo Kanner (1968) is credited with being the first person to describe autism disorder, and he was focused on classic autism.

Asperger's Disorder or Syndrome

Asperger's disorder or *syndrome* is a type of autism characterized by social and communication skill deficits, relatively normal language and cognitive development, and the presence of idiosyncratic interests. Hans Asperger first described

Asperger's in 1944 as a type of personality disorder (Asperger, [1944]1991). Individuals with Asperger's frequently use pedantic speech as well as scientific or technical vocabulary with an avoidance of slang. Because they often interpret things literally, they can appear socially awkward and have milder symptoms of autistic disorder. Although they generally test at an average to above-average intelligence level, they are usually perceived as immature and overly emotional. Often not understanding conventional social rules, people with Asperger's appear to demonstrate a lack of empathy by making limited eye contact, appearing to be unengaged in a conversation, and being confused by the use of gestures. However, rather than a lack of empathy, an individual with Asperger's explains that his "brain sometimes perceives things differently from other people, and often has different values and priorities.

Childhood Disintegrative Disorder

Childhood disintegrative disorder is a type of autism that develops in children who previously seemed to be developing typically by hitting the age-appropriate milestones until the child reached the ages of 3 to 5. These children stop talking, lose potty-training skills, and stop socializing. They may stop playing, lose motor skills, and fail to make friends. Children with this disorder usually develop severe intellectual disabilities. Although it is more common in boys than girls, it is nonetheless rare in either gender.

Rett's Disorder or Syndrome

Rett's disorder or *syndrome* is a unique developmental disorder that is first recognized in infancy and seen always in girls. It is caused by mutations on the X chromosome on a gene called *MECP2*. Since girls have two X chromosomes, girls can survive Rett Syndrome. The disorder was identified by Austrian physician Andreas Rett. It is a developmental disorder, not a degenerative disorder, and generally symptoms appear after an early period of what appears to be normal development. Then, the child displays a slowing down or stagnation of skills. Other problems may include seizures and disorganized breathing patterns, walking on the toes, sleep problems, a wide-based gait, difficulty chewing, slowed growth, seizures, and cognitive disabilities. In the early years, there may be a period of isolation or withdrawal where the child is irritable and cries inconsolably. Over time, motor problems may increase, but in general eye contact and communication generally improves and irritability decreases.

Pervasive Developmental Disorder Not Otherwise Specified (PDD-NOS)

Pervasive developmental disorder not otherwise specified (PDD-NOS) is a disorder that displays some of the characteristics of classic autism. Psychologists and psychiatrists sometimes use the term *pervasive developmental disorders* and *autism spectrum disorders* interchangeably. As such, during the time of *DSM–IV*, PDD-NOS became the diagnosis applied to children or adults who were on the autism spectrum but who did not fully meet the criteria for another ASD, such as classic autism or Asperger's. This disorder is often not as obvious as autism; people with PDD-NOS show symptoms of autism at various times, but not often enough to get a full diagnosis of autism. In these cases, there can be social and speech problems, as well as unusual sensitivities to specific sights and sounds.

Autism and Demographic Information in the United States

As was mentioned in Chapter 1, the Centers for Disease Control and Prevention (CDC) states that according to parent surveys approximately 1 in 50 children were born with autism between 2007 to 2012 (Blumberg et al., 2013).

The CDC is also using other tools to determine the prevalence of autism. Currently, the United States is participating in a large study administered by the Autism and Developmental Disabilities Monitoring (ADDM) Network (Baio, 2012). This network is an active surveillance system that estimates the prevalence of ASD and describes characteristics of 8-year-old children whose parents or guardians reside within 14 research areas in the United States. ADDM does not rely on professional or family reporting of an existing ASD diagnosis or classification to ascertain case status. Instead, information is obtained from children's evaluation records to determine the presence of ASD symptoms at any time from birth through age 8. ADDM focuses on children who are 8 years old because a baseline study conducted by the CDC showed that this is the age of identified peak prevalence.

The goals of the Network are to provide data about how common ASDs are in a specific place and time period (also known as prevalence) and describe the population of children with ASDs. Further, the CDC hopes to compare how common ASDs are in different areas of the country and to identify changes in ASD occurrence over time. In this way the CDC can help develop an understanding of the impact of ASD and related conditions in U.S. communities. Key findings from the CDC and ADDM's most recent report suggests that the number of children identified with ASDs varied widely across the 14 ADDM Network sites from 1 in 47 to 1 in 210.

As autism rates have climbed, researchers have begun to study where autism is most prevalent; for example, whether it is more prevalent among poor families and underrepresented ethnic minority families. They are looking for any clues as to the cause and the reason for the increase in the number of cases. One important study was large enough to show an association between autism risk and socioeconomic status (SES) (Baio, 2012). The differences found among the SES groups were observed in all four racial/ethnic groups studied. Overall, ASD prevalence was higher among non-Hispanic White and Asian children than among non-Hispanic Black or African-American and Hispanic children. In addition, when the results were organized by their economic status, the racial/ethnic differences in prevalence varied by SES. The lower prevalence among non-Hispanic Black or African American and Hispanic children was seen only in the low SES category. The fact that more non-Hispanic Black or African American and Hispanic children lived in poverty contributed to the lower overall prevalence among these groups. Researchers speculate that this difference is a result of children having access to diagnostic assessments. They believe that people with less money probably do not have access to professionals able to diagnose autism and recommend interventions (Baio, 2012).

It is also possible that children are diagnosed differently based on race. Morrier and Hess (2012) suggest that students from American Indian and Hispanic backgrounds were the most underrepresented compared to their proportions in the general populations. This was especially true in preschool. Preschool-aged children classified as Hispanic were consistently underrepresented in special education under autism eligibility, and those classified as Caucasian were consistently overrepresented in this eligibility category. Students from Asian backgrounds had the greatest overrepresentation when compared to the general population.

What Causes Autism?

Autism is not curable in that it is not a disease where individuals take medicine or engage in a treatment and then get well. Almost everyone would agree that genetics plays some part in the cause of autism (e.g., State & Sestan, 2012). Boys are five times more likely than girls to have autism. If parents have identical twins and one has ASD, then the other will be affected from about 36% to 95% of the time (Hallmayer et al., 2011; Ronald et al., 2006; Rosenberg et al., 2009; Taniai, Nishiyama, Miyahci, Imaeda, & Sumi, 2008). Parents who have one child with an ASD have a 2% to 18% chance of having a second child on the spectrum (Ozonoff et al., 2011; Sumi, Taniai, Miyachi, & Tanemura, 2006). Autism tends to occur more often in people who have certain genetic or chromosomal conditions, such as Down syndrome, fragile X, tuberous sclerosis, and other genetic and chromosomal disorders. Those who study autism and genetics suggest that the number of genes predicting risk for ASD has steadily increased, reaching well into the hundreds, with no single gene or gene sequence accounting for more than 1% of cases. People are still curious about what is causing the genetic mutations. A number of theories have been put forth to answer the question regarding the interaction of genetic mutations and factors that trigger those mutations. Scientists are studying many different environmental factors, from air pollution brought on by living close to freeways (Volk et al., 2013) to pesticides, viruses, and chemicals in household products (Hertz-Picciotto et al., 2006). Others have looked into the age of the mothers and fathers (Durkin et al., 2008) and whether maternal child abuse might also be risk factors (Roberts,

Lyall, Rich-Edwards, Ascherio, & Weisskopf, 2013). Some have speculated that there is a combination of environmental factors that affect children who are somehow vulnerable. There is still much speculation and few definitive answers.

Intellectual Disabilities

Particularly relevant for this book, the majority (62%) of children from the ADDM Network being born on the spectrum today do not have intellectual disabilities (Baio, 2012), which means that they have an intelligence quotient (IQ) that is greater than 70 (see Figure 2.1).

This is another change that people do not understand with regard to autism. In the past, 70% of children born with autism had severe intellectual disabilities. So, not only has autism been diagnosed at a higher rate starting in the 1980s and 1990s, but the symptoms of the condition have also changed. People point to changes in diagnoses, but changes in diagnoses cannot account for all the changes. The prevalence of diagnosed autism was 1 in 10,000 before the 1990s; now it is 1 in 50. Diagnoses alone could not possibly account for that increase, no matter how hard people keep hoping it is true.

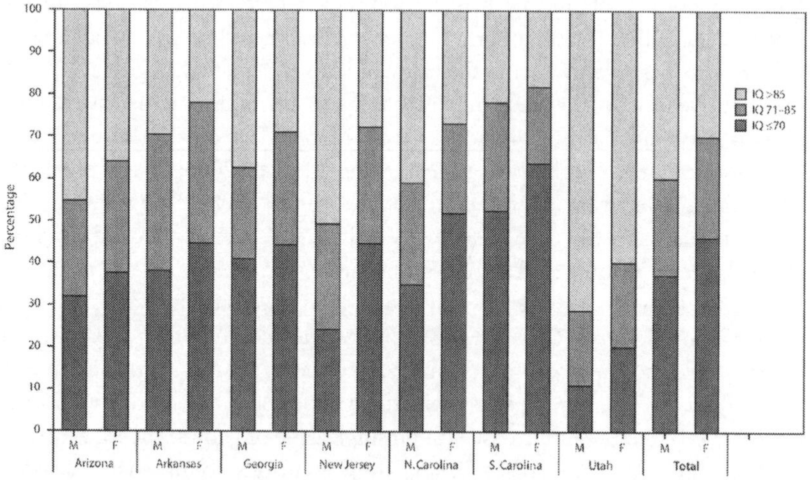

* N=1,981

† Includes sites having information on intellectual ability available for at least 70% of children who met the ASD case definition.

Figure 2.1 ADDM Network Identified Intelligence Quotient number of children in each state by intellectual ability.

Most recent intelligence quotient (IQ) as of age 8 years among children identified with autism spectrum disorders (ASD) for whom psychometric test data were available by site and sex. Autism and Developmental Disabilities Monitoring Network, seven sites, United States, 2008. Retrieved from http://www.cdc.gov/ncbddd/autism/data.html.

Does Autism Go Away?

We are at the beginning of a new era of educational advancement for a new type of child who will need to be understood and then nurtured. Although most experts agree that autism does not "just go away" (in the traditional sense), as the child gets older it is widely noted that the behaviors associated with autism can change so radically that a child might lose his or her diagnosis. Currently, researchers are examining improved outcomes in individuals with a history of autism (Fein et al., 2013). Preliminary findings suggest that some individuals demonstrate an overall level of functioning within normal limits as they get older. However, possible challenges in more subtle aspects of social interaction or cognition have not been ruled out. Further, this research does not describe optimal instructional and therapeutic interventions that lead to these outcomes.

When a child or an adult can no longer be diagnosed with autism based on symptoms, medical professionals refer to this as a *subclinical* case. However, even those children with a subclinical presentation of symptoms could as an adult suffer from anxiety, not only social anxiety, but anxiety related to performance and abilities at some time in their adulthood. Some of these adolescents have mild forms of obsessive compulsive disorder (OCD) or they develop phobias during their lifetime. In addition, they may have difficulties developing and maintaining relationships or holding down jobs because they have a low tolerance for frustration. These problems are often invisible, and although they may not be as obvious as some of the autistic behaviors apparent in childhood, they could still be debilitating in adulthood. Finally, if autism is a result of early genetic mutation, can it ever really go away? Even if the symptoms go away, the genetic material that caused the symptoms in the first place remains.

References

Asperger, H. ([1944]1991). Autistic psychopathy in childhood. In U. Frith (Ed.), *Autism and Asperger syndrome* (pp. 37–92). Cambridge, UK: Cambridge University Press.

Baio, J. (2012). Prevalence of autism spectrum disorders—Autism and Developmental Disabilities Monitoring Network, 14 sites, United States. *Surveillance Summaries, 61*(SS03), 1–19. Retrieved from http://www.cdc.gov/mmwr/preview/mmwrhtml/ss6103a1.htm?s_cid=ss6103a1_w

Blumberg, S. J., Bramlett, M. D., Kogan, M. D., Schieve, L. A., Jones, J. R., & Lu, M. C. (2013). Changes in prevalence of parent-reported autism spectrum disorder in school-aged U.S. Children: 2007 to 2011–2012. *National Health Statistics Reports, 65*, 1–11.

Durkin, M. S., Maenner, M. J., Newschaffer, C. J., Lee, L. C., Cunniff, C. M., Daniels, J. L., . . ., Schieve, L. A. (2008). Advanced parental age and the risk of autism spectrum disorder. *American Journal Epidemiology, 168*(11), 1268–1276.

Fein, D., Barton, M., Eigsti, I. M., Kelley, E., Naigles, L., Schultz, R. T., . . . Tyson, K. (2013). Optimal outcome in individuals with a history of autism. *Journal of Child Psychology and Psychiatry, and Allied Disciplines, 54*(2), 195–205.

Hallmayer, J., Cleveland, S., Torres, A., Phillips, J., Cohen, B., Torigoe, T., Risch, N. (2011). Genetic heritability and shared environmental factors among twin pairs with autism. *Archives of General Psychiatry, 68*(11), 1095–1102.

Hertz-Picciotto, I., Croen, L. A., Hansen, R., Jones, C. R., van de Water, J., & Pessah, I. N. (2006). The CHARGE study: An epidemiologic investigation of genetic and environmental factors contributing to autism. *Environmental Health Perspective, 114*(7), 1119–1125.

Kanner, L. (1968). Autistic disturbances of affective contact. *Acta Paedopsychiatry, 35*(4), 100–136.

Morrier, M. M., & Hess, K. L. (2012). Ethnic differences in autism eligibility in the United States public schools. *Journal of Special Education, 46*, 49–63.

Ozonoff, S. (2012). Editorial perspective: Autism spectrum disorders in DSM-5: An historical perspective and the need for change. *Journal of Child Psychology and Psychiatry, 53*(10), 1092–1094.

Ozonoff, S., Young, G. S., Carter, A., Messinger, D., Yirmiya, N., Zwaigenbaum, L., Stone, W. L. (2011). Recurrence risk for autism spectrum disorders: A Baby Siblings Research Consortium study. *Pediatrics, 128*, 488–495.

Roberts, A. L., Lyall, K., Rich-Edwards, J. W., Ascherio, A., & Weisskopf, M. G. (2013). Association of maternal exposure to childhood abuse with elevated risk for autism in offspring. *JAMA Psychiatry, 70*(5), 508–515.

Ronald, A., Happe, F. A., Bolton, P., Butcher, L. M., Price, T. S., Wheelwright, S., Plomin, R. (2006). Genetic heterogeneity between the three components of the autism spectrum: A twin study. *Journal of the American Academy of Child and Adolescent Psychiatry, 45*(6), 691–699.

Rosenberg, R. E., Law, J. K., Yenokyan, G., McGready, J., Kaufmann, W. E., & Law, P. A. (2009). Characteristics and concordance of autism spectrum disorders among 277 twin pairs. *Archives of Pediatric Adolescent Medicine, 163*(10), 907–914.

State, M. W., & Sestan, N. (2012). The emerging biology of autism spectrum disorders. *Neuroscience, 337*(6100), 1301–1303.

Sumi, S., Taniai, S., Miyachi, T., & Tanemura, M. (2006). Sibling risk of pervasive developmental disorder estimated by means of an epidemiologic survey in Nagoya, Japan. *Journal of Human Genetics, 51*, 518–522.

Taniai, H., Nishiyama, T., Miyahci, T., Imaeda, M., & Sumi, S. (2008). Genetic influences on the broad spectrum of autism: Study of proband-ascertained twins. *American Journal of Medical Genetics Part B: Neuropsychiatric Genetics, 147B*(6), 844–849.

Volk, H. E., Lurmann, F., Penfold, B., Hertz-Piccotto, I., & McConnell, R. (2013). Traffic-related air pollution, particulate matter, and autism. *JAMA Psychiatry, 70*(1), 71–77.

Chapter Three
Characteristics of Children With Autism

A parent once told us that her 6-year-old daughter with autism liked to laugh and sing and play with an umbrella in the rain by herself. However, when she did so a group of typically developing girls approached her and started teasing her. The principal told the mother that her daughter needed to stop singing and acting so odd. In this situation, and many others like it, we need to question our norms of appropriate behavior. When would it ever be appropriate for a group of older girls to make fun of a 6-year-old girl? Here, the phrase "making fun" minimizes the ugly truth of bullying, which is certainly what took place in this instance. When is bullying ever a socially appropriate behavior? It is times like these that remind us that it is sometimes the characteristics of the typically developing children that need to change, not those of the child with autism.

In this chapter, we talk about the characteristics of children with autism because recognizing and understanding these traits enables teachers and other professionals to better engage these students in the classroom. As educators, we know that increased engagement leads to learning (Marks, 2000). This is where children with autism differ from other children with learning disabilities, and also from typically developing children. The way they act, develop, and respond to the world is often counterintuitive, and this is often what causes problems for teachers. For example, children with autism can be so vulnerable that they have trouble adapting to teachers who do not believe they actually have the unusual challenges they have. Many teachers have never been around children who can solve a complex division problem in their heads one minute and in the next minute be flapping in front of a wall.

By understanding the complexities of how specific characteristics overlap, not only with each other but also with typically developing children, it is much easier to understand how these children see the world, how they appear to others, and why they act certain ways at different ages.

Because all children with autism develop differently depending on a number of factors, including what interventions they receive over the years, how their parents respond to their autism, and which schools they have attended, a teacher must get to know each child individually in addition to understanding the broad characteristics associated with autism. In this chapter, we explore the experiences of our families as well as the literature to better understand some of the challenges children face as they work to overcome barriers posed by autism.

Four Types of Social Interactions of Children with ASD

Wing and Gould's (1979) epidemiological survey of all children living in Camberwell, an area of South London, led to the finding that all children with social impairments had repetitive stereotyped behaviors and almost all had absence or abnormalities of language and symbolic activities. Their work gave rise to the concept of the triad of impairments: social interaction, social communication, and social imagination. In that study Wing and Gould (1979) described three social interaction groups: (a) social aloofness, (b) passive interaction, and (c) active, but odd, interaction. Later, a fourth category, overly formal or stilted, was added. In 1979 the aloof group was considered the most severely challenged in social interaction. Children in this group are indifferent to others, show little facial expression, and resist being touched or cuddled. They might act as though people do not exist and make little eye contact. In fact, sometimes they may not respond at all when someone speaks to them, especially strangers. These children are seen as being in a world of their own.

The passive group does not mind being approached socially, but they initiate few interactions. Those who are passive are content to be alone unless pressed to get involved in activities with others. These children usually need to be prompted and then encouraged to play. Passive children often have their own interests and would prefer to engage in their own activities, which are usually solitary activities. However, they do not usually object to getting involved in activities that involve other people; they just do not seem to prefer these activities, and they have a hard time connecting to the people around them. As a young child, their play, as well as their interactions and communication, are more often parallel, rather than reciprocal, with honest exchange and connection.

Children in the active but odd group make active approaches but have no real understanding of how to interact socially. Some tend to be very tactile and may have trouble with personal space or they may touch others inappropriately. They may shake hands or hug too long. They may want to be social, but only on their own terms. Although they seem to want friends, they pay little attention to other children's interests and usually have poor eye contact. Even when they are with other children, they often go off and play on their own, leaving their peers baffled as to why they wanted to play in the first place. They may talk about the same topic over and over again or want to play the same game (their game) and will melt down if other children want to do something else. They can verbally dominate or have problems communicating. Sometimes what they say doesn't seem to make a lot of sense unless you know how the child communicates. These children sometimes make inappropriate gestures or body noises (farting) because they think it is funny, even at an age where this may seem very immature to their peers. Children who are active but odd are usually more outgoing, but their odd behavior puts people off or scares other children away. Active but odd children are actually quite communicative, but their communication is sometimes one-sided or focused entirely on one isolated or obscure topic. Adults might find these children interesting or amusing for a while, but even they will tire of the banter, and peers are usually quite disinterested in this type of interaction.

The overly formal group was added later and is a pattern seen in adolescence. These teenagers try very hard to behave correctly, but have no true understanding of social rules. They tend to be very rigid about sticking to rules they have learned, whether or not they understand the rules. Many are excessively polite and formal. Most have a good level of language and are smart and do well in school because they follow the rules. They can be anxious because they are confused by the rules and are always afraid they may be doing something wrong.

All of the social interaction types, except the overly formal, tend to describe children much more accurately when they are in elementary school. Children tend to grow out of their odd behaviors and their isolationistic tendencies as they get older. Thus, these descriptions fit children more from elementary through middle school. In preschool, they may come across as very shy, unwilling to play with other children or even to go near other children.

In 1979 the aloof and passive types were described as being more severe along the spectrum and the active but odd types were seen as less severe. Today, these descriptions of social interactions have shifted. Many children with high-functioning autism and Asperger's come across as aloof or passive but do not demonstrate the exact characteristics as the children who were once put into those categories. In the next section we discuss some other areas of difficulty or impairment along the spectrum so a teacher can see the differences between the four types of social interactions in higher-level children and interactions of children who would be placed a little lower on the spectrum. It is important to note that children higher on the spectrum will often exhibit middle-spectrum abilities when they are younger (sometimes even on the lower end) and then move up toward the higher end as they grow up.

Characteristics of Children With High-Level Autism

Having a child with autism is not like having a child who is shy or withdrawn. Some kids who are shy or withdrawn can take a class, work with a peer mentor, or talk with a psychologist and after a few interventions show remarkable improvement. It is much more difficult to work with a child with autism. Only in extremely rare cases will a parent take a child on the spectrum to therapy and witness changes overnight. Children with high-level autism respond well to intervention, but they tend to progress slowly through developmental stages. Table 3.1 gives teachers some ideas of what aspects or characteristics of autism are more prevalent at different ages.

Movements: Stimming

Children with autism frequently engage in behaviors that are unusual; for example, engaging in repetitive movements called self-stimulatory behaviors, or *stimming*. Many people argue that all of us engage in stimming behavior to some extent. If you twirl your hair around your finger or you tap your foot on the floor, you are actually engaging in self-stimulatory behavior that helps you to address hidden anxieties.

Repetitive behaviors can include body movement, such as rocking back and forth; repetitive movement of objects, such as spinning the wheels of a toy car; staring at fans; wiggling fingers in front of their eyes; hand flapping; tensing the muscles of the arms or face; tapping surfaces; making repeated vocal sounds; or licking or placing unusual objects in their mouths. Some children with autism like jumping, walking on tiptoes, switching lights on and off, watching spinning objects, humming, singing, watching water or rain flowing down, placing objects in long lines or in stacks, or engaging in extensive bedtime (or morning) routines. In addition, some children might also want family members to sit in exactly the same places at mealtimes; they may also become attached to strange objects such as a piece of string or a remote control. These types of behaviors are certainly part of the autism experience. They happen a lot more in elementary school, and parents often try to extinguish these odd repetitive behaviors with behavioral therapy such as applied behavior analysis (ABA) in hopes of making their child look less obviously autistic.

Sensory Issues: Too Bright, Too Loud, Too Crunchy

According to Dunn (1997), many of the behaviors we observe in children can be attributed to an imbalance or poor modulation of sensory input in the brain; in other words, many children with autism are bothered by too much or too little sensory input. Children who are too sensitive to sensory inputs cannot complete classroom tasks because there are so many stimuli in the classroom environment. Some children with autism fixate on one sensory input, such as a tapping pencil, and be oblivious to other inputs. Dunn also discusses thresholds. When thresholds are too low, children respond too frequently to stimuli and can be distracted from their tasks. Alternatively, when thresholds are too high, children miss important cues about what is going on around them and can seem self-absorbed. Researchers have found that children with disabilities such as attention deficit hyperactivity disorder (ADHD), Fragile X, and autism have different patterns of sensory processing compared to their peers and each

Table 3.1 Characteristics of High-Functioning Autism Across Levels

	LOW LEVEL *Generally younger children, older preschool and early elementary, ages 4 through 8*	*MID LEVEL* *Comprised mostly of middle school grades 4 to 8, ages 8 through 12*	*HIGH LEVEL* *Generally older children, mostly high school, ages 13 through 20; note that this category could include some exceptional high functioning younger children in lower grades*
SPEECH	Speech delays to ages 4 to 5; receptive and expressive language difficulties.	Vocal pitch and volume differences (high pitch, loud volume for age, especially preteens); nasal speech is also common; odd accents (such as a cowboy or a New York accent despite no exposure to the geographic or cultural accent).	Speech can become more typical; however, some of the same speech differences present in early levels can be present.
LANGUAGE	*Echolalia* (immediate or delayed echoing or repetition of whole, unanalyzed expressions or reciprocation, depending on the ability to remember streams of auditory signals and to reproduce them; it may serve a number of functions, including conversation maintenance, communication, self-soothing and verbal rehearsal. This tendency to repeat phrases as unanalyzed wholes may persist into adulthood, even when language learning is presumably finished); misses words; forgets what he or she is talking about; seems to come in and out of his or her own world; has trouble verbalizing what he or she wants to say; can't express ideas; repeats the same statement or question or information over and over and over again; may choose never to talk (even though the child can).	Missing or skipping words; possible receptive or expressive problems that affect academic achievement; self-interest and off-topic speech; may not attend to other individuals' questions, answers the wrong questions; easily distracted when having conversations; changing subjects when he or she does not like (or is not comfortable with) a topic; able to communicate needs well; reasonable communication with a limited range of topics.	Invades personal space of others; talks too close; talks too much or too often; doesn't take turns; talks about odd topics and only topics he or she cares about; difficulty with initiating and carrying on a conversation (pragmatics); appears not to care about carrying on conversations; may have mild expressive and receptive (usually auditory) processing problems; difficulty with small talk.

(Continued)

Table 3.1 Continued

	LOW LEVEL *Generally younger children, older preschool and early elementary, ages 4 through 8*	*MID LEVEL* *Comprised mostly of middle school grades 4 to 8, ages 8 through 12*	*HIGH LEVEL* *Generally older children, mostly high school, ages 13 through 20; note that this category could include some exceptional high functioning younger children in lower grades*
SOCIAL	Says inappropriate and embarrassing things; appears mean to other kids; bossy or rude, inattentive or silly; appears less intelligent than he is; may be bullied and sometimes will fight back and be considered the bully; talk to him- or herself or the wall; hums or sings; tries to be humorous using childish body noises (farting); unaware of childhood body habits (e.g., picking nose).	Sees humor in nonsense and immature ideas; appears mean to other kids or disinterested; reject other children before they reject them; appears less intelligent than he or she actually is; talks about obsessions; rigid and only wants to do what he or she wants to do; has trouble showing interest in others; difficulty carrying on conversations and showing empathy; difficulty understanding his or her autism; slight understanding of nonverbal communication and misreads cues (e.g., typical kids may take advantage or a child with autism may read something negative into a neutral situation).	Difficulty discerning playful joking and teasing; difficulty trusting people, especially typical peers; difficulty communicating with peers, especially opposite sex; appears disinterested in peers; asks questions that appear naïve; difficulty with phone etiquette; better able to self-advocate; more willing to discuss autism but uncertain when and how to disclose it; sometimes withdrawn and quiet
IMAGINATION	Limited pretend and symbolic play; tends to stack or line up toys rather than play with them (e.g., lines up cars rather than pretend to drive them), plays games on the computer; concrete, rigid, and stereotyped interests.	Difficulty writing stories; stories tend to be more of a compilation of thoughts and ideas seen on TV or in books; difficulty generating original or imaginative ideas.	More use of imagination; imagination may be more developed in creative arts (ex., filmmaking and drama) rather than in playful activities or writing.

GROSS MOTOR	Difficulty with simple tasks (e.g., taking off shoes); difficulty climbing on monkey bars, swinging by him- or herself compared to typical peers.	Difficulty with competitive sports; clumsy; easily frustrated; jealous; difficulty understanding game rules.	Tends to be clumsy; dislikes competition; tends to have more typical motor skills
FINE MOTOR	Difficulty writing (dysgraphia), opening bottles, dressing, turning faucets on and off; difficulty pouring liquids.	Difficulty writing (dysgraphia), tying shoes, working zippers and buttons; difficulty with combination bike locks and lockers; difficulty getting dressed quickly (e.g., in PE class).	Difficulty writing (dysgraphia)
ACADEMICS	Difficulty with academics similar to learning disabilities (LD), especially in reading, math, and social studies; difficulty with executive functioning and motivation, like LD.	Strengths and fascinations with numbers, patterns, sequences/puzzles; strong number sense but difficulty with developing equations; early decoding reading skills but difficulty with reading comprehension and complex social issues (e.g., race relations) in social studies; difficulty with auditory, visual, and perceptual processing; requires more time to process information.	Typical or above average in academics; motivated to learn and achieve; improves over time; may surpass other children with splintered development; accomplished in reading or math, but struggles with social skills; may have problems with academics in a similar way to children with LD children
STEREOTYPIC MOVEMENT (unwanted movement that is inappropriate to the situation)	Demonstrates repetitive movements and behaviors; stares at clocks, flaps arms, wiggles fingers, rocks back and forth; hums or sings or chews on clothes.	Demonstrates some repetitive behaviors; drums on things with sticks or taps fingers, mostly controlled in public.	No repetitive behaviors or completely controlled in most settings, especially in public; engage in repetitive behaviors at home in private

(Continued)

Table 3.1 Continued

	LOW LEVEL *Generally younger children, older preschool and early elementary, ages 4 through 8*	*MID LEVEL* *Comprised mostly of middle school grades 4 to 8, ages 8 through 12*	*HIGH LEVEL* *Generally older children, mostly high school, ages 13 through 20; note that this category could include some exceptional high functioning younger children in lower grades*
SENSORY STIMULUS	Some sensory issues are a constant source of irritation and cause behavior problems; very picky about foods.	Avoids sensory issues that bother him or her.	Gets used to sensory issues that cause irritation; eats new foods
BEHAVIOR	Restless, destructive; aggressive; screams in public; temper tantrums; hitting, biting, banging on the walls; bothers other children by scaring or upsetting them.	Says inappropriate and embarrassing things; overly honest (you are fat); refuses to change activities; refuses to do work/homework or ignores homework; doesn't pay attention; appears not to listen; refuses to cooperate; wanders away, gets lost, hides; overly emotional; cries and yells out in class.	Generally age-appropriate behavior; anger management issues (ex., inappropriate comments to teachers and peers); inappropriate language; underdeveloped table and social manners (ex., interrupts conversations, chews with mouth open); refusing to do work/homework; refusing to go to school; attention problems

This table represents three levels within high-functioning autism and Asperger's. On occasion, these levels might represent younger and older children, because younger children often face more challenges even if they are higher functioning.

other (Ermer & Dunn, 1998; Myles et al., 2004). Children with autism are more likely to be sensitive to touch and to have auditory and oral sensory processing issues (Dunn, 1999; Ermer & Dunn, 1998; Kientz & Dunn, 1997).

Dunn (1999) identifies the following four types of sensory processing: seeking, low registration, sensitivity, and avoiding. Seekers add movement, touch, sound, and visual stimuli to every activity. They also make noise, fidget in their seats, touch everything, feel objects, touch and hang on to others, or chew on things. Some of these children may be impulsive to try to increase sensory input.

Children who have a low registration do not notice what is going on around them. They may seem dull, bored, or oblivious to their surroundings. They may withdraw and be difficult to engage, seeming apathetic and tired all the time.

Children who are sensitive tend to be hyperactive, distracted, and easily upset. They have a hard time completing tasks. They have more trouble learning because they are always distracted. These children often have trouble with peers because they are sensitive to how others around them are treating them.

Children who are considered the avoidant type work to reduce sensory input. They are resistant and unwilling to participate in activities. They experience a lot of discomfort and will withdraw to reduce it. They may feel overwhelmed and become aggressive so someone will take them out of the environment so they can reduce the sensory input.

In her chapter on sensory processing, Dunn (2008) provides four tables that list suggestions as to how teachers might adapt activities to meet the needs of each type of child. For example, for children who seek sensory input, she suggests allowing the child to change work positions (sitting, standing, going to a different part of the room), to use the chalkboard for some assignments, to color-code materials using bright colors, to open windows so the student can hear noises outside, and to clean the room with scented cleaners. For children who are low register, she suggests placing classroom materials out of reach so that students have to reach, walk, or move to get them; making mirrors available at the children's level; and arranging for the children to work on various surfaces (e.g., rug, desk, grass). For children with sensory sensitivity, she suggests that a teacher make heavy blankets available; provide ear plugs, ear muffs, and ear phones; organize discussion so that one child is talking at a time; limit the time they have to spend in loud places; and stick to routines. For children who are avoiding, Dunn (2008) suggests that teachers keep fans or vents from blowing on the children, use unscented materials, have students hold heavy doors while others file out of the room, and set aside some time for the child to be alone. These are all easy ways a teacher can be flexible and adapt to the sensory needs of a child with autism.

Obsessions and Fascinations: Should We Support a One-Track Mind?

A common question that both parents and teachers often ask about these children is: "Should we allow children with autism to focus on their obsession or try to get them to do something else?" Children with autism have so many different types of obsessions or fascinations at various times that it can be difficult to keep track. They may have obsessions with the weather, hurricanes, dinosaurs, bus schedules, train schedules, movies, TV shows, time (birthdays, people's ages, clocks), outer space, Google maps, volcanoes, puzzles/mazes/codes, weapons (ancient or modern), and calendars, to name just a few.

Children with high-level autism tend to like computers because they provide fast and easy access to information about their obsessions. They also like YouTube videos of movie trailers, silly animation, funny movie reviews, or the Annoying Orange (a YouTube animation whose star is an animated annoying orange). Girls tend to like anime and reading. In addition, children and adolescents with autism often enjoy video games and get very good at them because they spend a lot of time playing them. They tend to have high tolerance for engaging in activities over and over, and they are motivated to achieve a high level of skill in these games.

Again, different theorists have different beliefs about how to deal with these obsessions: Some groups suggest that children should be pushed to do the opposite of what they like to do because it helps develop the areas of the brain that are not yet developed (Vismara & Rogers, 2008). But, talk to any adult with high-level autism and he or she would likely tell you that not allowing a child with autism to engage in his or her obsessions would be damaging to his or her mental health. Forcing children to do what they can't do well, at the expense of what they love, can be very painful for any child. If the research ultimately shows that forcing children to do what they can't do well helps the underdeveloped parts of their brain develop, then we agree that is important, but it needs to be done in a way that is respectful, and the children also need to be allowed to equally engage in activities they love and can do well.

Motor Skills

Children with high-functioning autism do experience delays in motor performance compared to their typically developing peers, but we did not observe this to the same extent as what has been indicated in the literature (see, for example, Jansiewicz et al., 2006). It is possible that their motor development is only delayed, and as they grow older their delays are less prominent in high school or they perhaps receive intervention that helps them develop. Motor deficits seem to focus on execution of the tasks; however, motor learning may be affected as well, thereby impairing processing ability and subsequent execution of motor tasks (Jansiewicz et al., 2006). Children with autism are sometimes considered clumsy, but this could be the result of many different types of problems beyond motor problems; for example, some researchers claim that children with autism have difficulty with interval timing (Falter, Valdas, Wearden, & Bailey, 2012), which means that they may be off by just a fraction of a second in their internal timing. For most tasks, this is not a concern, but if you are trying to catch a ball, then having a delay in interval timing is going to make it difficult. Once again, note that autism does not manifest itself in all children with autism in this way. Many children with autism could be athletes if they chose, but as young children they have trouble negotiating the social aspect of team sports, including competition. They often shy away from sports opportunities that would allow them to practice certain types of skills that are more often carried out in team sports. This is another reason some of these children lag behind typically developing children with certain motor skills.

Comorbid Disorders

According to research, children with ASD are more likely to have comorbid disorders. Mazzone, Ruta, and Reale (2012) tell us that people with ASD are more likely to first have anxiety, especially social anxiety and obsessive-compulsive disorder and/or depression. Although it may appear that many children with ASD have ADHD, it is impossible at this time to differentiate between symptoms of ASD and ADHD. For example, many children with autism and typical development have difficulty focusing and paying attention in school, but that doesn't mean they have ADHD. For children with ASD, some researchers have concluded their hyperactivity and attention problems are a manifestation of their ASD, sometimes related to lower IQ levels and sometimes related to focused interests.

Developmental Stages for Children With Autism

Very few research studies have followed children with autism from birth through adulthood. However, there have been a few. In one of the rare long-term studies of the outcomes of a large sample of 152 children with ASD, children were followed into adolescence over a 10-year period (Baghdadli et al., 2012). The researchers used standard measures and parents' reports to study children's functioning as well as a group-based trajectory analysis to explore their developmental trajectories across their life course. These researchers identified the following distinct developmental patterns. While critical delays remained through adolescence in the adaptive abilities of children with ASD, changes in adaptive skills showed two distinct growth rates. Low growth patterns for both social and communication outcomes were associated with low cognitive and language skills, the presence of epilepsy, and the severity of autism at age 5. In addition, risk factors of low language and severity of autism for both social and communication were predictive of outcomes 10 years later. The amount of hours of early intervention was a protective factor for communication skills. Not surprisingly, lower numbers of hours of intervention during the first 3 years of the follow-up were also associated with a lower-level trajectory (Baghdadli et al., 2012). Higher prevalence of self-injurious behaviors was related to the lower levels of communication, but had no relation to socialization.

In other longitudinal studies, McGovern and Sigman (2005) demonstrated that the developmental path from early childhood to adolescence of 48 children with autism appeared to show positive change in social interaction skills. Shattuck and his colleagues (2007) found that despite the fact that a majority of individuals remained impaired in social reciprocity and communication, there was a tendency toward improvement in these same domains as children grew older. Consistent with the findings from previous studies, worst outcomes in socialization and communication were mostly confined to the lower-functioning children. Indeed, there was a strong association between this type of developmental pattern and several characteristics during early childhood: absence of language abilities, higher severity of autistic symptoms, and lower level of cognitive functioning that seemed predictive of whether and how much children changed over time in a number of studies (Anderson, Oti, Lord, & Welch, 2009).

From our own study, we found that children developed in three major blocks: in preschool, in primary years, and then in adolescence. According to parents, their children definitively improved over time in language, socialization, communication, and repetitive behaviors. Table 3.2 lists some of the ways we've noticed that children change over time.

Conclusion

Over the years, practitioners have worked to describe and label different types of autism in an attempt to bring order to a syndrome that has many crossover symptoms but manifests itself in different ways in different children and adults. Wing and Gould's (1979) descriptions of the aloof, passive, active but odd, and overly formal groups have endured the test of time. Practitioners still find those terms useful.

Children with autism are not only diagnosed based on symptoms of autism, but they are also taught based on how those symptoms manifest themselves (characteristics). In other words, how a professional relates to children with autism will be affected by whether a teacher understands them and responds to their needs. Although some teachers have good intuition about how to teach typically developing children, teaching children with autism is usually counterintuitive. Some strategies that a teacher might believe should work might actually set these children back or cause behavior problems. In addition, these characteristics are not static, so it is necessary to not only know how autism manifests itself in young children, but also in older children. Because their styles, academic capabilities, and social behaviors change over time, teachers need to understand how children with high-level autism, as opposed to classic autism, develop over time. Although it can be difficult, it is important for a teacher to see a 5-year-old child with high-level autism

Table 3.2 Development Pattern for Children With High-Level Autism From Pre-K–12

Preschool Years

1. Picky eater. The child may not accept a variety of foods in his or her diet.
2. The child may have unusual sensory responses with other people. The child may wish to be cuddled or may not want to be touched, especially by people they do not know. The child may come across as though he or she is treating people as objects.
3. The child may resist eye contact.
4. There may be constant crying or there may be an unusual absence of crying.
5. The child may tantrum often for what appears to be no reason.
6. The child often has marked repetitive movements, such as flapping, prolonged rocking, or spinning of objects.
7. The child may develop an obsessive interest in certain toys or objects while ignoring other things.
8. The child may have extreme resistance to change in routines and/or his or her environment.
9. The child may appear to avoid social situations, preferring to be alone.
10. The child may be limited in his or her development of play activities, particularly imaginative play. The child may resist play with other children or simply seem to ignore other children. The child may not engage in symbolic play.
11. The child may have sleeping problems or in other ways seem to not feel well, especially when it comes to the digestive system.
12. There may be an absence of speech, a regression of speech, or unusual speech, patterns such as repeating words and phrases (echolalia), failure to use 'I,' 'me,' and 'you,' or reversal of these pronouns.
13. There may be difficulties with toilet training.
14. The child may have problems with joint attention, sharing observations or experiences with others.
15. The child may be extremely distressed by certain noises and/or busy public places, such as shopping centers.
16. At this age, there may be no evidence of disability in the child's physical appearance. The child may also lack speech or seem unaware of what is going on around them.

Primary School Years

1. Parents may notice that a lot of the distressing behaviors of the preschool years decrease, especially tantrum behaviors.
2. There can be an increase in social interest. The child may be better able to tolerate playing beside other children and may begin to show attachments to certain people (often adults or younger children).
3. If echolalic speech is present, this decreases, and spontaneous speech emerges. Most of the higher-level children who were speech delayed in the preschool years will acquire relatively normal speech, but will consistently have language problems throughout their childhood.

(Continued)

Table 3.2 Continued

4. School behavior problems can occur because the child finds it difficult to concentrate on things he or she is not interested in and may have processing problems.
5. Behavior problems might also occur, because children with autism are having trouble socializing with other children.
6. Ritualistic and compulsive behavior patterns are very common.
7. Hyperactivity and a poor attention span are often observed, often because the child has trouble understanding instructions from the teacher or the classroom rules.
8. The child's difficulty in understanding other people and interpreting what is going on around them leads to significant levels of anxiety. This child might respond to this anxiety by acting out or withdrawing.
9. Many children with high-level autism will show a great motivation or desire to please others (especially teachers and parents) or a complete lack of motivation or desire to please others.
10. At this age, children have difficulty transferring skills learned in one setting to another setting (e.g., from therapy to the classroom).

Adolescence

1. The behavior disturbance and mood imbalance typical of teenagers can be exaggerated for those with autism. It may start a little earlier sometimes due to hormonal changes or from fear of transition at the end of elementary school, but eventually there is a resumption of calmer behavior.
2. Most adolescents show marked improvement in their behavior and skills and a few may show serious behavior regression due to anxiety and depression or other comorbid disorders if they do not get intervention.
3. Sexual development, physical development and interest, is normal but in general is delayed due to these teenagers lack of social abilities.
4. The commencement of menstruation and sexual drive are usually tolerated calmly but issues such as masturbation need to be dealt with openly and directly so that these children know the social norms around sexual behavior among children their age.
5. The presence of a disability can become more obvious as the child becomes older, especially when the voice changes or in their demeanor. Some come across as naive.
6. Increased levels of anxiety and the development of depressive symptoms often occur. Caregivers need to be alerted to this and seek professional help through counseling.
7. Adolescents need transition planning that includes work on executive functioning to better prepare them for adulthood.
8. Adults with ASD, if they have received specialist intervention, can overcome their difficulties but continue to require sensitive and sustained support.

with serious behavior problems and limited speech as a kindergartener who is on a developmental path to young adulthood fully capable of living independently and supporting himself with a good job if given the right supports and education. It is the kindergarten teacher's job to set this child down the right path.

References

Anderson, D. K., Oti, R. S., Lord, C., & Welch, K. (2009). Patterns of growth in adaptive social abilities among children with ASD. *Journal of Abnormal Child Psychology, 37*(7), 1019–1034.

Baghdadli, A., Assouline, B., Sonie, S., Pernon, E., Darrou, C., Michelon, C., Pry, R. (2012). Developmental trajectories of adaptive behaviors from early childhood to adolescence in a cohort of 152 children with autism spectrum disorders. *Journal of Autism and Developmental Disorders, 42,* 1314–1325.

Dunn, W. (1997). Implementing neuroscience principles to support habilitation and recovery. In C. Christiansen & C. Baum (Eds.), *Occupational therapy: Enabling function and well-being* (pp. 182–233). Thorofare, NJ: Slack.

Dunn, W. (1999). *The sensory profile manual.* San Antonio, TX: Psychological Corporation.

Dunn, W. (2008). Sensory processing: Identifying patterns and support strategies. In K. Dunn Buron & P. Wolfberg (Eds.), *Learners on the spectrum: Preparing highly qualified educators* (pp. 138–159). Shawnee, MI: AAPC Textbooks.

Ermer, J., & Dunn, W. (1998). The sensory profile: A discriminant analysis of children with and without disabilities. *American Journal of Occupational Therapy, 52*(7), 283–290.

Falter, C. M., Valdas, N., Wearden, J., & Bailey, A. (2012). More consistent, yet less sensitive: Interval timing in autism spectrum disorders. *Quarterly Journal of Experimental Psychology, 65*(11), 2093–2107.

Jansiewicz, E. M., Goldberg, M. C., Newschaffer, C. J., Denckla, M. B., Landa, R., & Mostofsky, S. H. (2006). Motor signs distinguish children with high functioning autism and Asperger's syndrome from controls. *Journal of Autism and Developmental Disorders, 36,* 613–621.

Kientz, M. A., & Dunn, W. (1997). Comparison of children with autism and typical children using the sensory profile. *American Journal of Occupational Therapy, 51*(7), 530–537.

Marks, H. M. (2000). Student engagement in instructional activity: Patterns in the elementary, middle, high school years. *American Educational Research Journal, 37*(1), 153–184.

Mazzone, L., Ruta, L., & Reale, L. (2012). Psychiatric comorbidities in Asperger syndrome and high functioning autism: Diagnostic challenges. *Annals of General Psychiatry, 11*(16). Retrieved from http://www.annals-general-psychiatry.com/content/11/1/16

McGovern, C. W., & Sigman, M. (2005). Continuity and change from early childhood to adolescence in autism. *Journal of Child Psychology and Psychiatry, 46*(4), 401–408.

Myles, B. S., Hagwara, T., Dunn, W., Rinner, L., Reese, M., Huggins, A., & Stansberry, S. (2004). Sensory issues in children with Asperger Syndrome and autism. *Education and Training in Developmental Disabilities, 3*(4), 283–290.

Shattuck, P. T., Seltzer, M. M., Greenberg, J. S., Orsmond, G. I., Bolt, D., Kring, S., . . . Lord, C. (2007). Change in autism symptoms and maladaptive behaviors in adolescents and adults with ASD. *Journal of Autism and Developmental Disorders, 37*(9), 1735–1747.

Vismara, L. A., & Rogers, S. J., (2008). The Early Start Denver Model. A Case of an Infant Practice. Journal of Early Intervention. 31 (1). 91–10.

Wing, L., & Gould, J. (1979). Severe impairments of social interaction and associated abnormalities in children: Epidemiology and classification. *Journal of Autism and Developmental Disorders, 9*(1), 11–29.

Chapter Four
Profiles of Families

As we mentioned in the first chapter, we interviewed parents of children with autism, and later interviewed their children, those who wished to participate. We asked the families to talk with us about what in their children's school experiences helped them to achieve and what hindered their progress. This book is based on both the themes that were generated by the family interviews and the research conducted over the last 30 years that can help teachers understand how to best work with children with high-level autism.

Methods

Demographic questionnaires and interview questions were developed to collect information about each family. Some of the information is simply facts about family members' age, race, gender, and geographic location. Some of the information is about how the parents perceive, manage, care for, love, and educate their children with autism. In this way, our study is qualitative in nature, focusing on personal interviews and summaries of pertinent research collected and disseminated by other researchers in the field.

Bogdan and Biklen (2006) state that qualitative research is the best method for studying human behavior and an important tool for studying human experience. Other researchers, such as Bronfenbrenner (1986), emphasize the importance of qualitative research because this design continues to generate and create knowledge. This means that findings are discovered rather than verified. It allows the researchers to present a complete picture of what is really happening in a natural setting rather than in a laboratory. In this book, we present deeply rich and descriptive experiences of children with autism and their parents. Using their own words and thoughts, these parents and children help us to understand the varied attitudes, beliefs, behaviors, motivations, opinions, and aspirations of children with autism.

Qualitative research has been criticized for its subjectivity, but we agree with Cohen, Manion, and Morrison (2000) that understanding a person's interpretation of the world is important because that is what drives human behavior. In this study, we not only focused on the specific memories of our research participants, but, more important, we valued what they remembered and we emphasized the meanings behind the events, processes, and structures of the families' lives. We gained insight from their perceptions, assumptions, prejudgments, and presuppositions and how each family connected those meanings to the social world around them (Miles & Huberman, 1994). In other words, we were interested in finding out what these families remembered as important and why, rather than asking them to remember everything about their lives from when the children were young during one interview.

Research Participants

Nineteen parents of children with autism and 12 teenagers with autism were interviewed for this study. Twenty teenagers with autism are represented in these 19 families. Two parents in one of the households interviewed together and in two of the families two of the teenagers had autism. Of the parents interviewed, 17 were mothers and 2 were fathers. Of the 20 teenagers, 9 were teenage boys and 3 were teenage girls. Of the 20 teenagers on the spectrum represented in this study, 14 were white, 4 were Asian or Asian mix, and 1 was Hispanic. We needed a translator with one of the families because not everyone in the family could speak English. All socioeconomic levels are represented in this study: three self-identified as lower income, four as working class, four as middle class, and six as upper-middle class. Three families chose not to respond to this particular demographic question. In four of the families, older or younger typically developing sisters were also available to talk while other family members were being interviewed. These young girls or older teenagers/women sometimes added comments as the rest of the family talked. A couple of the sisters were willing to answer some questions themselves about their own experiences growing up with a brother or sister with autism. Almost all families were interviewed in person; only a couple of parents were interviewed over the phone for their convenience. In Table 4.1 we provide demographic information about each child from a survey filled out by each parent.

Interviews

With the parents' permission, and each teen's assent, we completed 31 interviews. All participants were free to talk about whatever they were comfortable with and interested in talking about, although interview protocols were used. The criteria for the teenage participants was that they had a diagnosis of autism, PDD-NOS, or Asperger's and were between the ages of 13 and 22

Table 4.1 Children's Information Provided by Parents in the Demographic Questionnaire

	1	*2*	*3*	*4*	*5*	*6*	*7*	*8*	*9*	*10*	*11*	*11*	*12*	*13*	*14*	*15*	*16*	*17*	*17*	*18*	*19*
Parents	Lidia	Tamra	Kimberly	Donna	Lena	Dawn	Samatha	Ana	Maria	James	Rhonda	Rhonda	Emily	Joan	Jana	Elizabeth	Janine	Teresa	Teresa	Alonzo	Juanitaa
Teens	Rayne	Daniel	Austin	Mason	Ash	Rob	Chris	Gabriela	Alberto	Reese	John	Chet	Zack	Dennis	Steven	Parker	Jake	Lane	Linda	Juan	Juan
Gender	F	M	M	M	M	M	M	F	M	M	M	M	M	M	M	M	M	M	F	M	M
Age	13	15	15	15	15	15	15	17	18	15	22	19	14	16	16	16	14	18	17	14	14
Grade	8	10	10	10th	10	10	8/9	11	13	9	16	13	9	10	10	11	8	13	12	9	9
Diagnosed	Aut	Aut	Aut	Asp	Asp	Aut	PDD	Aut	Asp	Aut	Asp	Asp	PDD	Asp	Aut	Asp	Asp	Asp	Asp	Asp	Asp
Age of Diagnoses	5	2	3	9	7	2.8	3	2	17	1–2	18	10	4.5		2.4	7	6	6	12	3	3
Type of School	Public	Public	Public	Public	Public	Private Ld/Aut	Private SPED	Public	Public Jr.college	Public	Private college	Public Jr. college	Private Ld/Aut	Private Ld/Aut	Public	Public	Private Ld/Aut	Private Ld/Aut	Private Ld/Aut	Public	Public
# Mother	1	1	1	1	1	1	1	1	1	1	1	1	1	1	1	1	1	1	1	1	1
# Father	1	1	1		2	1	1	1		1	1	1	1	1	1	1	1	1	1	1	1
Lives with	Both	Mom	Both	Mom	M&SF	Both	Both	1	Mom	Both	Both	Both	Both	Both	Both	Both	Both	Both	Both	Both	Both
Siblings	1	2	2	0	1	1	0	1	0	0	1	1	2	1	2	1	1	1	1	1	1

(Continued)

Table 4.1 Cont inued

	1	*2*	*3*	*4*	*5*	*6*	*7*	*8*	*9*	*10*	*11*	*11*	*12*	*13*	*14*	*15*	*16*	*17*	*17*	*18*	*19*
Siblings age	16	1.5, 7	19, 21	–	22	17	–	18	–	–	19	22	12, 8	18	14, 13	11	27	–	–	11	11
Mother age	46	39	54	53	33	53	44	49	40	50	54	54	47	52	55	36	56			44	44
Father age	46	45	50	?	33	52	45	51	40	49	57	57	53	52	55	33	62			44	44
Income	A	C	D	B	A	D	C		B	D	D	D	A		D	C				B	B
Ethnicity	Asian/W	W	W	W	W	W	W	Asian-Mix	Asian	W	Asian/Jew	Asian/Jew	W	W	W	W	W	W	W	His	His
City	Belmont	Pacifica	San Mateo	SF/ Redwood City	Portola	San Mateo	Redwood City	Daly City	SF bay	Palo Alto	SD/ Oakland	SD/ Oakland	Burlin-game	Bay area	Redwood City	South Bay	Pacifica	South Bay	South Baby	South Bay	South Bay

The adults and teenagers who are highlighted in gray were interviewed.

Diagnosed: Aut, autism; Asp, Asperger's; PDD, pervasive developmental disorder.

Income levels: A, lower income; B, lower-middle class; C, middle class; D, upper-middle class; E, upper class; F, wealthy (born in the 1990s). Participants could also include teenage or young adult siblings.

After the individual interviews and demographic surveys were completed, parents were given the opportunity to supply additional information by e-mail or phone if they felt compelled to do so. Researchers called or e-mailed questions to participants if they needed additional information.

Ferguson (2009) talks about the importance of interviews and refers to them as generated narratives and in-depth oral histories. Our interviews were open-ended and served to provide structure for our conversations. Like their children, parents could talk about whatever they felt was relevant as we discussed their child's experiences, although we also had a set of questions to work from. The protocol was used to make sure that the same topics (at minimum) were covered with all parents. Parents were initially asked about when their child was diagnosed and what types of supports were provided in elementary, middle, and high school and how these supports helped their children move forward in their development.

We used a snowball sampling approach to recruit families for our study (Goodman, 1961). After getting approval from the university's Protection of Human Subjects Committee, we asked one agency and three school staff members to recruit participants from groups of parents from their programs that provide services for adolescents. The initial participants referred other interested individuals, and volunteers gave us more names as we pursued other leads. Our participants were recruited from the San Francisco Bay area, especially Silicon Valley in California (just south of San Francisco), including San Mateo, Santa Clara, and San Francisco Counties. These areas have large populations of children with autism.

A demographic survey was given to parents before the interview that asked questions about their child's gender, age, diagnosis, school, grade, and where the child grew up. It also asked about family income. This type of information is mentioned throughout the book as we discuss the results. As described previously, we talked to 19 families, of which 12 teens agreed to interview with us. Of these families, five of the children were ethnic minorities. At least 25% were low income.

To analyze interviews, we identified patterns across the 15 cases and constructed a framework to communicate the main idea. The challenge of analyzing interviews is to make sense of a massive amount of information by identifying themes (Patton, 2002). With this type of research, categories emerge out of the data—in this case interview answers and discussions—rather than being imposed prior to the study. In the final step, the interviews are interpreted, thereby going beyond description. Interpretation means attaching significance to what is found by offering explanations, drawing conclusions, making inferences, building linkages, attaching meaning, and imposing order.

The interviews were examined from different viewpoints (Cohen et al., 2000), which aids researchers in better understanding the results. In the various chapters, our conclusions are supported by examples of actual dialogue.

Interpretations are presented, and then the quotes that support these interpretations are listed in easy-to-identify categories following the interpretations. Some of the dialogue statements are not direct quotes; extraneous verbiage was eliminated to make important points easier to understand.

Some of the questions we had before beginning the interviews included:

1. Have the schools been a source of stress or a valuable resource for the families of high-level children with autism?
2. What do parents and children with high-level autism want from the school system in the way of support?
3. What are parents' perceptions of the school support?
4. What are the children's perceptions of school support?
5. How do schools support children with autism?
6. What types of interventions/instruction, including social and academic, do families see as most successful in helping their children achieve?

Context of the Area

The interviews took place in the San Francisco Bay area, and many of the families who participated live in the Silicon Valley area, a region where a particularly large number of children with high-level autism have been born over the last 20 years. California has a large number of children born with autism, the largest in the country, but that is mainly because of the state's size. Per capita, Oregon has the largest number of children being born with autism, at 1 per 10,000 infants (StateMaster.com, 2013). Table 4.2 lists the top 10 U.S. states with the highest number of children born with autism per capita.

Table 4.2 Number of Children With Autism per State per Capita Listed in Order of Highest to Lowest for the Top 10 States

1.	Oregon	12.054 per 10,000 people
2.	Minnesota	11.374 per 10,000 people
3.	Indiana	8.664 per 10,000 people
4.	Massachusetts	7.950 per 10,000 people
5.	Maine	7.703 per 10,000 people
6.	Maryland	7.292 per 10,000 people
7.	Michigan	7.172 per 10,000 people
8.	California	6.881 per 10,000 people
9.	Connecticut	6.715 per 10,000 people
10.	Wisconsin	6.627 per 10,000 people

Source: StateMaster.com. Retrieved from: http://www.statemaster.com/graph/hea_aut_num_of_chi_wit_aut_percap-autism-number-children-per-capita.

Introducing Families

Because we cannot provide a description of all 25 people in this study, we have chosen a sample to illustrate the diversity of children and parents who talked to us so that teachers will be able to better serve other parents and their children who will follow in their footsteps. To protect the identity of the families, we are not using real names. To make the dialogue throughout the book easier to read, we have deleted a lot of extraneous verbiage, such as "y'know" and "like I said" and "like you know."

Ash was diagnosed with Asperger's. He is not like most of the children with Asperger's that we know, who are often very articulate and use pedantic speech; many are very quiet and reserved and don't seem to care what their peers think of them, or at least don't notice. Ash does notice, and when he was young, he tried to get his peers to like him. In fact, that has been one of his problems over the years. As he tried to be funny and entertain or impress his peers, he only made his teachers frustrated with disruptions. In addition, he did entertain his peers, but more often in a way where they were laughing at him and not with him. Although many children with Asperger's also have one or two eccentric obsessions, Ash's interests were more typical and tended to change over time in a typical pattern. He told the interviewers that he had always done well in school. When we first started interviewing him, we thought perhaps he was diagnosed incorrectly. Later, however, his mother told us that when he was young he demonstrated repetitive movements (stimming behaviors) and ADHD-like problems at home and at school. When he opened up about his Asperger's, he told us that he always knew there was something different about him that made him somewhat of an outsider. In his mind there was no doubt he had autism.

Daniel is 15 years old and lives close to the beach. He was diagnosed with Asperger's when he was very young. He said that he had some troubles with teachers all the way through school, but not a lot. He just thought most teachers were boring and didn't understand him. Today Daniel is a very well-spoken young man in high school. He describes himself as being able to remember those things he wants to remember but has a hard time remembering things he doesn't care about. He says he does very well in history because he can remember every date, name, and event that he reads about if he goes over it a few times. He gets straight As and Bs in general education. A lot of his peers think he is very sweet.

Gabriella is a 17-year-old Hispanic adolescent who lives with her mother and father. She has an older brother named Donny who is in college. To her family, helping Gabby is a family affair. It is not clear whether Gabby has mild or more moderate autism. She has been involved in plays and filmmaking outside of her school, and she has friends who care about her. She has trouble making friends, because she sometimes makes comments that do not relate to what is being discussed or she talks about topics that nobody cares about. Gabby's family credits the interventions and help they have received over the years, saying that she has grown and changed significantly.

Rhonda is a parent and has two boys on the spectrum; both were diagnosed later than other children with autism. One was diagnosed when he was 10, the other when he was 17. Both of her boys are now in college and doing well. Talking about the past obviously brought up some difficult times for Rhonda. She feels bad that it took so long for her older boy to get diagnosed because he suffered socially through school, even though he did well academically. Her younger boy was diagnosed earlier and she was able to get him into a private school for children with high-level special needs, and she feels like he flourished in this environment and was happy. Although she had to convince her husband, who wanted to keep autism quiet when they first found out about the diagnosis with the younger boy, she decided early on that part of her duty was to help educate other people about autism.

Donna lives in a beautiful house in a lovely neighborhood. She talks about how lucky she was that there was one resource available for her when she first found out about her son's diagnosis. She gives this group a lot of credit for helping her son at an early age and moving him on a path toward proper development. Now her son is in high school and doing well. Her biggest question is how much she should push her son. She feels sometimes that he gets a bit lazy because he can do really well in school, but she doesn't want to stress him out too much and expect too much from him because that may set him back. Her son doesn't like to talk about his autism. He regulates his behavior in a way that makes it difficult for people to recognize he has it. In this way, he appears to be typically developing. In his view, why should he have to explain autism to people and talk about it? Donna wants to respect his wishes; therefore, the family doesn't talk about autism much outside their household. But she does explain her son's challenges to teachers and other professionals.

Results

We present the results of our interviews throughout the book to provide examples and family experiences that helped us think about what teachers need to know to teach children with autism effectively. However, when organizing the interview data and analyzing quotes, some broad themes emerged from the interviews, which we discuss briefly in this chapter. These themes include (a) early intervention and diagnosis, (b) emotional issues for children, (c) instructional issues, and (d) emotional issues for parents. The children's data were a bit different, and we found four themes, including: (a) teachers, (b) bullying, (c) what they think of themselves, and (d) friends.

Parent Interviews

Early Intervention

The parents talked a lot about early intervention and diagnosis. Some of the answers related specifically to the questions that we asked, and we always started out by asking them about when the children were diagnosed and how that happened (i.e., when and in what context). We then asked what types of early interventions the children had received. Only about half of the families actually had their children diagnosed before age 5, and most of those who had an early diagnosis received early intervention. For about 50% of the group who got early intervention, those families used applied behavior analysis (ABA), and they were happy with it. One parent said it was by far the most useful intervention. Some of the other families who didn't get early diagnoses did not know what ABA was. The few people who got an early diagnosis for their child felt that early intervention was important and were very happy that it was available for them. One parent in our study made this comment:

KIMBERLY: I will tell you he made such progress quickly; there was a lot of mutual respect. They respected how I approached things, and I respected how they approached things. And we worked very creatively together, and the program didn't look like a traditional ABA program. And what I meant by that is we ended up doing a lot of social stories. Tremendous amounts of social stories because he, got a lot more creative type of play, because they could see that he responded to that.

Based on our interviews, we found that some families with little money had trouble accessing intervention resources for their young children. The parents also commented on issues they experienced in classroom placement. Because very young children with autism often experience fairly serious challenges, whether they are high functioning or not, kindergarten placement can be difficult as parents wonder whether to place their child in a general education or special education class. There seems to be no "good" answer to this question. A special education program may provide more protection and encouragement. The classes will be smaller and the teachers more experienced. However, a general education track will encourage the student to succeed in the same way his or her peers are succeeding, and most parents know their children are very capable. They know that children will watch their peers and that it will help them to be socialized. They will have access to the mainstream curriculum, which progresses at an appropriate speed for their child's intellect.

This presents the parents with a tough decision; they have to choose between placing their children in special education—where they will be more supported academically and protected by special education personnel, but also sheltered in a way that breeds dependence—or placed in general education, which may prepare them for the real world and provide more inclusive social experiences, but could cause them to suffer self-esteem-damaging rejection from other children and academic decline when teachers don't have time for individual assistance. No placement is perfect.

Emotional Issues for Children

This category of parent concerns refers to the parents' comments about their children's anxieties, depression, and phobias and their inability to do common things that other children do, such as stay over at other children's homes, which for some children with autism can be very traumatic. They talked about how their children have accepted their status as "different." At a certain age, most have accepted their status and moved on. A few actually like being different. And a few don't like it at all and try to hide their autism and pass as typical to the rest of the world. In fact, some of the children in this category don't really like being with other children with autism. It reminds them of their differences. In addition, some children with autism are more difficult for them to get along with, and so they would rather hang out with typically developing children. However, this was not true of a majority of the children we interviewed. Most of them had friends on the spectrum and believed that they were more connected to those kids than some of their typically developing friends.

Parents also spoke to us about bullying. Bullying is now understood in a much more nuanced light than it used to be. Today, being intentionally ignored, perceptively rejected, or deliberately excluded can feel as much like bullying as outright teasing. When children are bullied at school, parents of children with autism often feel as though they are not protecting their children in an appropriate way. However, school personnel sometimes see bullying differently. School personnel view subtle teasing and verbal sparring as an inevitable part of a child's life because they see it all the time. They see typically developing children fighting and calling each other names and in the next minute walking down the hall arm in arm. But children with autism tend to experience verbal sparring as bullying and can be overly sensitive about any type of negative interaction.

When children get into high school, teenagers often joke with each other and tease each other, especially boys. For example, a typically developing teen may say to a friend after a class presentation, "Wow, Scott, that presentation really blew me away" in a very sarcastic tone to suggest it was lame. Scott might snap back, "Well why don't you show me how to do it then, Sam, you're so good at these things," once again in a sarcastic tone, suggesting he expects nothing better from his friend. Neither would think much of the interaction; in fact, in some ways this is a way for the two boys to bond around their lack of grace in presenting to the class, but for children with autism this is confusing. To them, people don't criticize each other and say mean things to each other and point out each other's weaknesses unless they are mad and dislike each other. This can be a source of confusion.

Instructional Issues

The instructional issues the parents brought up are discussed at length in later chapters. Within this category, parents talked about which teachers they thought were the best and which the worst and then shared instructional strategies they thought were helpful. The one common theme shared among all the parents is that they wanted teachers who liked and cared about their children and who worked hard to help them improve. They also wanted teachers who understood and acknowledged their children's challenges while simultaneously being able to recognize and support their children's potential. In some instances they thought teachers didn't believe these children were as challenged or as capable as they were.

Emotional Issues for Parents

Finally, the parents talked about the stress they experienced trying to educate their children. Some mentioned having to fight the school system, others mentioned feeling guilty for not providing enough extra support for their children. Other parents suggested that when their children felt rejected and left out with no friends it broke their hearts. Nobody mentioned that these children were "harder to raise" than other children. But many did say that they did get a lot of help from other parents once they met other parents of children with autism and realized they were not the only people who felt the way they did or experienced the schools the way they did. They said it was easier talking to other parents than to professionals because other parents understood their experiences in ways that could only be understood when a person spends every day and every year with a child. Professionals only get glimpses of children for short periods of time. Even teachers only know these children for one year at a time, and these children sometimes change a lot over the years.

Children

Teachers and Bullying

The children had a lot to say about the topics of teachers and bullying. Every single child who talked with us said that he or she had been bullied at some time to lesser or greater degrees except one, and we talk about that more in detail in later chapters. However, only a few of them had been in physical confrontations with other children, and those were usually the children who fought back, and so it was considered fighting rather than physical bullying.

For the most part, the children interviewed for this study, with a few exceptions, seemed to have fairly good self-confidence. We identified three types of teenagers who volunteered for this study: (a) some wanted to be heard and were perhaps just a bit angry about some of their experiences, (b) some believed it was their duty to educate teachers so that other teenagers and kids could have better lives in school, and (c) some were just nice kids who wanted to help us with our project and were interested in what we were doing.

Most of the teenagers claimed they were smart, even though some of them were not doing well in school, which suggested that they recognized that they were smart in other ways. A couple of the teenagers who weren't doing well in school (or were doing well in some classes and not in others), blamed the school and/or the teachers because they said they could do better but "couldn't stand certain classes" and therefore couldn't do well in those classes. But most of the rest of the teens earned fairly high grades and seemed to be perfectionists. Many spent hours completing homework and wanted it done right. School wasn't easy for any of the teenagers interviewed, but if they studied, most were able to get good grades given the general education curriculum.

While the students talked about how well they did in school, their assessment of their own grades and achievements were much more modest than their parents' descriptions of how well they were doing. When I asked them what grades they were getting, they would give me a breakdown and explain each grade. They would say something like, "An A in this class, B in that class, A– in that class, and right now I am getting a C+ in that class unless I bring up my grade to a B . . ." and so on. In contrast, their parents would say, "Oh he gets straight As all the time." Many of the children were getting a lot of As and Bs, surpassing their parents' expectations. As far as the parents were concerned, their kids were doing a fantastic job. However, for children who are perfectionists, a person only gets a 4.0 when they get straight As.

The teenagers liked most of their teachers, with one or two exceptions. However, those exceptions remained powerful memories of the great consternation and problems these teens faced when in those teachers' classes:

REESE: They think I am mentally retarded and that is kind of offensive. So I just wanna say that right away, you definitely shouldn't treat them like as if they're a 1-year-old, it's like, if they look like they're having trouble, maybe just give them a little bit of reassurance or just give them a tiny bit of help.

DANIEL: Yeah. Basically, if we didn't answer she'd more often than not insult us or call us stupid or completely humiliate us in front of the entire class in a way.

When the teenagers described the teachers they liked, the rhetoric was much more calm and natural, with a softer tone:

REESE: There's this one teacher in particular who really sticks out to me, who was in Jr. High; her name was Ms. Smith. I definitely think that Ms. Smith was the most understanding and nice teacher and she really helped me a lot and motivated me. So I really enjoyed having her throughout middle school.

ASH: Yeah, they were nice. They kind of treat us like our age group. Didn't treat us as younger or older.

CHRIS: Well, actually all of them I liked. I liked a lot.

I: You liked all of your teachers?

CHRIS: Yeah, like yeah.

I: Was there any you didn't like?

CHRIS: No, there really wasn't.

I: OK, and you can't think of a favorite, huh?
CHRIS: Not really, no.

Friends

The teenagers had a lot to say about friends, from the difficulties they had making friends to the types of friends they liked to how they made friends to whether they had friends and where they met these other teens. Many of them had friends because over the years they had learned how to develop friendships. Some of them were involved in an agency that helps children and teenagers make friends. Some of them joined clubs at school. Some of them found niches at school, such as chess club or a specialized language class such as Chinese, some joined sports teams and got to know other teenagers there. But most of them had had trouble making friends in elementary and middle school, and most of them still had trouble reading people and understanding how to interact with others. Also, most of them still had trouble introducing themselves to strangers and to groups of strangers. And it wasn't about being shy, it was about being anxious, and part of that anxiety related to their past experiences, such as being rejected by their peers. In many subtle ways, typical peers reject children with autism. The most common rejection is to simply ignore them, not necessarily on purpose, but because they have other friends they enjoy more. And when children with autism approach them and try to make friends, these children find ways (excuses) to separate themselves from children on the spectrum who they would rather not hang out with.

Most of the teenagers I interviewed felt good about their friends. One parent said that her son still had trouble finding friends to do activities with on the weekends. What seemed to be important was for each child to find at least one friend (or more) who they could connect with emotionally and then have other friends they could have fun hanging out with on the weekends:

I: What do you like doing with your friends?
GABRIELA: Working together or hanging out sometimes, sitting with them at lunch or in class, doing homework together.
I: Seems like you have a lot of friends.
CHRIS: Yeah, most likely. I don't wanna brag, so I'm just gonna leave it at that comment.
ASH: All the teachers are pretty awesome, but I guess there's stress with like friends and stuff like that I guess, kind of being accepted.
I: What about other things you liked about school or disliked about school?
DANIEL: I liked the amount of friends that I managed to make there.
RAYNE: And I would rather do bungee jumping with no bungee cord than be friends with the "it" crowd.
REESE: I don't really understand why myself, but I don't think it's ever been easy for me to approach people like in a large crowd if they're with a bunch of their friends.

Conclusion

In this chapter, we talked about how we interviewed families, who these families were, and what they said about how schools can more effectively work with children with high-level autism. In later chapters we discuss more topics addressed by both the parents and the children. For example, in Chapter 13 we present comments about what parents and teenagers really liked about teachers and their suggestions for improvement. In Chapter 15 the parents talk about whether and how they were supported. In the last chapter parents tell us what makes them proud of their children.

Ultimately, the parents all agreed that classroom teachers made the biggest impact on their children's progress over the years. The school environment, whether it was flexible and supportive of the children's special needs, was also important. For the children, their self-knowledge and ability to reflect on their situation was also considered impressive and important for their future success, and their help in solving the autism puzzle was much appreciated.

References

Bogdan, R., & Biklen, S. (2006). *Qualitative research for education: An introduction to theory and methods.* Upper Saddle River, NJ: Pearson.

Bronfenbrenner, U. (1986). Ecology of the family as a context for human development: Research perspectives. *Developmental Psychology, 26*(6), 723–742.

Cohen, L., Manion, L., & Morrison, K. (2000) *Research methods in education.* London: Routledge.

Ferguson, P. M. (2009). The doubting dance: Contributions to a history of parent/professional interactions in early 20th century America. *Research and Practice for Persons with Severe Disabilities, 33,* 48–58.

Goodman, L. A. (1961). Snowball sampling. *Annals of Mathematical Statistics, 32*(1), 148–170.

Miles, M. B., & Huberman, A. M. (1994). Drawing valid meaning from qualitative data: Toward a shared craft. *Educational Researcher, 13*(5), 20–30.

Patton, M. Q. (2002). *Qualitative evaluation and research methods* (3rd ed.). Thousand Oaks, CA: Sage.

StateMaster.com. Number of children with autism (per capita) (most recent) by state. Retrieved from http://www.statemaster.com/graph/hea_aut_num_of_chi_wit_aut_percap-autism-number-children-per-capita

Chapter Five
Cognition and Information Processing

Today, autism is most commonly associated with social problems, and rightfully so; all children with ASD have social challenges that affect every aspect of their lives, including academics, mental health, and potential for success. Whether these children can socialize appropriately will, in part, determine whether they will be able to function independently and work as adults. However, just as socialization for these children affects every aspect of their lives, every aspect of their lives affects their ability to socialize. There are reciprocal relationships among social impairments, communication, academic success, and cognition. Therefore, it is important to attend to the whole child, including cognition and information processing, things that are commonly overlooked.

Exploring the Myths

In this chapter, we examine some common beliefs about autism to separate truth from misperception. Do children with autism really have great memories? If that is the case, then why do so many struggle with academic content? Are parents of children with autism really more often engineers? As we try to separate myth from reality, we also provide suggestions on how teachers might focus on strengths rather than deficits when working with children on the spectrum.

Children With Autism and Technology

Technology Geeks?

The idea that some children with autism are technology geeks is not just a myth; it is a theory that was proposed by Simon Baron-Cohen, a well-known researcher in England. Baron-Cohen and his colleagues have proposed interesting theories to explain the affinity of many autistic students towards technology

(Baron-Cohen, 2008, 2009; Baron-Cohen et al., 2011). First, he suggests that there is a mating process in action, called "assortative mating," that brings people together with similar traits and is meant to help our society develop workers who have the complex analytical skills needed to succeed in a high-tech industry—for example a marriage between a computer whiz and a research scientist. Some of these people may be slightly socially awkward—the classic profile of the "computer geek." According to Baron-Cohen, the "geeks," although not fully autistic themselves, may be carrying some of the genes that contribute to autism.

Furthermore, Baron-Cohen suggests that these scientific parents of autistic children can be labeled as "systemizers." People who are systemizers are interested in systems because they prefer to follow rules that have predictable outcomes (Wheelwright et al., 2006). They are interested in repeatable, law-governed patterns. At the other end of the spectrum, someone who is an "empathizer" would rather focus on events that would be understood through the actions of people. The systemizer might look at a tie and notice the symmetry in the pattern of the tie; the empathizer might instead notice a soup stain and wonder if the person has a low regard for personal appearance (Ross, 2006).

Finally, because boys are far more likely to be autistic than girls, Baron-Cohen has also suggested that autism could be a kind of "extreme maleness," an amplification of a slight natural bias in many boys favoring analytical skills rather than social abilities (Baron-Cohen, 2002).

Parents as Engineers

Baron-Cohen and his colleagues have completed at least two studies that support his theories. He surveyed a number of parents of children with autism and found that a larger percentage of parents of children with autism are engineers compared to the general population (Baron-Cohen, Wheelwright, Stott, Bolton, & Goodyer, 1997). According to this study, 12.5% of fathers of children with autism were engineers, compared with only 5% of fathers of children without autism. Likewise, 21.2% of grandfathers of children with autism had been engineers, compared with only 2.5% of grandfathers of children without autism. The pattern appeared on both sides of the family. Women who had a child with autism were more likely to have a father who had been an engineer—and, of course, they were more likely to have married an engineer. The study did not look at the mother's occupations because too many of the women were not working.

In another study, Baron-Cohen looked at a large number of children in an area that was considered a technology hub in the Netherlands (Baron-Cohen, 2012a). He looked specifically at Eindhoven, a city in the Netherlands that has been compared to the Silicon Valley in the United States. He compared the number of children with autism in that city with the number of children with autism in Haarlem and Utrecht. He found that official rates of diagnosed autism among children enrolled in the Eindhoven schools were more than twice as high as those from Haarlem and Utrecht. In Eindhoven, the ASD rate was 2.3%, far higher than those in the other two cities (0.6% and 0.8%, respectively). The rate of the more narrowly defined classic autism was also higher. However, two control disorders (used as a comparison to see if just the autism factors were different)—dyspraxia and ADHD—were no different. The study was extensive; 369 schools took part, with over 60,000 children.

It should not come as any surprise that some engineers were not thrilled with the theory that they are geeks with autistic genes, or that women are emotional and not as systematic as men. A number or researchers have attempted to debunk Baron-Cohen and his colleague's controversial theories before they become widely accepted as absolute truth. These ideas are very preliminary, with few articles to provide evidence for their accuracy and other research to suggest they are wrong (e.g., Morsanyi, Primi, Handley, Chiesi, & Galli, 2012).

Do Children With Autism Have Savant Characteristics?

It is true that the populations of children and adults with autism have a higher percentage of savants than the normal population. A recent study of about 100 adults with autism shows that one-third have skills that stand out, both in comparison with their other abilities and with the skills of the general population. Previous studies put the prevalence of savantism in autistic people at around 1 in 10 (Howlin, Goode, Hutton, & Rutter, 2009). Savant capabilities are extraordinary skills in a specific area, often combined with lower than average abilities in other areas of development. The idea, however, that most savants have severe autism, or are "idiot savants," is not accurate. Very few savants have IQs below 50, and almost all of those tested for IQ have scores on some subtests in the normal range. A savant is simply a person who has a discrepancy between his or her performance in one area and his or her general level of functioning, for example, a child with an IQ of 70–80 who struggles in school but can sit down at a piano and start playing Chopin after hearing one song on the radio. Savant skills are more common in boys than girls by a 6 to 1 ratio, as compared to an approximate 4 to 1 ratio of boys to girls who have autism (Treffert, 2009).

The most commonly reported savant skills are in the areas of mathematics, music, art, and memory (e.g., for dates, places, routes, or facts). Less frequently reported areas are "pseudo-verbal" skills (hyperlexia or facility with foreign languages), coordination skills, and mechanical aptitude. Hyperlexia is the precocious ability to read words without prior training in learning to read, typically before the age of 5. Such children often can decode but have a harder time with comprehension; oftentimes, they can also spell very well.

It is important to remember that autism, particularly in the area of cognition, is characterized by uneven rather than simply delayed development. This means that it is common for a child with ASD to show splinter skills, appearing to be highly capable in some tasks (i.e., math computation) but unable to follow simple routines independently or to carry on a conversation. These discrepancies in skill development should be viewed as an opportunity to build on a child's strengths and extra abilities in one area while assisting him or her to improve or function independently in other areas. A talent for soccer, karate, or dance can provide a typical child with a sense of belonging and prestige. A splinter skill can do the same for a child with autism. It can also provide that child's parents with a clearer sense that their child, too, can shine.

In our study, we found that many of the teenagers we interviewed had some special abilities; for example, a few of them told us that they had very good memory, but only for things that they thought were interesting and really wanted to know and remember:

I: Do you feel like you have a good memory?
DANIEL: When I want to use it. If I don't wanna use it, I don't remember things.
REESE: It's not like I'm completely not interested anymore, it's just that I think I've kind of grown out of it a little bit.
I: Do you still have that kind of memory?
REESE: I think I could. I think it's very likely that I do.

Using a child's savant-like skills can be an important way to help enhance a child's self-esteem. Showing other children that the child has important intellectual gifts demonstrates that although the child is different, and at times might need directions repeated, that he or she can achieve where others might struggle. This provides credibility to the idea that children "think differently" and have both strengths and challenges. Teachers should make sure and emphasize these children's strengths so that everyone, including their parents, has a chance to see these strengths. Typically developing children can be very impressed with special abilities; such abilities should not be hidden, but instead promoted as the child learns, in front of his or her peers.

Recently, Baron-Cohen and colleagues suggested that "savantism may be nothing more than the end-product of good systemizing" (Baron-Cohen et al., 2007, p. 243). However, links between skills in music, art, memory, and systemizing performance have yet to be established (Baron-Cohen et al., 2007). Savantism could also be related to the autistic child's ability to focus on one topic for long periods of time and to be able to go over the same topics repeatedly without getting bored. Baron-Cohen is interested in investigating whether specific ASD-like traits are associated with special abilities. So far his results indicate that nonsocial ASD-like traits, such as repetitive and restricted interests and activities, are showing the strongest association with special abilities (Baron-Cohen et al., 2007).

Vital, Ronald, Wallace, and Happe (2009) agree that it is possible that some autistic children's obsessions are associated with special abilities through practice and repetition. Children with autism have the capability to practice something over and over without pause for hours, days, months, and years; typically developing children would find this to be almost unbearable. According to Vital and colleagues (2009), "detail-focus" was a better predictor of special ability than was "special interests" or "insistence on sameness," which may reflect obsession-like behavior. Parental report of attention to, and memory for, detail increased more than twofold the likelihood of reported special abilities. This finding, if replicated, might support the suggestion that special skills result from a cognitive style or bias towards featural versus configural processing (focusing on details rather than the whole), which may contribute to understanding the increased incidence of special abilities among this population. Thus, some children with autism tend to process information in detailed parts as opposed to a whole, sometimes called weak central coherence, and this might be what helps them in their savant or savant-like splinter characteristics.

Weak Central Coherence

Weak central coherence, no matter the name, seems to provide both advantages and disadvantages. It is the ability to synthesize an array of information, such as verbal and nonverbal cues in conversation. In other words, some people may say that children who have weak central coherence "can't see the forest for the trees." The flip side of an inability "to see the forest for the trees" is being very, very good at seeing the trees (Wolman, 2010).

Frith (1989), one of the first researchers to study weak coherence theory, suggests that it is based on an understanding of how information processing typically occurs in most people. In their interactions with the environment, or in recalling information, most individuals will recall an overall impression or the gist of something, such as a story or a conversation. Individuals on the autism spectrum tend to be more, sometimes overly, focused on details; this can often be at the expense of understanding the actual meaning or appreciating the nature of a situation or context. The basis of this theory is that this detailed processing is suggestive of weak central coherence (Roth, 2010).

The word "weak" in connection with central coherence does not necessarily mean inferior. Weakness in this situation can be an asset. Some postulate that it can be useful to filter out external stimuli if a person is writing an e-mail in a noisy coffee shop or searching for a camouflaged insect in a rainforest. Recasting weak central coherence as attention to detail and resistance to distraction suggests a mode of thought that could have advantages (Wolman, 2010). The notion of weak coherence as a processing style, rather than deficit, lends itself to a continuum approach in that weak coherence is seen as one end of a continuum, and people with ASD are placed at a more extreme end of this continuum. By contrast, the opposite cognitive style, strong coherence, might be characterized as a tendency to process concepts and the big picture at the expense of attention and memory for detail and structural form. In this way, the person with weak coherence may be poor at seeing the bigger picture and the person with strong coherence may be a terrible proofreader. Because these ideas are part of a working hypothesis, we need to recall that these styles represent only biases and it is possible that an individual with strong coherence can focus attention on details such as remembering unconnected facts for an exam by force of will and determination. In addition, the individual with weak coherence can, by necessity, extract the main ideas of a long speech (Happe & Frith, 2006).

A converging body of evidence suggests that weak coherence may be the result of reduced connectivity throughout the brain (Happe & Frith, 2006). Happe and Frith explain several variations of these findings. They propose that the brain develops without normal cross-talk between regions, and that weak coherence emerges due to lack of synchronization of neural activity necessary to bind parts into wholes.

As a cognitive style, weak central coherence is a contender for the aspect of autism that is transmitted genetically and characterizes the relatives of individuals with autism. One study is currently comparing cognitive style in parents of children with autism, with dyslexia, and without developmental disorder (Vital et al., 2009). Some of the preliminary results suggest that parents, and especially fathers, of children with autism show significantly superior performance on tasks favoring local processing: they excel at an (unsegmented) block design and at accurately judging visual illusions. They are also more likely than fathers in the other groups to give local completions to sentence stems such as, "The sea tastes of salt and . . . ?" (pepper). In all respects, these fathers resemble individuals with autism, but their detail-focused cognitive style is usually an asset, not a deficit. These initial findings fit well with the work of Baron-Cohen et al. (1997), which showed that fathers and maternal grandfathers of children with autism are possibly overrepresented in professions such as engineering. However, although they explain their results in terms of superior "folk physics" (intuitive understanding of physical systems), the hypothesis of weak central coherence predicts that people with autism and their relatives will be characterized by expertise only with those systems where focus on detail is an advantage. Weak central coherence also stretches beyond the visual-spatial domain, and predicts piecemeal processing in verbal tasks not easily accounted for by superior "folk physics."

In might seem counterintuitive, but those children who had more special abilities showed significantly more ASD-like traits than those without such abilities (Vital et al., 2009). Specifically, special abilities were more strongly associated with restricted and repetitive interests and activities. What might the association between nonsocial traits of autism and special abilities signify? One obvious possibility is that their obsessions might be associated with special abilities through practice and repetition. The type of nonsocial traits most strongly associated with parental reports of special abilities suggest a link to weak coherence theory, or what some call featural information processing style or, more simply, a focus on detail. (Vital et al., 2009). So, although consistent practice and intense interest are also elements of the tendency toward obsession, detail focus, or weak coherence theory, was the better predictor of special abilities.

Today, Baron-Cohen (2012b) has moved away from his earlier research and has started looking specifically at empathy and its relationship to cruelty. One of his findings is that children who had more testosterone in their amniotic fluid when they were in utero had less empathy when they were older. He theorizes that part of what makes a person cruel is lack of empathy. At times he has also characterized adults with autism as having zero empathy, but he does admit that adults with autism are not prone to violence or cruelty, and so therefore uses them as a counterexample. He, therefore, admits that other factors must affect what makes people cruel, including how people are treated as children. According to his research, women are slightly less cruel than men.

In our study, some of the children seemed less interested in (or caring toward) other people, whereas others were overly concerned about how others thought of them. Some were smart, and others struggled with school. Some engaged in repetitive behaviors; others did not. Some were very funny and responded to humor, and some seemed to have no sense of humor at all. Some found ways to make friends, and some had very few friends. Some had behavior problems in schools, and some were the sweetest kids you would ever want to know. Some were incredibly sensitive to the point that they would cry at sad movies, and some seemed incredibly self-centered (and felt guilty about it). As we interviewed families, we did not come across children with no empathy, quite the opposite. Below, we have presented a few comments from children with autism that suggest they have empathy, both intellectual and emotional:

I: OK, and how do you like ASC, what do you like about the program?

DANIEL: It lets me interact with those who are similar to me. I understand all their pasts and we can assist each other.

I: Do you have advice for how teachers should work with children on the spectrum?

DANIEL: If they're actually struggling? One thing I would say is encourage them to question the material if they don't understand it? I understand that some high-functioning autistic people could be a little scared of asking questions 'cuz they don't wanna look like morons. At least that's in my case. But I encourage, if you don't understand something, just ask whatever you need to ask. It'll help you out in the long run.

RAYNE: I also cried when I saw *Les Miserables.*

I: Oh yeah?

RAYNE: Yeah, I'm proud to say I cried.

I: And why was that?

RAYNE: Because so many innocent people died and to see how old they were, is just like, oh my God, sick and twisted people. And the officers are sick and twisted, which reminds me of Batman, Year 1, because the police in there suck butts, like the teachers.

I: Have you guys always been able to talk so openly and be so self-reflective?

LINDA: Yes, we don't talk heart to heart often because you know sibling relationships are often awkward talking heart to heart, but if we need to we can.

I: Do you find it helpful?

LINDA: Ya, granted, I don't know any other way of living.

I: Is it because she understands your Asperger's and your autism?

Rayne: Well she understands that I want a life.

I: Oh, so she understands you just being a teenage girl too?

RAYNE: Yeah.

ASH: I don't think anyone can really notice now (his autism).

ASH: Because my mind is developed more.

I: Do you think you developed out of it, kind of changed?

ASH: Even though I still kind of do some autistic things at home, I kinda feel safe there.

I: And it's conscious, or it's really easy?

ASH: It's easy just to be like, "Wow, I have to think of this," just act how people expect you to act outside and inside, do whatever.

MASON: Kids don't pick on you in high school, most so called bullies just don't really care anymore. They just wanna do their own thing. And like be in their inner circle. And it's really easy because some kids I haven't really seen in years since like in elementary school. I got to know them a little more. One of my friends, he really grew his hair long like a rock star and surprisingly enough, most of the kids didn't really change that much compared to elementary school.

I: How can teachers help kids with Asperger's or autism succeed?

REESE: With kids with Asperger's and autism, well first of all, I'd like to say right off the bat that it's really important to not treat them like they're mentally retarded; don't treat them too much like they're babies because that's actually kind of offensive. Because to be honest, that kind of happened to me sometimes, and it kind of makes me feel like they're underestimating my intelligence.

Adults with autism (in the past) may have demonstrated less cognitive empathy, as measured in some surveys, but for children with high-level autism who are growing up today the concept of empathy seems perhaps more complex.

For children with autism to understand how someone else may seem different or stand out in a crowd seems easier for some of them to recognize than for them to recognize these traits in themselves. This is why, for example, using video modeling to either provide social skill development or to model appropriate behavior as a conversation starter can be a place to begin talking to children about their own behaviors or actions. It is easier for them to see how someone in a video is acting differently than to start all at once admitting they need to change. For children to reflect on their behavior, they need to be ready; many children with autism seem very sensitive to criticism and upset when someone points out how different they are in comparison to typically developing children. Some children with autism, especially when they are younger, do not want to be different, so they need their differences pointed out delicately. Below are some comments from the parents in our study:

DAWN: So, it was a very difficult transition and he didn't wanna go to this special ed school because he immediately saw that the kids were, either like him, or more pronounced. And he immediately was aware of that, and he didn't understand why he had to be there.

MARIA: So the psychiatrist, she says, "We need to address the depression first."

MARIA: They diagnosed him with Asperger's.

MARIA: Why was he depressed? Lack of friends?

MARIA: Him feeling different, too.

DONNA: Yeah, he just resented being different. Yeah, because I think he understands it enough now to know that there's other kids like him. I think he felt singled out.

Memory

When assessing memory, researchers often talk about different types of memory skills. For example, Williams, Goldstein, and Minshew (2006) looked at complex visual memory, complex verbal stimuli, associative learning ability, verbal working memory, special memory, and recall. Findings from that study suggest that the profile of memory abilities in children with autism is substantially different from that of typically developing children (Williams et al., 2006). Children with autism had poor memory for both complex visual (design memory and picture memory) and complex verbal (sentence memory and story memory) information, with relatively intact associative learning ability (sound/symbol), verbal working memory (number/letter), and recognition memory (story memory). Spatial working memory (temporary storage) of the children with autism was also impaired relative to the control group; however, spatial memory, as defined as memory for location (visual learning), was not. Delayed recall was not generally different for children on the spectrum, with the exception of thematic verbal material as assessed by recall of stories. The researchers concluded that children with autism had a very different memory ability structure from that demonstrated by the typically developing control group as well as the norming sample of children used to standardize the test.

Finally, we ask, is memory better in children with autism? According to formal research, children with autism have memory that is not as well developed in some areas as their typical peers, whereas some areas of memory are the same. However, as suggested by the participants in our study, it is possible that children with autism simply have a better memory for things that truly interest them.

Interval Timing: What Is It, and Why Do We Care?

Autism is associated with some challenges, including perceptual delay, that affect motor coordination (clumsiness). Some parents told us that their children used to stare at clocks for hours as they watched the minutes tick away, seemingly fascinated with the passage of time or with the clock itself. Other children become anxious with transitions, especially when they are in the middle of finishing a task they want to finish. Sometimes it seems as if time has no meaning for these children or, conversely, that it is extremely important and when they are given time limits it can be very stressful. These children cannot understand why they should start math when they haven't finished their science project. The idea of putting aside one project before the other is complete can cause a tantrum.

Other children with autism might tell a teacher what time it is every 30 minutes. The teacher assumes the child is bored and wants to move on, but in reality this particular child has an obsession with time. Rather than getting irritated, the teacher should make that child a time keeper for the class so that the child can use the obsession in a productive way.

Children with autism have enough issues with time for us to recognize that there is a problem to be solved here. Some scientists think that these quirks may be related to abnormal neuronal timing and clock-gene mechanisms (Welsh, Ahn, & Placantonakis, 2005; Wimpory, Nicholas, & Nash, 2002). In other words, the brain's internal clock is a bit off due to the fact that the genes meant to run this clock are not working in the same way they do in typically developing children.

Even though phenomenological observations and anecdotal reports suggest atypical time processing in individuals with ASD (Zukauskas, Silton, & Assumpcao, 2009; Boucher, 2001), very few studies have investigated interval timing, and those that have often report contradictory findings.

Falter, Elliott, and Bailey (2012) sought to clarify which timing processes functioned atypically in children on the spectrum and whether these processes were related to the typical autism profile. They looked at interval timing in 18 individuals with autism. Their findings suggest that children with autism have reduced sensitivity for temporal interval differences. The researchers conclude that these individuals have a decreased sensitivity for the perception of time.

This does not mean that children with autism think slower; it means that their internal clock is different than that in children without autism, which may explain why some children are obsessed with time and other children's savant-like splinter abilities are associated with time. One way our bodies use interval timing is in knowing when to eat; our bodies have an internal clock that tells us when we are supposed to eat. A person who has problems with his or her internal clock may not know when to start or stop eating. The time intervals involved can also be very short; for example, it might be more difficult for a child to catch a ball if his or her internal clock is off just a fraction of a second. Some children with autism may be very good at catching balls. When we speak of a child with autism's internal clock perhaps being less sensitive than a typically developing child's, it does not mean that the child is inferior, it just means the child is different, especially given the way some neurotypicals focus on time.

Cognition Style Meant to Explore and Discover?

Another way that children with autism may think differently and benefit from that difference is in how they make choices about repetitive tasks. In one study, researchers wanted to find out if individuals with autism had a cognitive style that facilitated exploration and discovery (Yechiam, Arshavsky, Shamay-Tsoory, Yaniv, & Aharon, 2010). The researchers were interested in what motivated children and adults with autism to make certain types of choices. In the past, experimenters have used a repeated-choice task instrument to assess for exploration, discovery, and motivation. What is an example of a repeated-choice task? People often use repeated-choice tasks when gambling. For example, if a person is given a choice to use a certain slot machine when gambling and then loses, some would keep using the same machine over and over, hoping that sooner or later he or she would win with this same machine ("I've got to win off this machine sometime!"). Others might change machines every time they lose a game (a completely different strategy). This would be an example of a repeated-choice task, and the question in this case would be, "What strategy do you use to try to win those gambling dollars from your slot machines?"

Recent studies have reported a tendency of individuals on the spectrum to change their choices when making choices on a repeated task (Yechiam et al., 2010). Using formal reinforcement learning models, the researchers compared three possible explanations for this pattern of change. The first explanation was that individuals on the spectrum made choices at random. This was consistent with the idea that complex tasks required generalization skills and posed a challenge to people with autism because of their difficulty in recognizing relationships between features of the task and identifying the general patterns that form. A second explanation was that the adaptation process of individuals on the spectrum involved more trial-and-error exploration. This argument was consistent with findings that showed that adolescents on the spectrum rated higher on perseverance and drive for perfection (e.g., Ashburner, Ziviani, & Rodger, 2008; Gillberg, 2002). A third, related, explanation of difference in exploration was qualitative rather than quantitative in that while individuals on the spectrum explored more than typically developing individuals, it was possible that their exploration did not conform to a conventional reinforcement pattern because of their adaptation process. To test this last possibility, a more conventional model of reinforcement was compared with two new models of reinforcement based on the assumption that exploration, and not the pursuit of outcomes, was the main incentive motivating the learning process for individuals on the spectrum.

Yechiam and his colleagues (2010) reported that for the typical group the likelihood of switching choices after gains was 56%, and after losing it was 68%. This increase in switching choices following their losses was a significant difference. For the spectrum group, the likelihood of switching following gains was 74%, and after losing it was 73%. Thus, the switching likelihood for spectrum participants was almost equal following gains and losses, indicating that they were unaffected by previous losses in their switching decisions. This finding is consistent with the third alternative: that adaptation implies that outcomes matter less in sampling decisions for individuals with autism.

It also shows that participants on the spectrum were just as predictable as typically developing individuals. So the theory that individuals on the spectrum were more unpredictable was not upheld in this study. In addition, there were no significant differences between the spectrum and typical groups in exploring. This indicates that what appears to be driving the differences between individuals on the spectrum and the control sample was not just one psychological parameter, such as the extent of the exploration. Rather, the adaptive learning style appeared to be different in most of the spectrum participants, with exploration replacing value or reward as the main driver in the motivation to sample choice alternatives. This demonstrates that individuals on the spectrum have a tendency to continuously shift between choice alternatives in complex repeated-choice tasks and that some individuals on the spectrum have a form of adaptation characterized as being less sensitive to the immediate incentive structure and by an intensive exploratory search of the available alternatives (Yechiam et al., 2010). Their findings also suggest that individuals on the spectrum show low reward dependence, which denotes heightened self-directedness, which has been demonstrated in other studies (e.g., Anckarsäter et al., 2006; Sizoo, van den Brink, van Eenige, & van der Gaag, 2009; Soderstrom, Rastam, & Gillberg, 2002). Additionally, a number of studies have found that individuals with autism are more distracted by novelty than typically developing individuals (e.g., Sokhadze et al., 2009) and that they have trouble processing novel information (e.g., Gomot et al., 2006). These previous studies suggest that the exploratory adaptation patterns of people with autism represent a drive towards solving a problem, rather than seeking novel situations.

Brain Imaging

Some scientists have questioned how ASD might result in differences on brain scans of individuals with and without autism. The technologies of the late twentieth century provided anatomical displays and gross electrical measures (EEGs) in which children with autism were shown to have relatively "normal" brain anatomy and indistinguishable EEGs. However, newer technologies have changed what we know about the brain, brain activity, and areas of activation during varied tasks between individuals with and without autism. Within the past decade, neuroscience research has enabled functional brain imaging as well as views of brain pathways during activity (Minshew & Keller, 2010). MRI and functional brain imaging technology now points to marked developmental differences in the brain connections of individuals with autism. Researchers have reported findings that support the cortical underconnectivity theory of autism (Just, Cherkassky, Keller, & Minshew, 2004). Simply put, this theory maintains that individuals with autism have trouble connecting sight to sound, sound to meaning, or one thought with another because the long fiber tracts that process and integrate complex information across brain territories are not developing in a typical way. Wass (2011) suggests that the short fiber tracts are overconnected and overused in individuals with autism, possibly explaining why these individuals demonstrate stereotypical, but not very useful, repetitive behaviors. This more recent body of research suggests that the heterogeneity of behaviors and learning problems that we observe in students with autism are not so much variable as they are unique. The specific repetitive behaviors we observe, although different from child to child, likely still represent the same underlying problem, that the integrative highways needed for most learning are scuttled by short traffic circles with no off-ramps (Wass, 2011). According to Wass (2011), it appears that a student with ASD now enters school with some or most of the longer highways underdeveloped so that the child's brain detours incoming information to something akin to cul-de-sacs or circular, unending off-ramps. Traditional approaches to education simply cannot work because the information cannot be processed adequately (Wass, 2011).

Wass (2011) and his contemporaries suggest that there are two lines of research for investigating interventions designed to examine brain development in children on the autism spectrum. One approach is in use at the University of California–Davis MIND Institute. It is attempting to identify children at risk for autism at an early age in hopes of providing maternal guidance in ways to play and interact with young children to stimulate development of these long fiber tracts (Vismara & Rogers, 2008). Parents have a natural tendency to do things with toddlers that the toddlers enjoy and to avoid activities that they do not enjoy. A toddler at risk for ASD, for example, may enjoy electronics more than blocks or inanimate toys, such as trains, and may also be less interested in toys such as stuffed animals. That same toddler may also reject being read to or being cuddled. However, these are the very activities that the underconnectivity theory suggests are necessary to build the longer integrative neural pathways. By teaching parents how to encourage activities the child is not drawn to, but nonetheless needs, these researchers hope that children at risk will develop in a more typical way. If this research is useful and demonstrates success, it could have a powerful effect on approaches toward early intervention.

The other intervention is a different application of neuroscience and neuroimaging in relation to interventions developed for school-aged children. Within the past 15 years, neuroscientists at University of California–San Francisco have been designing and revising game-like exercises specifically designed to drive development of the long left hemisphere fiber tracts essential for language, reading, and mathematics (Merzenich et al., 1996). They have developed a suite of 11 programs—the Fast ForWord® family of products marketed by Scientific Learning Corp.—that systematically targets those long fiber specific pathways through entertaining games. The Fast ForWord programs also include unique speech stimulation exercises that are acoustically enhanced to conform to the perceptual needs of children with auditory processing problems. In addition, all exercises are performed on a computer, which is very compelling to children on the autism spectrum.

Comparing Boys and Girls

We looked at one last study to see what researchers were doing to compare boys and girls with autism, because boys and girls seem to be very different in the way their autism symptoms manifest. One study we found indicated that girls and women with ASD show better emotionalizing in terms of multiple conceptual tracking capacities and foresighted planning than males with ASD, and this was associated with fewer stereotypic behaviors and interests (Bölte, Duketis, Poustka, & Holtmann, 2011).

Bölte and colleagues (2011) found that males were superior on visual attention to detail (ATTD) in terms of visual spatial performance. This study can only be considered as the start of work addressing cognition in females versus males with ASD. The identified association between emotionalizing and stereotypic behaviors and interests is indeed one area of interest. The study was not able to distinguish whether these cognitive and clinical variables are driving each other or whether they represent a broader underlying neurological sex difference. The study was limited to higher-functioning individuals, which in most ASD samples are not evenly distributed among girls and boys (Bölte et al., 2011). There are marked differences between boys and girls with ASD, and researchers are just now starting to look at these differences and to explore why boys and girls may be so different along the spectrum.

Intelligence Testing

Children with autism, whether higher functioning or more challenged, generally take longer to hit milestones such as talking and becoming toilet-trained. When they are adults, many still struggle to fit into society. The mainstream medical view of autism is that it represents a form of developmental brain damage.

WISC-III

However, is it true that children with high-level autism have lower IQs, or do some simply have processing problems? Are they smarter than other children, similar, or challenged intellectually? Children with autism have been tested for intelligence with a number of different types of intelligence measures, most notably the WISC-III, the third revision of psychologist David Wechsler's classic 1949 test for children, which was modeled after army intelligence tests developed during World War I (Wechsler, 1949). Researchers have tested children and adults with autism for many reasons, including educational, vocational, and clinical diagnostic applications. Intelligence tests have been used in autism research to separate high-functioning from low-functioning autism, for differential diagnostic purposes within the autism spectrum, and, perhaps most significantly, for delineating the pattern of cognitive function in autism. The problem is that it is not possible to be sure these tests are valid. In fact, we are not even sure that intelligence tests are valid for any children. For nearly 100 years researchers and psychologists have been using standardized intelligence testing, and some have referred to it as one of psychology's greatest successes. It is one of the field's most continuing and widely used inventions. However, intelligence testing has often been accused of unfairly stratifying test-takers by race, gender, class, and culture and of minimizing the importance of creativity, character, and practical know-how. In this way, it promulgates the idea that people are born with an unchangeable amount of intellectual potential that determines their success in life.

Stanford–Binet

The Stanford–Binet has also been used to assess the intelligence of children with autism. Coolican, Bryson, and Zwaigenbaum (2008) first looked at the cognitive profiles of the entire sample of participants and found that autistic children's nonverbal IQs were higher than their verbal IQs. With regards to the nonverbal subtests, the main finding was that children with ASD demonstrated relative strengths in fluid reasoning, quantitative reasoning, and visual-spatial processing skills (versus knowledge and working memory skills). On the verbal subtests, the main finding was a relative strength in quantitative reasoning skills.

These researchers then looked at the cognitive profiles of each diagnostic subgroup (Coolican et al., 2008). The researchers compared children with Asperger's, autism disorder, and PDD-NOS. The pattern of the children's performance between the diagnostic subgroups was surprisingly similar. The large variability in subtest performance within the various subgroups was consistent with the possibility that there is as much, or even more, differences within each diagnostic subgroup as between subgroups.

Raven's Progressive Matrices

Raven's Progressive Matrices and Vocabulary Scales are used in the assessment of general cognitive abilities in children and adults. The Progressive Matrices provide an assessment of nonverbal ability, an important feature in ethnically diverse populations. However, children with autism do not present the same results consistently. When researchers use the Raven's Progressive Matrices, children with autism score much higher than when they are given the WISC-III, and these two tests should correspond to each other to be valid. In fact, in a study by Dawson, Soulieres, Gernsbacher, and Mottron (2007), children with autism scored on average 30% higher (and up to 70% higher) on the Raven's Progressive Matrices as opposed to the WISC-III. A similar contrast was observed when a sample of autistic adults was compared with a sample of typical adults (Caron, Mottron, Berthiaume, & Dawson, 2006). Dawson and colleagues were some of the first to challenge the mainstream view by examining the association between autism and low IQ. The researchers concluded that intelligence has been underestimated in people with autism.

How Can Teachers Use This Unique Cognitive Profile to Improve Instruction?

In an educational context, a test that focuses on nonverbal ability is used as an indication of a student's ability to understand and assimilate novel information independent of language skills. Scores on these tests can indicate a student's ability to learn new material in a wide range of school subjects based on his or her current level of functioning (DeThorne & Schaefer, 2004). These tests might require recognition of similarities, analogies, and patterns in unfamiliar designs. For example, if a person has better nonverbal skills, he or she might be better at constructing maps (travel direction, distance in miles), playing computer games (players must navigate from one area to another using grid references, distances, or directions), making models (visual analysis, spatial judgment, and manual dexterity), and sketching and drawing (ability to estimate lengths, heights, angles, and relative proportions).

How can this type of information be used to help children? If children are better at nonverbal learning tasks, this suggests that there may be more understanding and ability than we understand given the child's expressive language abilities. It is important never to underestimate a child's intelligence and to always explain social situations, as well as content, before making assumptions that these children do not understand what you are saying. Sometimes when you talk to the child it may seem as though he is not paying attention, and then a few days later he will repeat back to you what you told him a few days ago.

After getting to know a child on the spectrum and making sure that this particular child is truly good at systemizing, better at seeing details rather than the big picture, or has an interesting splinter skill, how can the teacher use these strengths to the child's advantage? Knowing a child's strengths and challenges is important. Parents know a child's strengths and weaknesses, so it is impressive to them when teachers understand these details.

It is important to use these skills to elevate the child's status in front of the other children. It might not seem that important, but a lot of children with autism have social anxiety because they think there is something wrong with them in comparison to the other children around them. They think they are not as smart, as talented, as liked, or as fun to be around as other children. Every time a teacher holds up something a child with autism does as being special, it tells other children in the class that this child is on equal footing with the typically developing children, the child is just "different," as everyone keeps saying.

When doing group work, let the child with autism do the work he or she is good at, during peer interaction is not the time to help children get better at their worst skills. It holds the other children back, which embarrasses the child with autism and frustrates everyone in the group. When interacting socially with the rest of the group, children with autism should always be doing their best work so that everyone can see that they can do good work. If a child is good at picking out details, that should be his job. If the child is not so good at seeing the bigger picture, then maybe that is something to do on his own in a short paper that he works on with the teachers and other staff. Be aware that if you ask a child with autism to write a summary of a story plot, you might get more about the details of the environment, which is what may have been more interesting to him than the plot. Who cares about Alice if the story was about Wonderland? It is important to understand that this is common for a child on the spectrum, not something to simply mark as "wrong," leaving the child confused and upset.

It is important for teachers to focus on children's strengths, especially their splinter skills and their interests, as opposed to their deficits. Parents of typical children do not expect their children to do math at the exclusion of everything else when their children dislike math and are not good at it. In contrast, parents of the typically developing children embrace their children's special abilities and help them move forward in areas that are difficult for them.

Parents of children with special needs are expected to push their children in areas that are difficult because many believe that areas of weakness represent the parts of the child's brain that are underdeveloped. Therefore, to make a child "more typical," it is necessary to work on the child's deficits. For children with autism to live and work independently, they also need confidence, they need to make friends, they need to feel good about who they are, and they need to understand their strengths as well as their challenges. These emotional developments also help their brains to develop.

In Table 5.1 we have tried to capture what we believe are the strengths discussed in this chapter, as opposed to the deficits, and how a teacher might take advantage of a child with autism's cognitive strengths.

Table 5.1 Building on Areas of Strength

Areas of Strength	*Building on Areas of Strength*
Cognition	
• Understands concrete concepts well. Can recall visual images and memories. • Thinks in a visual way. Better with nonverbal learning tasks. • Can learn to decode written text at an early age • Some read very young (hyperlexia). • Sometimes has spelling skills. • Excellent long-term memory. • Some have splinter/savant strengths (memory). • Some are precise and detail oriented. • Good concentration for interests. • Good memory for things they like. • Can work well with details, as opposed to focusing on the big picture. • Average to above average IQ and many like to learn.	• Use concrete language to provide explicit directions for home and classroom activities. • Build on prior experiences using familiar language when encouraging generalization to similar but new tasks. • Utilize expertise in rote tasks like multiplication tables and spelling; call on the resident expert to demonstrate talent. • Use visualization to improve reading comprehension and mathematical reasoning. • Use oral reading skills to demonstrate and encourage others to read. Start with decoding. • Spelling and multiplication tables memorization can be strengths. • Use splinter skills and interests as expertise.
Social and Emotional	
• Perfectionist in approach to task. • Can be very genuine; may not appreciate the motive behind trying to impress others. • Can be very honest. • Can maintain schedules and to be on time. • Can be very focused on tasks. • Can be charming in their innocence. • Have a strong sense of integrity. • Can follow rules and comply with directives. • Many have a sense of humor. Some are perfectionists. • Can handle repetition (for things they like). • Interested in helping others.	• Quality-control member in group work. • Evaluation and rubric checks. • Fashion monitor (with training). • All children to be timekeepers. • Precision and attention to detail. • Willing to do less desirable tasks. • Appreciates simple humor. • Follows rules. • Willing to perform menial tasks that can lead to more meaningful tasks. • Class paper shredder. • Ask them to help young children or volunteer. • Ask them to write humorous stories.

(Continued)

Table 5.1 Continued

Areas of Strength	*Building on Areas of Strength*
Flexibility of Thought/Imagination	
• Understands and uses concrete rules. • Have some specific and unusual interests. • Has a different perspective on our social world. • Are interested in drama and the arts. • Can understand suffering. • Many can learn to regulate personal traits.	• Helps others to use words more accurately. • Understands complex concepts and may be able to explain in simple concrete language. • Sharing differing perspectives creates richness in classroom discussions. Creative arts can segue into other areas.
Skills	
• Some good public speakers. • Some good in drama. • Some are good in art. • Some are good with numbers. • Can reflect on their own behavior (older). • Some have memory for what they like. • Some have splinter skills such as playing piano. • Many learn through experience. • Many learn to think about what others think. • Many learn to get along and work at it.	• Class presentations (UDL). • Practice social skills. • Focus on specific, mundane tasks. • Utilize memory for spelling and multiplication tables. • Reflect on behavior of self and others. • Use visuals. • Use experiential learning. • Use metacognition and reflect on experiences. • Use splinter skills as expertise.

Conclusion

Most researchers dismiss the idea that autism could be part of an evolutionary process, because evolution is usually a very slow process; however, there are some exceptions. Enriquez and Gullans (2011) have suggested that perhaps we are witnessing the evolution of a new species of human. Theorists point to the fact that humans have grown taller, about 1.9 inches since 1900; in addition, Olympic swimmers have grown 4.5 inches, and Olympic runners have grown 6.4 inches since the 1900s (Charles & Adrian, 2009). Certainly, some of the changes associated with autism make sense given that the genes associated with autism are inherited, and some of the traits that children with autism have seem adaptive to the type of society we might need someday. For example, today's world is so information rich that it makes sense that people will need to start focusing on only a few topics to the exclusion of many others. It makes sense that we need to adapt to a more computerized, systematic way of living as we move further away from socializing like the way we did before technology. It makes sense that in order for our species to survive men will no longer need to fight ground wars and hunt, but instead focus repetitively on virtual problems and challenges.

If this is some type of fast-moving change, then something seems to be going wrong. Perhaps the process is moving too quickly, because there are some children whose minds don't seem to be able to accept these genetic shifts and are somehow closing in on themselves and shutting themselves off. Some researchers might suggest that these children are shielding themselves from the social disapprobation they experience.

All of these theories are controversial, but we must think outside the box to answer our most pressing questions about autism, such as what is causing such a rapid rise in ASD and how can we more effectively teach children who are born with ASD. Many parents have been putting their children into private schools for children with high-level autism and Asperger's because they believe their children have potential that is not being supported in public schools. In private schools for children with autism, teachers are specially trained to work with these children, and they are familiar with strategies for helping them achieve, stay calm, and focus.

Parents believe they are helping their children get the best education they can get by moving them into these specialized environments. Given the choice, however, most parents would still rather their children be in good public schools, not only because of the lower financial cost, but also because their children would be learning how to interact with typically developing children. They would be integrated and in a position that would more accurately simulate the situations they will encounter after high school when they enter the world of higher education and work.

References

Anckarsäter, H., Stahlberg, O., Larson, T., Hakansson, C., Jutblad, S. B., Niklasson, L., . . . Rastam, M. (2006). The impact of ADHD and autism spectrum disorders on temperament, character, and personality development. *American Journal of Psychiatry, 163,* 1239–1244.

Ashburner, J., Ziviani, J., & Rodger, S. (2008). Sensory processing and classroom emotional behavior and educational outcomes in children with autism spectrum disorder. *American Journal of Occupational Therapy, 62,* 564–573.

Baron-Cohen, S. (2002). The extreme male brain theory of autism. *Trends in Cognitive Sciences, 6,* 248–254.

Baron-Cohen, S. (2008). Sex differences in the brain: Implications for explaining autism. *Science, 310,* 819–823.

Baron-Cohen, S. (2009). Autism: The empathizing–systemizing (E–S) theory. *Annals of the New York Academy of Sciences, 1156,* 68–80.

Baron-Cohen, S. (2012a). Autism and the technical mind: Children of scientists and engineers may inherit genes that not only confer intellectual talents but also predispose them to autism. *Scientific American, 307*(5), 72–75.

Baron-Cohen, S. (2012b). *The science of evil: On empathy and the origins of cruelty.* New York: Basic Books.

Baron-Cohen, S., Bor, D., Billington, J., Asher, J., Wheelwright, S., & Ashwin, C. (2007). Savant memory in a man with Colour Form-Number Synaesthesia and Asperger syndrome. *Journal of Consciousness Studies, 14*(9–10), 237–251.

Baron-Cohen, S., Lombardo, M. V., Auyeung, B., Ashwin, E., Chakrabarti, B., & Knickmeyer, R. (2011). Why are autism spectrum conditions more prevalent in males? *PLoS Biology, 9*(6), 1–10.

Baron-Cohen, S., Wheelwright, S., Bolton, S., & Goodyer, I. (1997). Is there a link between engineering and autism? *Autism, 1*, 153–163.

Bölte, S., Duketis, E., Poustka, F., & Holtmann, M. (2011). Sex differences in cognitive domains and their clinical correlates in higher-functioning autism spectrum disorders. *Autism, 15*, 497.

Boucher, J. (2001). Lost in a sea of time: Time-parsing and autism. In C. Hoerl & T. McCormack (Eds.), *Time and memory* (pp. 111–137). Oxford, UK: Clarendon.

Caron, M. J., Mottron, L., Berthiaume, C., & Dawson, M. (2006). Cognitive mechanisms, specificity and neural underpinnings of visuospatial peaks in autism. *Brain, 129*, 1789–1802.

Charles, J & Bejan, A., (2009). The evolution of speed, size and shape in modern athletics. The Journal of Experimental Biology, 212, 2419–2425.

Coolican, J., Bryson, S. E., & Zwaigenbaum, L. (2008). Brief report: Data on the Stanford–Binet Intelligence Scales (5th ed.) in children with autism spectrum disorder. *Journal of Autism and Developmental Disorders, 38*, 190–197.

Dawson, M., Soulieres, I., Gernsbacher, M. A., & Mottron, L. (2007). The level and nature of autistic intelligence. *Psychological Science, 18*(8), 657–662.

DeThorne, L. S., & Schaefer, B. A. (2004). A guide to child nonverbal IQ measures. *American Journal of Speech-Language Pathology, 13*, 275–290.

Enriquez, J., & Gullans, S. (2011). *Homo evolutis.* New York: TED Books.

Falter, C. M., Elliott, M. A., & Bailey, A. J. (2012). Enhanced visual temporal resolution in autism spectrum disorders. *PLoS ONE, 7*(3), e32774.

Frith, U. (1989). *Autism: Explaining the enigma.* New York: Blackwell.

Gillberg, C. (2002). *A guide to Asperger syndrome.* Cambridge, UK: Cambridge University Press.

Gomot, M., Bernard, F. A., Davis, M. H., Belmonte, M. K., Ashwin, C., Bullmore, E. T., & Baron-Cohen, S. (2006). Change detection in children with autism: An auditory event-related fMRI study. *Neuroimage, 29*, 475–484.

Happe, F., & Frith, U. (2006). The weak coherence account: Detail focused cognitive style in Autism Spectrum Disorders. *Journal of Autism and Developmental Disorders, 36*(1), 5–25.

Howlin, P., Goode, S., Hutton, J., & Rutter, M. (2009). Savant skills in autism: Psychometric approaches and parental reports. *Philosophical Transactions of the Royal Society B: Biological Sciences, 364*(1522), 1359–1367.

Just, M. A., Cherkassky, V. L., Keller, T. A., & Minshew, N. J. (2004). Cortical activation and synchronization during sentence comprehension in high-functioning autism: Evidence of underconnectivity. Brain, 127, 1811–1821.

Merzenich, M. M., Jenkins, W. M., Johnston, P., Schreiner, C., Miller, S. L., & Tallal, P. (1996). Temporal processing deficits of language-learning impaired children ameliorated by training. *Science, 271*(5245), 77–81.

Minshew, N. J., & Keller, T. A. (2010). The nature of brain dysfunction in autism: Functional brain imaging studies. *Current Opinion Neurolology, 23*(2), 124–130.

Morsanyi, K., Primi, C., Handley, S. J., Chiesi, F., & Galli, S. (2012). Are systemizing and autistic traits related to talent and interest in mathematics and engineering? Testing some of the central claims of the empathizing–systemizing theory. *British Journal of Psychology, 103,* 472–496.

Ross, P. (2006). When engineers' genes collide: Could modern patterns of marriage be concentrating the genes that predispose people to autism? Retrieved from http://spectrum.ieee.org/biomedical/ethics/when-engineers-genes-collide

Roth, I. (2010). *The autism spectrum in the 21st century: Exploring psychology, biology and practice.* London: Jessica Kingsley in association with The Open University.

Sizoo, B., van den Brink, W., van Eenige, M. G., & van der Gaag, R. J. (2009). Personality characteristics of adults with autism spectrum disorders or attention deficit hyperactivity disorder with and without substance use disorders. *Journal of Nervous and Mental Disease, 197,* 450–454.

Soderstrom, H., Rastam, M., & Gillberg, C. (2002). Temperament and character in adults with Asperger syndrome. *Autism, 6,* 287–297.

Sokhadze, E., Baruth, J., Tasman, A., Sears, L., Mathai, G., El-Baz, A., & Cassanova, M. F. (2009). Event-related potential study of novelty processing abnormalities in autism. *Applied Psychophysiology and Biofeedback, 34,* 37–51.

Treffert, D. A. (2009). The savant syndrome: An extraordinary condition. A synopsis: Past, present, future. *Philosophical Transactions of the Royal Society B, 364,* 1352–1357.

Vismara, L. A., & Rogers, S. J. (2008). The Early Start Denver Model: A case of an infant practice. *Journal of Early Intervention, 31*(1), 91–110.

Vital, P. M., Ronald, A., Wallace, G. L., & Happe, F. (2009). Relationship between special abilities and autistic-like traits in a large population-based sample of 8-year-olds. *Journal of Child Psychology and Psychiatry, 50*(9), 1093–1101.

Wass, S. (2011). Distortions and disconnections: Disrupted brain connectivity in autism. *Brain and Cognition, 75*(1), 18–28.

Wechsler, D. (1949). *Wechsler intelligence scale for children.* New York: The Psychological Corporation.

Welsh, J. P., Ahn, E. S., & Placantonakis, D. G. (2005). Is autism due to desynchronization? *International Journal of Developmental Neuroscience, 23,* 253–263.

Wheelwright, S., Baron-Cohen, S., Goldenfeld, N., Delaney, J., Fine, D., Smith, R., Wakabayashic, A. (2006). Predicting autism spectrum quotient (AQ) from the Systemizing Quotient-Revised (SQ-R) and Empathy Quotient (EQ). *Brain Research, 1079*(1), 47–56.

Williams, D. L., Goldstein, G., & Minshew, N. J. (2006). The profile of memory function in children with autism. *Neuropsychology, 20*(1), 21–29.

Wimpory, D., Nicholas, B., & Nash, S. (2002). Social timing, clock genes and autism: A new hypothesis. *Journal of Intellectual Disabilities Research, 46,* 352–358.

Wolman, D. (2010). The advantages of autism. *New Scientist, 206*(2758), 32–35.

Yechiam, E., Arshavsky. O., Shamay-Tsoory, S.G.G., Yaniv, S., & Aharon, J. (2010). Adapted to explore: Reinforcement learning in Autistic Spectrum Conditions. *Brain and Cognition, 72,* 317–324.

Zukauskas, P. R., Silton, N., & Assumpcao, F. B. (2009). Temporality and Asperger's syndrome. *Journal of Phenomenological Psychology, 40,* 85–106.

Chapter Six
Socialization

The one common characteristic that all children with autism face is social problems. Many will avoid social gatherings as well as individual social encounters. Some of these children are afraid of crowds, some don't like to change their routines; others feel out of place in unfamiliar settings. Still others may be afraid of planes or hotels. They may miss objects at home that give them a sense of security and comfort. Children and parents can become more isolated as a child with autism grows up. One parent from our study commented:

DAWN: He sat on the couch, swung his arm over the back of the couch and he said, "I don't think I wanna go to the county fair. I just wanna stay home and watch it on TV." And that was really the way he is and has always been. We constantly push him out of his comfort zone. We constantly take him on trips and take him places. And he will say the first day of like a three- or four-day trip, "Can we go home a day early?" I took him to the Grand Canyon. We were supposed to stay three nights, we walked to the edge of the Grand Canyon—we were looking at it for the first time. Both of us, we've never seen it before. It was obviously, incredibly beautiful. And he looked at me, and he started crying and he said, "When can we leave? When can we go home? When can we go back to Phoenix?"

Research suggests that social challenges contribute to the quality of life and future outcomes for individuals with autism, including academic achievement and social adjustment for school-aged individuals and underachievement in occupation, independent living, marriage, and relationships for adults on the spectrum. (Odom et al., 2006; Howlin, Goode, Hutton, & Rutter, 2004). Developing social skills can contribute to better outcomes (Strain, 2001).

Social Development

Children move through various stages of social development. We found this in our study, both in socialization and in other skill areas. This also has been shown in other studies (Baghdadli et al., 2012). In our study, we found that many of the children seemed to move through five major stages of social development that were linked loosely to age and grade levels. The five stages that we discovered as we conducted discourse analysis with our interview data included: (a) social isolation and play (in preschool), (b) intense self-focus and repetition (ages 5–8), (c) rejection and setback (ages 9–12), (d) self-awareness and regulation (ages 12–15), and (e) fragile friendships and identity development (ages 15+). These five stages are described further on.

1. **Social isolation and play (prekindergarten).** In this stage, the children are younger than 5 years old. Parents are interested in helping their children learn how to interact with typically developing peers. Many children with autism (high or low) resist social interaction at this age. They often need to be taught how to play with other children. They resist imaginative play and prefer stereotyped play.
2. **Intense self-focus and repetition (early elementary, ages 5–8).** At this level, children have an intense focus on themselves; many have obsessive interests and repetitive movements. They do not have as much difficulty playing alongside other children in parallel play, but they do have problems making connections with these children. Although typically developing children this age might play with them and invite them to their houses, children with autism are often rejected by their typically developing friends later on in elementary school, so these friendships often do not last.
3. **Rejection and setback (late elementary and middle school).** Children with autism in late elementary school (fourth, fifth, and sixth grades) start to recognize that they are different. Other children also begin to recognize and understand that they are different. During the fourth and fifth grades, typically developing children start wanting to fit in with the group and feel accepted. They are too young to understand that rejecting friends with disabilities is wrong, yet old enough to want to fit in with their peers. Therefore, they start rejecting other children around them who might seem odd or exceptional in some ways. This is about the time that some parents tell their children with autism about their disabilities and challenges. This is a difficult time for children on the spectrum. Some of their friends might start rejecting them, and their symptoms become more noticeable. Academics become harder in fourth grade in anticipation for middle school coming up in sixth or seventh grade. Typically developing children often continue their rejecting behaviors for another few years, until about eighth grade, when they start maturing.

4. **Self-awareness and regulation (late middle school and early high school).** In middle school, children with autism start thinking about what it means to be autistic and begin to understand how they might act differently than other children. This is when many start trying to regulate their behaviors in a more conscious way. Children sometimes develop more social anxiety around this time, which can manifest itself in depression or phobias. Social anxiety or depression might be brought on by self-awareness, peer rejection, or hormonal changes. They still have trouble making friends.
5. **Fragile friendships and identity (high school and early college).** In high school, children with autism are often more accepted for who they are; they have learned to regulate their behaviors more. Most have some friends, but these friendships seem fragile, and the teens are a bit nervous about losing friendships they have developed. They may develop friendships with typically developing children, but often these friendships are confusing and trust is often an issue, because children with autism cannot read body language or subtle cues and many don't understand the culture of typical teenagers who seem to move in and out of relationships all the time based on the circumstances or context of their lives (e.g., sports, academics, girlfriends/boyfriends). Many children have been rejected in the past by typically developing children, so this can cause lack of trust. Self-confidence is an issue as is academics. Below we have some interview comments from both parents and children that provide some information about the development patterns we just discussed.

Parent Comment

JAMES: In second grade, they had a fall and spring play and in the spring one, he was one of the stars and did really well. And I think even impressed some of the typical kids. I think they were a little surprised to see how well he did in second grade. So his second-grade teacher was great. His third-grade teacher really liked him a lot, too. And I think made him feel good. His fourth-grade teacher was not so good unfortunately. She just, I think she was pregnant, about ready to have her first child, and I don't think her heart was really in the classroom, and I just don't think she really understood or connected that well with Reese, or knew how to deal with kids like him so he had a harder time academically and socially in fourth and fifth grade. Middle school seemed to actually improve the quality of the instruction, although he still was isolated socially, but he started doing better in junior high, especially in eighth grade. High school gets more academically rigorous so for the first year, they have multiple classes, you've gotta deal with different teachers. In high school so far he has done well, he was able to join sports teams which has helped him socially.

MARIA: I mean Albert just, y'know, sort of like poker face. It was like one emotion, either he was just OK, or he was like, when he's a toddler running around screaming and laughing and just going around and around in circles. And then, OK, so I had two emotions, the I'm OK, or I'm really, y'know, excited and happy. And then later when he gotten to fourth or fifth grade, then he was I'm just OK. Right, and that's all I got.

Teen Comments:

RAYNE: Once I got into third grade, all hell broke loose.

I: So before that it was OK, but then after third grade it wasn't.

RAYNE: Because there are rules, and rules, and rules. And then fourth grade was a little better, but yeah, and then fifth grade, I was stupid. I was trying to be popular and such, which is the stupidest thing anyone can ever do, it'll just ruin you. In sixth grade I got some sense, but some people thought that I was crazy for some reason. And then in seventh grade, it got worse. A rumor was spread about me that I liked this guy, and then people kept asking me if I cut myself because I wear black. And since I cut my hair short, they're asking if I was a lesbian, which is annoying. And yes, I did want to beat them and rip them to shreds, but I didn't.

MASON: Junior high was good starting seventh grade. Sixth grade, I was really not getting along with a lot of people. But during seventh, during the summer between seventh grade and sixth grade, I really started to learn more social skills. So then at seventh grade, I really started to get along with a lot more people.

I: That's good. Why do you think you had problems in sixth grade?

MASON: Sixth grade, it's a mixture between fifth grade. I had problems like social skills. Plus the stress of like so much to do. And well, a lot of the kids usually have a lot of friends and like older siblings that could teach them other things. I was just on my own. So I didn't really fit in as much.

Mind-Blindness and Theory of Mind

Mind-Blindness

Mind-blindness can be described as a cognitive disorder where a person is unable to attribute mental states to one's self and others. As a result, the person is unaware of others' mental states. The individual is not capable of attributing beliefs and desires to others. This ability to develop a mental awareness of what is in the mind of an individual is also known as theory of mind (ToM). It allows a person to attribute behaviors and actions to various mental states, such as emotions and intentions. People with mind-blindness are said to have deficits in social insight.

Theory of Mind

Generally speaking, the mind-blindness theory asserts that children with ASD are delayed in developing a theory of mind, which allows typically developing children to put themselves into someone else's shoes and to imagine their thoughts and feelings. Thus, it theorizes that autistic children often cannot conceptualize, understand, or predict emotional states in other people. Some claim that theory of mind deficits occur in people not only with ASD, but also those with schizophrenia and ADHD, as well as neurotoxicity due to alcohol abuse.

A number of researchers in England formulated and studied what they call theory of mind (e.g., Baron-Cohen, Leslie, & Frith, 1985). Uta Frith (2003) was one of the first cognitive neuroscientists to study autism and wrote the book *Autism: Explaining the Enigma.* Simon Baron-Cohen and Tony Attwood, both important researchers in the field of autism, were PhD students in Frith's lab. Frith was also one of the first scientists to suggest that individuals with autism have weak central coherence, in that they are better at processing details than they are at integrating information from many different sources (Happe & Frith, 2006)

Many social skills training models used with higher-functioning students with autism focus on social cognition or understanding the principles behind social behavior based on theory of mind. Although research indicates that individuals with autism can improve performance on false-belief tests and perspective-taking tasks with training, these improvements often do not translate into progress in everyday interactions (Ozonoff & Miller, 1995). A false-belief test (FBT) is used to test theory of mind. In the classical version of FBT, the location change task (Baron-Cohen et al., 1985; Wimmer & Perner, 1983) is presented with a scene in which a puppet puts an object in a box and leaves the room to play. While the puppet is away, another character moves the object from the box to another place. When the puppet returns, the child is asked: "Where will the puppet look for the object?" If the child points to the box, this demonstrates the ability to consider the puppet's belief about the object's old position as opposed to relying on his or her own knowledge of its real position.

Social Skills Development

As mentioned before, difficulties with social skills are a defining characteristic of autism, and challenges with socialization are present in all individuals with autism regardless of cognitive or language ability (Carter, Davis, Klin, & Volkmar, 2005). Reviews of research on social skills intervention describe an abundance of program models and services; however, common challenges to intervention include the generalization and maintenance of skills (Rogers, 2000; White, Keonig, & Scahill, 2007). This is especially challenging when interventions do not target meaningful skills taught in the context of natural settings (Rogers, 2000; White et al., 2007; Gresham, Sugai, & Horner, 2001; Bellini, &

Akullian, 2007). However, researchers have identified practices that foster generalization and maintenance, including outings to community settings, opportunities for families to practice skills, and activities outside of the intervention and regular meetings with families (LePage & Courey, 2011; Mackay, Knott, & Dunlop, 2007).

Marans, Rubin, and Laurent (2005) suggested using environmental supports that include social skills instruction within preferred activities through a familiar and predictable home or community setting that limits unpleasant sensory stimulation and includes support and involvement of families. Other recommendations for improving the effectiveness of social skill programs include matching strategies and tailoring programs to the individualized needs of the student (Gresham et al., 2001; Bellini & Akullian, 2007).

What are social skills classes? Most classes, therapy sessions, or group opportunities are meant to help children learn specific social skills, such as looking others in the eye when they are talking to them, showing interest in what others are talking about, and waiting to see if a friend is interested in a particular topic before jabbering on about it.

Many of these programs try to use fun activities to teach children these skills; for example, they might have a child explain to another child how to draw a picture. The child with autism has to draw a picture from a friend's description of the scene in his or her head. This forces the child who is drawing to really listen (active listening) to the other child and try to understand what he or she is trying to describe. It forces the other child to articulate a good vision. The child drawing might have to ask questions, and the child giving instructions might have to explain more steps.

These programs might also have children act out specific scenarios; for example, they might have children act out a scene where a group of children are playing and the child with autism has to go ask if he or she can play with them in order to help the child learn how to initiate interaction. These programs can be made to be quite fun, but whether they really have any effect, or at least whether it is possible for children to transfer those skills, is questionable. Some children can do these tasks quite well in social skills groups but not at all in school.

These groups have also been criticized for focusing almost completely on "changing the child." Researchers suggest that caution should be taken with any program that forces children on the spectrum to constantly reflect on their social weaknesses or make them evaluate themselves in negative ways, because that type of attitude can impact their anxiety levels and ultimately make them worse, if not right away, perhaps in the future when they become preteens (Mundy, Henderson, Inge, & Coman, 2007). Concerns about anxiety are especially significant, because individuals on the spectrum have been found to exhibit significantly higher levels of anxiety than neurotypical individuals or individuals with learning disabilities (Bellini & Akullian, 2007). Researchers suggest addressing socialization needs that are unique to autism due to higher levels of physiological arousal reducing social anxiety while teaching self-regulation and relaxation strategies and emphasizing the importance of group participation with peers (Bellini, 2006).

We also suggest that teachers and therapists make clear what the goal is for these programs. Sometimes these programs are set up and the children have fun, but teachers and therapists really don't connect the message to the children's challenges. The autistic children really don't know why they are there, because they do not know how they are different from other children and they do not know that these differences are why their peers reject them. When children are older and more self-aware, some will be able to reflect on these issues and discuss them. But when they are young, it is difficult. People seem to fear talking to children about their need for social skills. However, social skills programs can help children better understand their strengths and weaknesses. For interventions to work and be transferable, teachers need to be explicit with the children while at the same time emphasize their strengths.

Cognitive Social Interventions: Social Thinking

Social thinking is one cognitive approach to social skills development that has been designed, used, and perfected by Winner and Crooke (2011). This intervention is built on the idea that children and adults need to understand theory of mind. Others have started to do some research on Michelle Garcia Winner's program (Crooke, Hendrix, & Rachman, 2008). These researchers conducted a large multiple baseline single-subject design study that looked at the effectiveness of using a social cognitive (social thinking) approach with six males with Asperger's or high-level autism. The data were collected from pre/post comparisons of verbal and nonverbal social behaviors. Structured treatment and semistructured generalization sessions occurred over 8 weeks. Results indicated significant positive changes from pre- to post-measures on both verbal and nonverbal "expected" and "unexpected" behaviors. Study participants had significant increases in the subcategories of (a) expected verbal, (b) listening and thinking with eyes, and (c) initiations. They also had robust decreases in unexpected verbal and nonverbal behaviors. Table 6.1 lists what each of these categories represents, as described by Crooke et al. (2008).

An example of an unexpected response was described by Emily, a parent we interviewed, who talked about how her son, Will, doesn't like when other teenagers or adults snap their fingers. Will says he doesn't like it because he can't snap his fingers. Being annoyed by snapping fingers may not be that odd; many others could be annoyed by snapping fingers, but Will takes it a bit further and goes a little crazy when he hears people snap their fingers. It distracts him, takes him off task, and when he was young it might have caused a tantrum. Is the real reason he is bothered by someone snapping their fingers because he cannot snap his own, or does the sound bother him? At one point, did someone snap his or her fingers as a gesture meaning that he should work faster? In any case,

Table 6.1 Expected and Unexpected Behaviors in Michele Garcia Winner's Cognitive Approach

Garcia Winner's Verbal and Nonverbal Expected versus Unexpected Behaviors
Expected vs. Unexpected: Verbal and Nonverbal Actions Have Thought Consequences
Participants are taught that verbal and nonverbal actions have consequences in terms of how other people think about them and that "expected" actions can generate good thoughts and "unexpected" actions can generate weird thoughts. Participants are also taught that they can change others' thoughts by changing their own actions.
Whole Body Listening: Bodies and Eyes are a Part of Listening and Conversation
Participants are taught that listening occurs with more than just ears. People also listen with their eyes, shoulders, hands, feet, and body. Whole body listening reflects keeping all parts of one's body "in the group." This relates back to the kinds of thoughts others have about you and is connected to expected versus unexpected nonverbal behaviors.
Social Files: Brains Make Social Memories That Give Us a Strategy for Initiations
Participants are taught that social files are "brain files" for people to learn and remember things about each other. Storing information about others occurs in the form of social memories. "Social files" provide a framework for initiations.
Knowledge and Opinions: What to Keep in & Let Out: Filtering Verbal Behavior Influences the Thoughts That Others Have About You
Participants are taught that certain types of knowledge and opinions should stay in one's head if it is off-topic, a data dump of facts, or if it is to correct someone. Participants are taught that opinions should not always be stated aloud.

it is not "typical" to have such an angry response to finger snapping. This is an odd response that people do not expect.

Rhonda, another parent in our study, told us that one of her two sons with autism had been involved in a Michelle Garcia Winner's social skills program and this is what she said about it:

RHONDA: They've been in social skill groups privately, which were more like facilitated play and sometimes with a physical component. One of them was in a social skills group with a Michelle Garcia Winner–trained therapist. He really didn't like that. He liked the theoretical framework, going deeper, it's not just about making eye contact, but why do you make eye contact. Try to understand theory of mind. So he loved the theoretical framework. But he didn't like the "try to pass" [as typical] focus of the class. Yeah, so that was why he dropped out of that.

Play-Based Socialization in Naturalistic Settings

Socialization Groups

Many of the teenagers that we interviewed had been involved both in playgroups as young children and also in social groups as older children and teenagers. From our research, the most popular and effective socialization programs seemed to be those that were interest based, content specific, and project oriented; for example, a few children attended film groups on the weekends. The following is what a few of the teens said about that program and one teen told us about a dance class:

I: So, you make short films with other kids, ok, and that has helped you, in what ways has it helped you?

REESE: Well it's helped me in a sense that, it's helped me meet some people like Jack and Blake and Daniel and I've been their friends for a long time because of it, and I definitely wanna make sure I don't lose those guys 'cuz I really like being their friend. So it really is important for me that I gotta stay with them.

I: What do you think about the movie-making group? You think that's helped you? You like it?

MASON: Yes, I really think it's helped make some friends and really pointed out some things. It's taught me a lot about stories and I really like that you get to learn a lot and have fun while doing it. So, in a way, it's almost like school, but more specialized, which I like.

I: What do you do in dance class?

GABRIELA: We do warm-ups, and then we try to practice our dance moves for the dance performance in May.
I just did Jazz, and Pop-Rock, and . . . and great dances.

I: So how have you been liking acting?

RAYNE: I love it actually.

I: Good.

RAYNE: I'm just waiting for a female to finally join. It's like, OK.

I: So what do you like about it?

RAYNE: I like some of the people. The people are very nice except one! And I'm looking up on the Internet how to use After Effects so I can keep going and it's also really fun acting. I mostly like doing death and killing scenes, which those are exciting.

The socialization groups that were most effective were those that allowed children to learn and accomplish something creative together that was important to them. Children with autism are often creative. Many like technology, art, drama, and music. The children like to create something they can hold in their hands and take pride in. Even for drama, dance, or music programs, many wanted the performances video or audio taped so they could see what they had produced. In these groups, the children got to know each other. They learned about each other's strengths and weaknesses, and they learned to depend on each other. A few children liked sports, and those who did really enjoyed being on sports teams and believed that it was a good way to get to know typically developing kids. Most children with autism don't like sports teams because they have fine and gross motor challenges and feel they are not very good in sports. Also, many are competitive and get angry when they lose, especially in the earlier grades when they don't understand the complex social guidelines associated with competitive sports for young children (which are competitive, but not really competitive). Also, some did not understand the rules of the games, which sometimes did not make sense.

We concluded that an effective naturalistic socialization program must have seven specific components. The groups must:

1. Be integrated to the best extent possible with children who are compatible in age, level of ability, and interest (with or without autism).
2. Be focused on interest-based, content-specific areas that are tailored for each child.
3. Emphasize identity development and self-awareness for children with autism, but do not force them to talk about autism or their challenges (unless the group chooses), but rather allow them to develop self-awareness in their own way and in their own time.
4. Teach autism awareness and diversity appreciation to typical peers.
5. Focus on helping children build connected friendships inside and outside the program.
6. Develop a caring community that includes both children and parents.
7. Make sure the children are having fun!

Identity Awareness

Another important aspect of social development is identity awareness. We have never seen a program that is focused on this specific area, but most of the cognitive, social skills, and naturalistic play-based groups all include aspects of identity development. Identity development is important for a number of reasons. It is important for children to build confidence. People are drawn to other people with confidence, whether they are different or not. In our opinion, the problem with a lot of social skills and cognitive social programs is that they are too focused on changing children with autism instead of helping children with autism understand how they are different and embracing their difference.

This focus on "what is wrong with children with autism" and how they "need to change" in our opinion has been one of the factors that has contributed to parents being shy about disclosing their children's autism to family, friends, and professionals.

As discussed in an earlier chapter, Baron-Cohen (2009) proposed a theory that children with autism are more often systematizers, rather than empathizers, and that this may be a type of "extreme maleness." Men historically have not liked being told how to act, who to be, or how to fit in with the norm; this is something they have always resisted. And, girls with ASD can have trouble socializing when they are young because they like to have things done their way, or they want people to do what they like to do. They find it difficult to compromise and let others lead and make decisions. Although research is lacking on girls and women with autism, it has been our experience that girls and women with autism and Asperger's are less conformist than their typically developing peers; they, too, need to be supported in developing their identity and self-confidence in who they are and want to be.

Autism Awareness

If you work with children to accept themselves, you also need to work with typically developing peers to accept children with autism. This is what one teenager said:

REESE: So, for one last tip of advice for teachers out there, if they wanna hear what I have to say, I would just basically say, always make sure that kids without autism are treating kids with autism with respect. If not, make sure to bring them over and tell them to not be mean to them, and then explain to them what autism is so that they will understand, and be nicer to people with autism.

Schools need to develop a plan for autism awareness, demystification, and/or understanding. People can come into the school and provide autism awareness in a number of different ways. For example, some people use puppet shows to help children who are younger and might not understand the complexities of disabilities and autism. Kids on the Block is a popular (www.kotb.com) puppet show for children. It has different puppet shows and uses large puppets to act out stories about children who don't fit in. The puppet show might talk about how a child makes strange noises or can't walk very well, but how the child still wants friends and to play. The shows are often set up at different agencies in different areas, and schools can ask for them to provide disability awareness programs for young children. These programs, however, will not make an impact unless the people providing the puppet show help the children in the schools make direct connections from the puppets on the stage to some of the children in the school. Children will go away thinking they should include children with autism in play, but they have no idea which children have disabilities (including autism) at their school. So, it won't change their behavior if they go away thinking this was a show about the one child in the school who is in a wheelchair—that is not going to have a big impact. This can happen even if the puppeteers make a point to talk about invisible disabilities, and these demonstrations need to be connected to the children at the school if at all possible. This can be handled in a number of different ways. Some children may be willing to talk about their autism, and a plan can be discussed with the children with autism and their parents. Further, it is important to have follow-up discussions.

Another way to provide autism awareness is to get teenagers or adults with autism together and have them present about their experiences. This allows other children with autism to see teenagers open about their autism, and it allows typically developing children to see older children who seem perfectly normal talk about what their autism was like and how they wished they had more friends when they were younger.

One way teachers can provide autism awareness for older children is to have them experience sensory overload. Some people put typical peers (for example) in 3-D dark glasses, spin them around, put on bright lights, and then have the children try to write something. Sensory overload experiences can be simulated in a number of different ways. These simulations allow typically developing children to get an idea of how children with autism who have sensory issues may be feeling when they try to do class work and are overloaded with sensory input such as too much noise. The Anne Arundel County Chapter of the Autism Society of America's website provides descriptions of some of these types of sensory experiences (http://mysite.verizon.net/hamiltonal/awareness/autawareness.html).

For older children, it may also be helpful to have the class read a book about a child with autism and then let the child discuss the book. Today a number of autobiographies by children with autism are available, including *Middle School—The Stuff Nobody Tells You About—A Teenage Girl With High-Functioning Autism Shares Her Experiences* by Haley Moss (2011) or *Running on Dreams,* which was an Eric Hoffer Award winner (Heiman, 2010). A brief description of the book follows:

> This is the story of Brad, a track star at his high school who gets assigned a buddy, and Justin, a 15-year-old boy with autism who is starting his first semester in a mainstream school. Thrown together in a story of teenage angst, confusion and friendship, Justin and Brad share their individual perspectives as an adolescent with autism and of a neurotypical teen struggling to understand each other and themselves. The book captures many bittersweet and humorous moments that bring new insight to a familiar world—two boys whose relationship starts out quite turbulent, but evolves into a friendship of loyalty and trust. (Heiman, 2010)

Levels of Participation in Activities

We identified four levels of participation in activities as children with autism learn to make friends with other children: (a) rejection, (b) group activities only, (c) intervening, and (d) true friendships.

At the rejection level, bullying is commonplace. Children tease other kids when the teachers turn their backs. Children with autism may go home crying and/or angry. Teachers/counselors often call the parents and tell them that their children are not getting along with other kids and ask parents to take their children home. Children with autism are often seen as having behavior problems, when, in fact, typical children may be provoking outbursts.

At the group activities level, the children on the spectrum are included in group activities, but otherwise ignored. Besides being involved in structured group activities, little else is done to help the child develop relationships. In situations where there is no large group activity being facilitated, the child is generally left to play alone. He is not teased or bothered when he plays alone, and when he joins other kids in group activities, he has fun, but otherwise he plays alone.

At the intervening level, adults spend time and energy to include children with autism in various group activities, in small groups or dyads. They make it clear that all children should be included and that it is not okay for children to be excluded. Adults often talk to children both separately and in groups and teach them how to negotiate and solve problems. Children with autism are usually included and happy in these situations, but there is a sense that typically developing children are encouraged to accept their autistic peers because they need to be good citizens, not because they have had the chance to get to know their autistic peers and like them as friends. In these situations, the adult sometimes replaces the child's peers and becomes the child's friend. Adults in these situations actively look for ways to integrate the child, and they care that these children feel happy and included, but they don't really know how to help these children connect with their peers.

At the fourth level, children with autism develop real connections and make friends. For example, in content-specific groups, the idea is for children to connect with each other around a specific interest and for the child's peers to see the child in a context where he or she excels and for the child without autism to learn to like and enjoy being with the child with autism. So, the goal is to set up a situation where typically developing peers can learn to understand and know children with autism.

Research on Social Interactions at School

Most of us believe that children with autism have fewer friendships than their typically developing peers, but to test this assumption researchers at UCLA observed children with ASD in general education first- through fifth-grade classrooms. They found that the children with high-level autism were most often on the periphery of their classroom social networks. Their social networks were smaller than their typical classmates, the friendships they identified were less often reciprocated, and the quality of their friendships was poorer (Kasari, Rotheram-Fuller, Locke, & Gulsrud, 2012; Chamberlain,

Kasari, Rotheram-Fuller, 2007). The 2007 study found that none of the children were completely isolated, but they were more often on the periphery of their social networks (Chamberlain et al., 2007). Moreover, a gender effect was noted, with boys with ASD primarily connected to the social networks of girls. The 2012 study (Kasari et al., 2012) used a larger sample of 60 children with ASD from a diverse set of classrooms (half were from Title I schools). The researchers found that children with ASD were mostly peripheral in their classroom social networks, and some were completely isolated (approximately 13% of the sample). The gender effect was not noted; boys were connected to boys and girls to girls, and these findings were consistent for younger and older children with ASD.

These researchers also found that the reciprocity of friendships was particularly low for the children with autism, who only had 18% of their relationships reciprocated, as compared to 64% of their typical classmates, and also lower than a previous study of 34% of second and third graders with ASD in the earlier study (Kasari et al., 2012). Because friendships in the school context are important given the amount of time children spend in school and the importance of friends in promoting social and academic outcomes, the researchers wonder if unilateral friendships might satisfy similar needs as reciprocal friendships for children with ASD.

Some of the children in our study were actually very sensitive, not only to how people felt, but also to subtle gestures and facial expressions that told them when and if someone was being rude or obnoxious. Emotional empathy is when you understand how someone feels because you feel the same along with them. With compassionate empathy, we not only understand a person's predicament and feel with them, but are spontaneously moved to help.

One study examined the links between peer, self, and teacher reports and observations of children in their natural environment at school (Kasari et al., 2012). One might expect that children whose peers see them as more socially connected to other children in the class would also be more engaged on the playground. Yet, contrary to their expectations, there was little association between playground engagement and peer nominations of social connections. Regardless of social status in the classroom, children with ASD were just as likely to be unengaged on the playground if they were rated as popular or isolated. Moreover, even with a reciprocal friendship, children with ASD were no more engaged on the playground than were children with ASD who did not have a reciprocal friendship.

Children with autism can interact well and play and socialize with children in a class and then go home at night and tell their parents they have no friends. Why is this? Much of it depends on how a person defines a friend. Most children and teenagers who are friends will visit each other's home and go places (like movies) together. Children with autism often feel no bond with their classmates and rarely do they get invited to go on play dates or to hang out as teenagers. So, to the children with autism, these kids at school are nice, but not friends.

Just because a child with high-level autism is talking and laughing with other kids and people are saying hello and kids in the class like him and he works well with others does not mean he has friends. Children with autism need real friends who care about them. It is possible that Dr. Kasari was told by the children with autism that they had all those friends that were not reciprocated because those children were embarrassed to tell her the truth. Children with autism are embarrassed they don't have friends; it makes them feel there is something wrong with them. They are smart enough to make up stories to make themselves look better. It is not that they lie. When asked about friends when they are young, they will name a few children in their classroom who are nice to them, because to them that is what a friends is—someone who is nice. For many (not all), this has been their experience of friendship.

Helping Children Make Friends

Every teacher has children in their class who have no friends. It breaks everyone's heart to see a child with no friends, but what can a teacher do? Forcing children to do things that are uncomfortable is not going to help children connect. First, these activities often are set up during lunchtime, and there are problems with that. Many children in elementary school like to spend time with their friends at lunch, and even if you offer typically developing children an incentive, many still want to play with their established friends.

Second, it takes too long for these children to connect; even if they could connect, the activities provided often don't last long enough for children who have trouble connecting to slowly make friends. A child with ASD should engage in an activity for at least a year to connect with another child and then another year to solidify the relationship. Both children also need to get together outside the one activity to enhance their relationship. The teacher should not give up in a month or so, but if it is obvious that the children are not getting along or they just are not connecting in any way after 3 to 6 months, then it is probably time to try another match.

It is important to find the right match with another child, one who might share a sense of humor or common interests. This doesn't mean the previous dyad shouldn't be friends, unless they annoy each other and are mean to each other, and that should be worked out at a different time. But if they get along and they just don't seem to connect well, that doesn't mean they can't be friends, just not perhaps best friends. Even children who have nothing in common and are not particularly interested in each other might start connecting if they are active together for a long period of time, simply because they've known each other for so long. Typically developing children have some friends that they connect with more and some less; the same is true for children with autism, it just takes them a lot longer.

Third, in elementary school many children on the spectrum still have a lot of their autistic quirks. If they do talk, they might talk only about their obsessions.

They might come across as very immature and naive. Or, they may never talk. In these cases, typically developing children may not be interested in forming a friendship with their autistic classmates outside a structured setting. In such instances, it is helpful to have children with autism start connecting with each other and allow typically developing children more time to get to know the children with autism. When children with autism are very young, they connect better with typically developing children because those children are more flexible and can play in ways that is more accommodating to children with autism. When children get older, they often bond more with others who have autism, because they have more in common with those like themselves and they share some similarities in interests, thinking, and humor.

It would also help a child if the school were to provide peer buddies (or a peer buddy group) to interact with the child with autism when he or she first arrives at school. Not just for a day, but for a long enough period of time so the child who is the buddy can really get to know his or her new friend and to introduce him or her around to supportive and accepting people. With the child with ASD's full knowledge and participation, a high school–aged teenager who is the buddy may work with him or her and an adult social coach and provide clues as to when and how this child sometimes presents outside the norm. Children with autism can be nice friends, but it takes them awhile to open up, and it takes a while for typically developing children to get used to their differences. A school needs to establish a community where children know that all children are treated with respect, no matter how they look or act.

Children need to know that you never turn someone away from a game. Everyone should feel included. This needs to be constantly reinforced and emphasized. Children with autism often need to be forced, or at least heavily encouraged, to be involved in a game they enjoy; they can't be expected to break into other children's play until they are ready and that often doesn't happen in elementary school. There should be a few games where adults supervise and these adults should help facilitate socialization and communication among children. Fourth, all adults, aides, recess aides, teachers, and others need to be trained on how to facilitate inclusive play and social communication between children for best affect. The easiest way to get a child with autism playing is not for an adult to press the issue, but for a child to come take the hand of the child with autism and say, "Will you come play with us?" and for the child to take his hand and lead him over to where the other children are playing.

In a recent study, children with ASD did not differ from typically developing children in the number of rejection nominations they received from their peers (Humphrey & Lewis, 2008). This finding, along with the relatively low levels of isolated children nominated on the social networks measure, suggests that children with ASD have more potential for fitting into their typical school classrooms than other data-based and anecdotal reports would suggest (Humphrey & Lewis, 2008). Rather than active rejection, children with ASD may fall into the class of neglected children, often overlooked as potential playmates by other children in the class. Here is a comment from a teen:

REESE: Well, I think they should help sort of lead people without Asperger's to people with Asperger's, introduce them to people without autism and stuff. And maybe help them get a relationship started, just see if you can get them to talk to each other and see if they have things in common.

I: OK, maybe help find ways that they can talk to each other, that kind of thing.

REESE: Yeah, exactly.

That children have more opportunities for play than they realize but teachers need to be careful not to assume that children in the classroom are all willing to play with a child with autism. There are situations where parents get pulled aside by other parents and told, "My child doesn't want to play with your child. I am sorry; I've tried to get him to change his mind, but he is not willing." Most children do not like for adults to force them to be with other children that they really do not want to be with. Forcing children together or being naive (thinking that any child will play with any other child) is exactly how children with autism get actively "rejected," or bullied, which can break their hearts. If the child with autism is with a typically developing peer who doesn't really want to be there, the peer often acts snippy and mean, and this can cause more problems than it solves. Better engagement on the playground is associated with more get-togethers of children outside of school (Frankel, Gorospe, Chang, & Sugar, 2011). However, social integration needs to be well thought out before setting up a scenario.

Bullying

In research studies involving adolescents with Asperger's syndrome, individuals report fewer friends and more incidents of bullying (Storch et al., 2012; Twyman et al., 2010). Bullying causes depression and anxiety in children (Storch et al., 2012). All but one of the teens in our study said they had been bullied sometime in their lives, mostly verbally, and to lesser and greater degrees:

CHRIS: I have to admit though, growing up, because I had autism and stuff, some kids, some stupid kids like have been mean to me and stuff and that's led me to not trust a lot of people. So, that's the only reason I'm afraid to go, I'm afraid of high school, well not afraid, I'm just nervous.

CHRIS: Yeah, but I learned only be friendly to the people who deserve it. And people who are just mean, just say, "F you!" and walk away. No, it's only, yeah, it happened at school and it's happened a couple of times, but eventually as I got older, I actually started to ignore them. And when they did it, tell the nearest adult. Um, and eventually, it actually helped me. Like the last time that someone made fun of me, um, I told the director and he ended up getting kicked out of choir. He spent way too long flipping me off for no apparent reason, whatsoever, and making really rude remarks.

DANIEL: Yes, I didn't have to transition from a different school; however, that's when I started having even more bullying problems. I know bullying is constantly shown in front of kids in TV shows and movies a lot, but you gotta experience it first hand to really understand how terrible it is. I know some friends of mine that actually committed suicide 'cuz of bullying.

I: So were you physically bullied or verbally bullied, emotionally bullied?

DANIEL: They'd use the teachers and staff to their advantage. Basically, there's this one day, sixth grade when I was just sitting at my desk, minding my own business, when this guy puts a dirty magazine on my desk. He got the teacher's attention, but you should've seen me. I grabbed the dirty magazine, ran to the door, and threw it out before she could see it.

I: So they were trying to get you in trouble with the teacher.

DANIEL: Yeah.

REESE: I do remember for the first few years there was one kid named Lee who was really mean to me. And there were some kids who tried to exclude me sometimes because of the fact that I seemed different. That definitely wasn't everybody.

I: Was this Lee, would you call him a bully?

REESE: Yeah, I kind of would.

I: How did he bully you?

REESE: Well he would constantly degrade me and would always say mean things to me, and sometimes he'd also push me down or something, and also one time even tried to push me off my bike.

I: Was he the same age as you or older?

REESE: He was like way older.

I: OK.

REESE: Like, when I was in kindergarten, I think he was like in third or fourth grade.

I: OK, and the school, did you tell the school that he was bothering you?

REESE: Yeah, I'm pretty sure I did.

I: Did they do anything about it?

REESE: I think they tried, but I feel like he was just like so much of a dick that he just wouldn't really listen and that whenever they weren't looking, he would take advantage of it.

Bullying is much more complex than people realize, and that is why it is hard to control. According to the families that we interviewed for this book, many of the children were bullied at some point in their school career. Some were bullied in middle school, and an even larger number were bullied in elementary school. A few were bullied in high school, but almost all of the parents said the bullying had decreased quite a bit in high school.

Why are children bullied? Well, an easy answer is that school personnel let it happen. It is very important that when it comes to bullying that we do not blame the children or the families. Whether children get bullied tells us something about how well the school is monitored before, during, and after school. It also tells us something about the culture of the school. It tells us whether children feel safe to be honest with adults at the school. It tells us that children know what it means to bully in all its different forms. If a school is monitored well, the culture of the school is that bullying is wrong and is not tolerated, that if someone is caught bullying then they are punished (suspended). If children feel safe to report bullies, then bullying doesn't happen.

Bullies are often portrayed in black and white, rather than in shades of gray, however, children don't always know what it means to bully another child. Most children think that being a bully means hitting another child or beating him up, when that is the least common form of bullying. The most common form of bullying is verbal or nonverbal bullying. For example, if children in a class are constantly rolling their eyes and laughing at someone behind their back, that is a form of bullying. These children with autism are smart enough and sensitive enough to know this is happening.

Children also need to be taught directly how to be nice to their peers, and that includes all of their peers. For example, for the members of the football team to constantly be calling each other "gay" all the time is not appropriate. They need to be taught how this can affect children in the room who may be gay and also other children who may be different and feel they need to keep quiet about their differences. Children with autism are not the only children in schools who are learning how to navigate the social world. Children with autism are, actually, the children who are helping us to recognize and finally do something about the fact that all children need to learn how to communicate, to interact, to stand up for themselves, to share, and to accept and acknowledge the contributions of others.

In schools where there is no tolerance for bullying, where children know what bullying is, and where children who define themselves (or have been defined) as bullies or as victims can communicate in appropriate ways, then bullying doesn't happen.

It is simple to say that school culture is the cause of bullying, and certainly adults at the school have to take responsibility for developing a culture of conflict and anger. However, bullying also happens outside the schools. Sometimes it is not just about how the schools monitor their students; it is also important for schools and parents to teach children right from wrong.

One of the parents we interviewed told us about how some kids at her son's high school created a Facebook account in her son's name and pretended to be her son. She found out about it because she herself was on Facebook and she knew that her son did not have a Facebook account. In her words:

> A lot of people had "friended" this "fake" Facebook page, including old teachers and relatives and friends at his school. I knew the kids who set this up. The kids were punished by their parents and by the school; and I threatened to call the police if something like that ever happened again. And, when the people who had "friended" him from school found out about it, everyone was really mad about it. But still, I will never tell him about this. Never! It would break his heart!

Bullying was such a painful topic for both the kids and the parents as they were being interviewed in some ways I could tell neither the parents nor the kids really wanted to talk about it. And, in some ways they all avoided it as much as they could. Most of the boys hadn't been picked on for a while, since they were younger, and they wanted to put those memories behind them. For many people we were interviewing, this topic brought back bad memories.

To completely eradicate bullying, it is important to look at the causes. We can't just say that children who bully are bad. Everyone knows that children who get bullied sometimes become the bullies. A teacher once told us that she felt that it was the children with autism who were the bullies. This is a rare view, but there are children with autism who are angry and aggressive, who scare other children because they are forceful in their presence.

One of the children I interviewed once told me that he would rather have people be scared of him than simply have no friends because at least it made him feel powerful. Bullies are made in the same way victims are made, by being disliked, ostracized, and left out. Different children respond in different ways to alienation.

Another reason bullying is difficult to completely eliminate is because there is a fine line between bullying and peer socialization, which is part of all cultures. Our society is changing. We no longer want people to "bully us" into conforming to act in certain ways and to look or express ourselves in certain ways, especially in relation to disability, gender, sexual orientation, religion, or culture. However, if groups of teenagers are drinking, smoking, and taking drugs, we still want peers to respond negatively to those children and give them the message that "the majority of us" don't want to be around other teens who engage in that behavior. It is a form of socialization, which is the same in schools. Most faculty are tenured, which makes it difficult to be fired after many years of service. Therefore, if a person is not pulling his or her weight, following the rules, or treating students with respect, after direct communication fails many believe there is no other option than for the group to give subtle messages that his or her behavior is unacceptable. This methodology can be abused; for example, if the group is trying to push a person out who wants to make positive change and the rest want to protect the norm. What once was considered group socialization is now being reexamined for its potential to be abused.

Children socialize each other to act within the norm as they grow up, and many adults still agree with the underlying philosophy of "let the children work things out for themselves." Girls have complicated relationships and develop best friend scenarios, and they especially have trouble navigating triads. For a child with autism to experience a typically developing girl showing interest in her and then suddenly moving on to another friend, leaving her to wonder what happened, can be devastating, especially if the child does not have any other friends. This could provoke a physical or verbal outburst from the child with autism, which only makes things worse. Passive aggressive behavior, however, is problematic among all girls, not just between those with and without autism:

ANA: When the psychologist observed, they noticed how she was being picked on, taken advantage of, outside of class. The teachers did find her being very stressed, it was very stressful for her because she felt she had to keep up and had to catch up, and it was too much for her, especially like the history class so they took her out of general education.

Building a Community of Parents

Developing community among parents is important for a child's social development. Whether children will become friends has a lot to do with whether the parents can get together and bring the children together outside their playgroups, social skills groups, or afterschool programs. One parent in our study who has had a lot of contact with parents of typically developing children and also parents of children with autism told us the following:

DONNA: The biggest difference between parents of teens with autism and parents of teens without autism is that parents of autistic kids are so involved in their children's social lives and other parents are not. In fact, when I take Mason's autistic friends somewhere, the parents (of children with autism) will ask if I need help driving, or if I need money, or if there is anything they can do. His other friends [typical] show up at our door, with no money, and I have never met their parents.

When parents complain to school professionals that their children do not have friends at school, we've heard teachers tell them, "What you need to do is set up play dates." Parents often just stare in response. They don't know what to say. Telling a parent to go set up a play date does seem like the obvious answer. But it is important to remember that the reason autistic children have problems making friends is because other children do not want to play with them. It never seems to cross a teacher's mind that it takes an assertive parent to ask other parents (who may be uncomfortable with an autistic child) for a play date. And, it never seems to cross their minds that if these children have no scaffolding and are left to play alone they will likely grow further apart because the autistic child will come across as odd and disinterested and the typical peer will come across as snippy and mean. Thus, many parents of autistic children are uncomfortable setting up play dates with typical peers. And, most parents are embarrassed to admit to a teacher that they are uncomfortable setting up a play date with another parent because it sounds so silly. Don't most parents set up play dates all the time? When a teacher says something like, "Just go set up a play date with another parent" to a parent with a child with autism it shows just how little that teacher knows about autism and what their child needs. Their child has social problems; they need social scaffolding and social skills training. You don't just "go set up a play date," as if that child is just like any other child. It is frustrating to parents that special education teachers come across as so uninformed. It is like a special education teacher telling a parent of a child with learning disabilities (who just flunked a math test), "Tell your daughter she can take the test over again," with no acknowledgment that obviously this child needs more instruction because she doesn't understand the material!

Some parents will try to set up play dates, but families often live in different areas, so getting the children together takes some time and effort. It is often easier for programs to facilitate play dates. There is skill to facilitating play dates, and, although there are parent-training programs, some parents are just not comfortable facilitating interactions between their children and other children. This is especially true as children get older and may get into arguments with other children. Parents often have to work with their children on conflict resolution, and they need to understand the social idiosyncrasies of other children as well. For example, many children with autism get tired of social interaction and when they are done, they are done, and they need to go home or be by themselves. Parents must understand this of both children when they facilitate play between two children with autism, otherwise they could encounter a meltdown.

So, setting up a community of parents to get to know each other, support each other, and get to know each other's children through conversations is helpful. Parents of children with autism often accompany their children to all of their social events and stay with them so that they can facilitate any problems their children may have with other children or parents. This is unusual for parents of typically developing kids, who expect to simply drop off their children and leave. Most of the time high-level children with autism are fine, and it is hard for other parents to understand. The parents are afraid that something could happen, for example, a meltdown could occur or the child might run off and play by himself in another room and become insistent on staying there. Once Tamra, one of the parents in this study, talked about her neighbor who invited her son, Daniel, over to her house after she had invited the neighbor's two boys over many times. One day her son had a meltdown and the neighbor called and asked Tamra to come get him. The neighbor never asked Daniel to come play at her house again. Parents don't want their autistic children to squander a perfectly good social opportunity just in case something bad happens and their child never gets asked over again.

Conclusion

In this chapter, we talked about a number of issues that children have with socialization and how a teacher might work with children to overcome social problems in and out of the classroom. Social challenges are common to all children and adults with autism or Asperger's, and they start when a child is young and continue until a child is an adult:

DAWN: Every single weekend is groundhogs day because every single weekend is, well, can we find a playmate, can we find an activity, can Rob do something enjoyable with a peer? And every weekend is a brand new story; brand new weekend—brand new struggle.

We talked about different types of interventions that can be used to help children work on social issues. For example, play is an important aspect of early socialization for young children, and in our chapter about early childhood (Chapter 9) we talk more about play as an aspect of early intervention.

We also talked about how children in our study seemed to develop socially over their childhood during their school-aged years, having the most trouble in middle to late elementary school and early junior high school. In high school, many of the teenagers were doing better, but some still wanted to learn how better to interact socially and to make friends.

We talked about socialization, including how younger elementary-aged children are often exposed to someone directly teaching basic social skills, and we also talked about a cognitive approach, including Michelle Garcia Winner's social thinking method. We suggested that identity awareness is important and how naturalistic, play-based approaches often allow children to have fun and learn to socialize through peer-mediated activities.

Finally, we talked about autism awareness and the difficulty of connecting children with autism with their typically developing peers and how teachers might try various strategies. We also talked about the complexity of bullying and how parent support, training, and connection can help with socialization.

References

Baghdadli, A., Bassouline, B., Sonie, S., Pernon, E., Darrou, C., Michelon, C., . . . Pry, R. (2012). Developmental trajectories of adaptive behaviors from early childhood to adolescence in a cohort of 152 children with autism spectrum disorders. *Journal of Autism and Developmental Disorders, 42,* 1314–1325.

Baron-Cohen, S. (2009). Autism: The empathizing–systemizing (E–S) theory. *Annals of the New York Academy of Sciences, 1156,* 68–80.

Baron-Cohen, S., Leslie, A. M., & Frith, U. (1985). Does the autistic child have a theory of mind? *Cognition, 21*(1), 37–46.

Bellini, S. (2006). The development of social anxiety in high functioning adolescents with autism spectrum disorders. *Focus on Autism and Other Developmental Disabilities, 2*(3), 138–145.

Bellini, S., & Akullian, J. (2007). A meta-analysis of video modeling and video self-modeling interventions for children and adolescents with autism spectrum disorders. *Exceptional Children, 73,* 264–287.

Carter, A. S., Davis, N. O., Klin, A., & Volkmar, F. R. (2005). Social development in autism. In F. R. Volkmar, R. Paul, A. Klin, & D. Cohen (Eds.), *Handbook of autism and pervasive developmental disorders: Vol. 1. Diagnosis, development, neurobiology, and behavior* (pp. 312–334). Hoboken, NJ: John Wiley & Sons.

Chamberlain, B., Kasari, C., & Rotheram-Fuller, E. (2007). Involvement or isolation? The social networks of children with autism in regular classrooms. *Journal of Autism and Developmental Disorders, 37*(2), 230–242.

Crooke, P. J., Hendrix, R. E., & Rachman, J. Y. (2008). Brief report: Measuring the effectiveness of teaching social thinking to children with Asperger Syndrome (AS) and High Functioning Autism (HFA). *Journal of Autism and Developmental Disorders, 38*(3), 581–591.

Frankel, F., Gorospe, C. M., Chang, Y., & Sugar, C. A. (2011). Mothers reports of play dates and observation of school playground behavior of children having high-functioning autism spectrum disorders. *Journal of Child Psychology & Psychiatry, 52*(5), 571–579.

Frith, U. (2003). *Explaining the enigma* (2nd ed.). Hoboken, NJ: Wiley-Blackwell.

Gresham, F. M., Sugai, G., & Horner, R. H. (2001). Interpreting outcomes of social skills training for students with high-incidence disabilities. *Exceptional Children, 67,* 331–344.

Happe, F., & Frith, U. (2006). The weak coherence account: Detail-focused cognitive style in autism spectrum disorders. *Journal of Autism and Developmental Disorders, 36*(1), 5–25.

Heiman, H. (2010). *Running on dreams.* Shawnee Mission, KS: AAPC Publishing.

Howlin, P., Goode, S., Hutton, J., & Rutter, M. (2004). Adult outcome for children with autism. *Journal of Child Psychology and Psychiatry, 45,* 212–229.

Humphrey, N., & Lewis, S. (2008). Make me normal: The views and experiences of pupils on the autistic spectrum in mainstream secondary schools. *Autism*, 12, 1362–3613.

Kasari, C., Rotheram-Fuller, E., Locke, J., & Gulsrud, A. (2012). Making the connection: Randomized controlled trial of social skills at school for children with autism spectrum disorders. *Journal of Child Psychology and Psychiatry, 53*(4), 431–439.

LePage, P., & Courey, S. (2011). Filmmaking: A video-based intervention for developing social skills in children with autism spectrum disorders. *Interdisciplinary Journal of Teaching and Learning, 1*(2), 88–104.

Mackay, T., Knott, F., & Dunlop, A. (2007). Developing social interaction and understanding in individuals with autism spectrum disorder: A group work intervention. *Journal of Intellectual and Developmental Disability, 32,* 279–290.

Marans, W. D., Rubin, E., & Laurent, A. (2005). Addressing social communication skills in individuals with high-functioning autism and Asperger's syndrome: Critical priorities in educational programming. In F. R. Volmar, R. Paul, A. Jin, & D. J. Cohen (Eds.), *Handbook of autism and pervasive developmental disorders, diagnosis* (pp. 947–977). Hoboken, NJ: John Wiley Sons.

Moss, H. (2011). *Middle school—The stuff nobody tells you about—A teenage girl with high-functioning autism shares her experiences.* Shawnee Mission, KS: AAPC Publishing.

Mundy, P. C., Henderson, H. A., Inge, A. P., & Coman, D. C. (2007). The modifier model of autism and social development in higher functioning children. *Research and Practice for Persons with Severe Disabilities, 32,* 124–139.

Odom, S. L., Zercher, C., Li, S., Marquart, J. M., Sandal, S., & Brown, W. H. (2006). Social acceptance and rejection of preschool children with disabilities: A mixed-method analysis. *Journal of Educational Psychology, 98,* 807–823.

Ozonoff, S., & Miller, J. N. (1995). Teaching theory of mind: A new approach to social skills training for individuals with autism. *Journal of Autism and Developmental Disorders, 25,* 415–433.

Rogers, S. J. (2000). Interventions that facilitate socialization in children with autism. *Journal of Autism and Developmental Disorders, 30,* 399–409.

Storch, E. A., Larson, M. J., Ehrenreich-May, J., Arnold, E. A., Jones, A. M., Renno, P., . . . Wood, J. J. (2012). Peer victimization in youth with autism spectrum disorders and co-occurring anxiety: Relations with psychopathology and loneliness. *Journal of Developmental and Physical Disabilities, 24,* 575–590.

Strain, P. S. (2001). Empirically based social skill intervention: A case for quality-of-life improvement (ZIP). *Behavioral Disorders, 27*(1), 30–36.

Twyman, K. A., Saylor, C. F., Saia, D., Macias, M. M., Taylor, L. A., & Spratt, E. (2010). Bullying and ostracism experiences in children with special health care needs. *Journal of Developmental and Behavioral Pediatrics, 31,* 1–8.

White, S., Koenig, K., & Scahill, L. (2007). Social skills development in children with autism spectrum disorders: A review of the intervention research. *Journal of Autism and Developmental Disorders, 37,* 1858–1868.

Wimmer, H., & Perner, J. (1983). Beliefs about beliefs: Representation and constraining function of wrong beliefs in young children's understanding of deception. *Cognition, 13*(1), 103–128.

Winner, M. G., & Crooke, P. J. (2011). Social communication strategies for adolescents with Aspergers. *ASHA Leader, 16*(1), 8–11.

Chapter Seven

Evidence-Based Practices: Looking at Research Critically

Before we talk about what types of autism interventions are considered evidenced based, we need to take a few minutes to critically look at what it means for an intervention to be labeled "evidence-based." We also need to talk about the word "intervention" so that we can better understand the language of special education and educational research.

In this chapter, we are going to talk specifically about what types of instruction in the field of autism have been described as being evidenced by research. Later in the book we discuss other strategies that teachers have been using, for example, letting children have quiet time when they are feeling stressed or overwhelmed during class time. This is a simple strategy that teachers of children with autism have used successfully for years to prevent behavior escalation, but this strategy has no research evidence that it "works." However, it has been used enough and discussed enough anecdotally by teachers that it is certainly worth trying in a classroom for those children for whom it might be appropriate.

As far as evidence-based practices are concerned, this topic is more complicated than is often presented in textbooks. For those who use the words "evidence based" to describe their interventions, they believe that their instructional techniques have been proven to be effective to help children learn. The need to use evidence-based practices seems both intuitive (why use something that hasn't been proven?) and necessary given the hundreds of educational approaches that have been tried in the past and then vacated after the excitement dies down because the program is really only moderately successful for some children.

Using evidence-based practices makes perfect sense, and of course teachers should use proven methods whenever possible. There are a number of problems, however, with our quest for using evidence-based practices. First, some researchers and self-proclaimed experts in the field say that their work is evidence based, when it has not been proven to be so, or at least they are the only ones making that claim. Their evidence is often based on their own unpublished and non-peer-reviewed research that may be a bit suspect, especially if they have a conflict of interest in seeing this research become evidence based.

Second, according to a National Autism Center report written in 2009 there are only 11 evidence-based practices for autism (Wilczynski & Pollack, 2009). Thus, it would be fairly restrictive if a teacher had to stick to this limited number of "proven methods" to teach their classes.

Third, most autism research over the last 50 years has been conducted predominantly with children with classic autism and/or a mix of children on the spectrum. Children with classic autism are very different from children with high-functioning autism or Asperger's. To qualify as evidence based, the research must be conducted with the same population or group of students for whom the intervention was designed.

Fourth, there is very little funding for research from the federal or state governments, and conducting the type of research that is considered evidence based is very expensive. To conduct quality research studies on every possible educational strategy known to the world of autism would be utterly impossible due to cost and time limitations. In addition, when people conduct research on specific strategies, they often set up experiments in specific ways so that the research is convincing to outside critics. They must demonstrate that the positive outcomes were a result of only the intervention or strategy in question and not some other variable that was not controlled for in the experimental environment. Often research is conducted in a laboratory or non-natural setting and may not account for variations and environmental factors in a real classroom. This limits the questions researchers will ask. And, if a teacher uses a strategy or educational model in a different way than was otherwise intended (the teacher modifying the strategy to suit his or her particular needs), the strategy is not being implemented with fidelity, and thus the strategy can no longer be called evidence based. Finally, the term "evidence based" is not a static term that everyone agrees upon. Different groups use different criteria to determine eligibility when deciding what is or is not evidence based. For example, the U.S. Department of Education has determined the "gold standard" for research as a randomized controlled trial (Whitehurst, 2003), which includes quantitative analysis of large sets of data. Randomized controlled trials are studies that randomly assign individuals to an intervention group or to a control group in order to measure the effects of the intervention. Random assignment is important, because with randomization each group is a sample of the larger population from which the study hopes to draw. Random assignment helps the researcher to evaluate whether the intervention itself, as opposed to other factors, such as differences in academic achievement or socioeconomic status or ethnicity, caused the observed differences in outcomes.

At one time, The U.S. Department of Education's What Works Clearinghouse developed such stringent criteria for evidence-based practices that even well-accepted and promising practices were turned away as unacceptable due to lack of adequate evidence. Just recently, the What Works Clearinghouse has broadened its definition of "gold standard" research to include nonexperimental designs. This will enable researchers to offer more evidence-based and promising interventions and practices to the field of education (Sparks, 2010). To more narrowly address the unique needs of students with autism, the National Standards Project (NSP), a primary initiative of the National Autism Center (NAC), designed guidelines to determine what interventions are to be considered evidence based in their field.

The National Autism Center

The National Standards Project examined and quantified the level of research supporting interventions that target the core characteristics of ASD in children, adolescents, and young adults (younger than 22 years of age) on the autism spectrum. Ultimately, it designed a rubric that included guidelines to determine to what extent various interventions were evidence based and then labeled them as established, emerging, unestablished, or harmful (Wilczynski & Pollack, 2009). We have listed the criteria the Committee used to determine whether the various practices were evidenced based in Table 7.1. This classification system was adapted from the National Standards Project Report (Wilczynski & Pollack, 2009).

Table 7.1 Categories for Evidence-Based Criteria According to National Standards Project

Established	*Emerging*	*Unestablished*	*Ineffective or Harmful*
This category requires several published, peer-reviewed studies.	These studies have a few published, peer-reviewed studies.	The outcomes from these studies may not be based on research.	This category could have several published, peer-reviewed studies that show poor outcomes.
The Scientific Merit Rating for articles are rated at 3, 4, or 5. These studies may be supplemented by others with lower scores on the Scientific Merit Rating Scale.	The articles may be rated on the Scientific Merit Rating Scale with scores of 2. These studies may be supplemented by others with higher or lower scores on the Scientific Merit Rating Scale.	Beneficial treatment effects reported based on very poorly controlled studies (scores of 0 or 1 on the Scientific Merit Rating Scale). The claims are based on testimonials, unverified clinical observations, opinions, or speculation.	No beneficial treatment effects reported. Considered ineffective or adverse treatment effects reported.

See National Standards Report for more detailed criteria.

Best Practices

The National Autism Center (NAC) came up with 11 evidenced-based practices in autism. These established practices and interventions have been well researched and proven to be effective for children with ASD. As you can see from Table 7.2 although one or more studies might suggest that a treatment produced favorable outcomes for individuals with ASD, high-quality studies must have consistently demonstrated effectiveness before the NAC deemed the treatment to be evidence based. Table 7.3 includes the name of the practice, the number of research studies providing evidence of effectiveness, a brief description of the practice, and examples of the practice. For more detailed information, see the National Standards Project Report (Wilczynski & Pollack, 2009).

Emerging, Unestablished, or Harmful Research

If the strategies were not deemed good enough to be called evidenced based, the NAC Committee identified many strategies and interventions that it called "emerging." That meant it didn't quite have enough research behind it to be thoroughly vetted, but these practices show some promise and should be studied further to establish validity. But, for an intervention to be labeled as evidence based, at least three good research studies had to back the intervention's effectiveness. Beyond emerging, you have unestablished and then harmful (Wilczynski & Pollack, 2009).

The National Professional Development Center

The NAC was one of two organizations seeking to establish criteria and assess whether various interventions were evidence based in the field of autism over the last 5 to 6 years. The second organization was the NPDC, the National Professional Development Center (Odom, Collet-Klingenberg, Rogers, & Hatton, 2010). This group's criteria for an intervention being evidence based were different. For individuals with ASD, efficacy must be established through peer-reviewed research in scientific journals using:

1. **Randomized or quasi-experimental design studies.** Two high-quality experimental or quasi-experimental group design studies.
2. **Single-subject design studies.** Three different investigators or research groups must have conducted five high-quality single-subject design studies.

Or

3. **Combination of evidence.** One high-quality randomized or quasi-experimental group design study and three high-quality single subject design studies conducted by at least three different investigators or research groups (across-the-group and single-subject design studies).

Table 7.2 Established Evidence-Based Practices

Established Evidence-Based Practices

	Strategies (Number of Studies Providing Evidence)	*Descriptions*
1	Antecedent Package (99 Studies)	These interventions involve the modification of situational events that typically precede the occurrence of a target behavior. These alterations are made to increase the likelihood of success or reduce the likelihood of problems occurring. Treatments falling into this category reflect research representing the fields of applied behavior analysis (ABA), behavioral psychology, and positive behavior supports.
2	Behavioral Package (231 Studies)	These interventions are designed to reduce problem behavior and teach functional alternative behaviors or skills through the application of basic principles of behavior change. Treatments falling into this category reflect research representing the fields of applied behavior analysis, behavioral psychology, and positive behavior supports.
3	Comprehensive Behavioral Treatment for Young Children (22 Studies)	This treatment reflects research from comprehensive treatment programs that involve a combination of applied behavior analytic procedures (e.g., discrete trial, incidental teaching, etc.), which are delivered to young children (generally under the age of 8).
4	Joint Attention Intervention (6 Studies)	These interventions involve building foundational skills involved in regulating the behaviors of others. Joint attention often involves teaching a child to respond to the nonverbal social bids of others or to initiate joint attention interactions.
5	Modeling (50 Studies)	These interventions rely on an adult or peer providing a demonstration of the target behavior that should result in an imitation of the target behavior by the individual with ASD. Modeling can include simple and complex behaviors. This intervention is often combined with other strategies such as prompting and reinforcement. *Examples include live modeling and video modeling.*
6	Naturalistic Teaching Strategies (32 Studies)	These interventions involve using primarily child-directed interactions to teach functional skills in the natural environment. These interventions often involve providing a stimulating environment, modeling how to play, encouraging conversation, providing choices and direct/natural reinforcement, and rewarding reasonable attempts.

(Continued)

Table 7.2 Continued

Established Evidence-Based Practices		
	Strategies (Number of Studies Providing Evidence)	*Descriptions*
7	Peer-Training Package (33 Studies)	These interventions involve teaching children without disabilities strategies for facilitating play and social interactions with children on the autism spectrum. Peers may often include classmates or siblings. When both initiation training and peer training were components of treatment in a study, the study was coded as "peer-training package." These interventions may include components of other treatment packages (e.g., self-management for peers, prompting, reinforcement, etc.).
8	Pivotal Response Treatment (14 Studies)	This treatment is also referred to as PRT, Pivotal Response Teaching, and Pivotal Response Training. PRT focuses on targeting "pivotal" behavioral areas — such as motivation to engage in social communication, self-initiation, self-management, and responsiveness to multiple cues, with the development of these areas having the goal of very widespread and fluently integrated collateral improvements. Key aspects of PRT intervention delivery also focus on parent involvement in the intervention delivery, and on intervention in the natural environment such as homes and schools with the goal of producing naturalized behavioral improvements.
9	Schedules (12 Studies)	These interventions involve the presentation of a task list that communicates a series of activities or steps required to complete a specific activity. Schedules are often supplemented by other interventions such as reinforcement.
10	Self-Management (21 Studies)	These interventions involve promoting independence by teaching individuals with ASD to regulate their behavior by recording the occurrence/non-occurrence of the target behavior, and securing reinforcement for doing so. Initial skills development may involve other strategies and may include the task of setting one's own goals. In addition, reinforcement is a component of this intervention with the individual with ASD independently seeking and/or delivering reinforcement.
11	Story-Based Intervention Package (21 Studies)	Treatments that involve a written description of the situations under which specific behaviors are expected to occur. Stories may be supplemented with additional components (e.g., prompting, reinforcement, discussion, etc.).

Table 7.3 Emerging Evidence

Emerging evidence		
	Strategies	*Descriptions*
1	Augmentative and Alternative Communication Device	These interventions involved the use of high or low technologically sophisticated devices to facilitate communication. Examples include, but are not restricted to, pictures, photographs, symbols, communication books, computers, or other electronic devices.
2	Cognitive Behavioral Intervention Package	These interventions focus on changing everyday negative or unrealistic thought patterns and behaviors with the aim of positively influencing emotions and/or life functioning.
3	Developmental Relationship-based Treatment	These treatments involve procedures that are based on developmental theory and emphasize the building of social relationships. All of the studies falling into this category met the strict criteria of: (a) targeting the defining symptoms of ASD, (b) having treatment manuals, (c) providing treatment with a high degree of intensity, and (d) measuring the overall effectiveness of the program. These treatment programs may also be referred to as the Denver Model, DIR (Developmental, Individual Differences, Relationship-Based)/Floortime, Relationship Development Intervention, or Responsive Teaching.
4	Exercise	These interventions involve an increase in physical exertion as a means of reducing problem behaviors or increasing appropriate behaviors.
5	Exposure Package	These interventions require that the individual with ASD face anxiety-provoking situations while preventing the use of maladaptive strategies used in the past.
6	Imitation-based Interaction	These interventions involve directly teaching individuals with ASD to initiate interactions with their peers.
7	Language Training	These interventions have as their primary goal to increase speech production. Examples include, but are not restricted to, echo relevant word training, oral communication training, oral verbal communication training, structured discourse, simultaneous communication, and individualized language remediation.
8	Massage/Touch Therapy	These interventions have as their primary goals to increase both speech production and understanding of communicative acts. Examples include but are not restricted to: total communication training, position object training, position self-training, and language programming strategies.
9	Multi-component Package	These interventions involve a combination of multiple treatment procedures that are derived from different fields of interest or different theoretical orientations. These treatments do not better fit one of the other treatment "packages" in this list nor are they associated with specific treatment programs.

(*Continued*)

Table 7.3 Continued

Emerging evidence		
	Strategies	*Descriptions*
10	Music Therapy	These interventions seek to teach individual skills or goals through music. A targeted skill (e.g., counting, learning colors, taking turns, etc.) is first presented through song or rhythmic cuing and music is eventually faded.
11	Peer-mediated Instructional Arrangement	These interventions involve targeting academic skills by involving same-aged peers in the learning process. This approach is also described as peer tutoring.
12	Picture Exchange Communication System	This treatment involves the application of a specific augmentative and alternative communication system based on behavioral principles that are designed to teach functional communication to children with limited verbal and/or communication skills.
13	Reductive Package Scripting	These interventions rely on strategies designed to reduce problem behaviors in the absence of increasing alternative appropriate behaviors. Examples include but are not restricted to water mist, behavior chain interruption (without attempting to increase an appropriate behavior), protective equipment, and ammonia.
14	Sign Instruction	These interventions involve the direct teaching of sign language as a means of communicating with other individuals in the environment.
15	Social Communication Intervention	These interventions seek to build social interaction skills in children with ASD by targeting basic responses (e.g., eye contact, name response) to complex social skills (e.g., how to initiate or maintain a conversation).
16	Structured Teaching	Based on neuropsychological characteristics of individuals with autism, this intervention involves a combination of procedures that rely heavily on the physical organization of a setting, predictable schedules, and individualized use of teaching methods. These procedures assume that modifications in the environment, materials, and presentation of information can make thinking, learning, and understanding easier for people with ASD. All of the studies falling into this category met the strict criteria of: (a) targeting the defining symptoms of ASD; (b) having treatment manuals; (c) providing treatment with a high degree of intensity; and (d) measuring the overall effectiveness of the program. These treatment programs may also be referred to as TEACCH (Treatment and Education of Autistic and related Communication-handicapped children).

17	Technology-based Treatment	These interventions require the presentation of instructional materials using the medium of computers or related technologies. Examples include but are not restricted to Alpha Program, Delta Messages, the Emotion Trainer Computer Program, pager, robot, or a PDA (Personal Digital Assistant). The theories behind Technology-based Treatments may vary but they are unique in their use of technology.
18	Theory of Mind Training	These interventions are designed to teach individuals with ASD to recognize and identify mental states (i.e., a person's thoughts, beliefs, intentions, desires and emotions) in oneself or in others and to be able to take the perspective of another person in order to predict their actions.
Unestablished		
1	Auditory Integration Training	This intervention involves the presentation of modulated sounds through headphones in an attempt to retrain an individual's auditory system with the goal of improving distortions in hearing or sensitivities to sound.
2	Facilitated Communication	This intervention involves having a facilitator support the hand or arm of an individual with limited communication skills, helping the individual express words, sentences, or complete thoughts by using a keyboard of words or pictures or typing device.
3	Gluten- and Casein-Free Diet	These interventions involve elimination of an individual's intake of naturally occurring proteins gluten and casein.
4	Sensory Integrative Package	These treatments involve establishing an environment that stimulates or challenges the individual to effectively use all of their senses as a means of addressing overstimulation or understimulation from the environment.

Ineffective or harmful. At this time, there are no treatments that have sufficient evidence specific to the ASD population that meet these criteria.

Using these criteria, the NPDC found 25 interventions to be research based; these are listed on Table 7.4 and compared with the strategies that the NAC determined were evidence based (Odom et al., 2010). The NPDC identified six interventions evidence based that the NSP categorized as emerging. Two interventions (Joint Attention Intervention and Comprehensive Treatment for Young Children) were found to be evidence based by the NSP, but not by NPDC. However, the two agencies had significant crossover agreement about what constituted evidence-based practices even though they used different criteria to determine what was or was not evidence based as you can see on Table 7.4.

Interagency Autism Coordinating Committee

The Interagency Autism Coordinating Committee (IACC) is a federal advisory committee that coordinates all efforts of the U.S. Department of Health and Human Services (HHS) concerning autism in the U.S. This committee was created to ensure that a wide range of ideas and perspectives were represented and discussed in a public forum.

The IACC's mission is to:

- Provide advice to the secretary of Health and Human Services regarding federal activities related to ASD.
- Facilitate the exchange of information on and coordination of ASD activities among the member agencies and organizations.
- Increase public understanding of the member agencies' activities, programs, policies, and research by providing a public forum for discussions related to ASD research and services.

IACC meetings are open to the public and include presentations and discussions on a variety of topics, including activities and projects of the IACC, recent advances in science, and autism policy issues. A portion of each meeting is reserved for public involvement.

Each year the IACC writes a Summary of Advances in Autism Spectrum Disorder. It has been providing these publications since 2007. The Summary of Advances sheds light onto the causes of autism, potential risk factors, diagnosis, and promising early intervention strategies. The Summary of Advances also addresses the prevalence of ASD, both in the United States and internationally, as well as the service needs of people with ASD across the lifespan. The Summary of Advances lists what the IACC thinks are the most influential articles published about autism that year. Most of the articles listed are related to medical issues concerning the causes or treatments of autism. Only a few are related to educational interventions. In 2012, the IACC chose to write about the Denver Early Start Program developed at the MIND Institute as part of its summary of advances. It selected two articles that it believed moved the field forward, these

Table 7.4 Overlap Between Evidence-Based Practices Identified by the National Professional Development Center (NPDC) and the National Standards Project (NSP)

Evidence-Based Practices Identified by the National Professional Development Center (NPDC) on ASD	Established Treatments Identified by the National Standards Project (NSP)										
	Antecedent Package	Behavioral Package	Story-based Intervention Package	Modeling	Naturalistic Teaching Strategies	Peer Training Package	Pivotal Response Treatment	Schedules	Self-Management	Comprehensive Behavioral Treatment for Young Children	Joint Attention Intervention
Prompting	X			X						The NPDC on ASD did not review comprehensive treatment models. Components of The Comprehensive Behavioral Treatment of Young Children overlap with many NPDC-identified practices.	The NPDC on ASD considers joint attention to be an outcome rather than an intervention. Components of joint attention interventions overlap with many NPDC-identified practices.
Antecedent-Based Intervention	X										
Time delay	X										
Reinforcement		X									
Task analysis		X									
Discrete Trial Training		X									
Functional Behavior Analysis		X									
Functional Communication Training		X									
Response Interruption/Redirection		X									
Differential Reinforcement		X									
Social Narratives			X								
Video Modeling				X							
Naturalistic Interventions					X						
Peer Mediated Intervention						X					
Pivotal Response Training							X				
Visual Supports								X			
Structured Work Systems								X			
Self-Management									X		
Parent Implemented Intervention	The NSP did not consider parent-implemented intervention as a category of evidence-based practice. However, 24 of the studies reviewed by the NSP under other intervention categories involve parents implementing the intervention.										
Social Skills Training Groups	Social Skills Training Groups (Social Skills Package) was identified as an emerging practice by the NSP.										
Speech Generating Devices	Speech Generating Devices (Augmentative and Alternative Communication Device) was identified as an emerging practice by the NSP.										
Computer Aided Instruction	Computer Aided Instruction (Technology-based Treatment) was identified as an emerging practice by the NSP.										
Picture Exchange Communication	Picture Exchange Communication System was identified as an emerging practice by the NSP.										
Extinction	Extinction (Reductive Package) was identified as an emerging practice by the NSP.										

National Professional Development Center on Autism Spectrum Disorders. (2013). Retrieved from: http://autismpdc.fpg.unc.edu/content/national-standards-project.

included Dawson et al. (2012) and Rogers et al., (2012). In one study, Dawson et al. (2012) evaluated brain activity in children with autism while they were engaged in the Denver Early Start Program and compared it with that of children who were taking part in other community programs. Researchers evaluated electrical brain activity recorded in response to social (faces) versus nonsocial (toys) used as stimuli for 4-year-old children with ASD. Four-year-old typical children served as a comparison group for both of the ASD groups. Results indicated that when viewing images of faces versus objects, children who received The Denver Early Start Program showed brain activity patterns that were similar to the typical group, characterized by greater brain activation while viewing the social rather than the nonsocial stimuli. Furthermore, the improved pattern of brain activity in the Denver group was also found to be associated specifically with improved social behaviors. In contrast, children in the community intervention group demonstrated the reverse pattern of brain activation, with delayed neural response to social stimuli and increased brain activation during the viewing of object images.

The IACC makes it easy to access up-to-date articles on research that has been vetted by experts and that has important implications for autism.

Meta-Analysis

Although the U.S. Department of Education stipulates that randomized control groups are the gold standard, Spaulding (2009) argues that meta-analysis is "considered by many to be the 'gold standard' of research in special education" (p. 6). Meta-analysis isn't a method of empirical data collection. Researchers perform a meta-analysis by combining the quantitative research that has been published on a topic and then analyzing the data across the various studies together. They weigh the effects of each study based on its strengths (e.g., number of participants) to see the effect size once the studies are combined and analyzed.

Meta-analysis relies on the basic statistic of effect size (ES) and involves averaging effect sizes across a large number of research studies examining a similar phenomenon in order to determine either the level of differentiation between a group (e.g., students with disabilities versus students without) or the magnitude or strength of an instructional intervention. Effect size is simply a way of quantifying the size of the difference between two groups. Effect sizes can be applied to any measured outcome in education or social science. It is especially well-suited for quantifying the effectiveness of a particular intervention relative to some comparison. Instead of simply answering the question, "Does it work or not?" the effect size can tell us how well it works in a range of contexts (Coe, 2002). Through meta-analysis, researchers can determine the magnitude of an intervention or the amount of differentiation among groups, main effects, interactions, and covariation.

Reichow and Wolery (2009) used a meta-analysis technique to examine the efficacy of early intensive behavioral intervention (EIBI) for young children based on the University of California at Los Angeles Young Autism Project methods. They calculated the standardized mean difference effect size for 10 comparative studies to analyze the differences between EIBI and comparison groups. The effect sizes suggested that children receiving EIBI made more gains than children receiving minimal behavioral intervention, eclectic treatment, or treatment as usual. However, the authors cautioned the reader that although these findings were strong, the lack of adequate comparison groups and the nonrandom assignment of participants to groups limited their conclusions about the superiority of EIBI to other treatments.

Limitations

One limitation to research is that a small sample (the number of participants in a research study) of a population (all children with autism) is supposed to represent the larger population. If a practice is effective with the smaller sample, we then generalize the results to the larger population. However, there is a continuum of effectiveness, and not everyone in the sample benefits the same way. Parents and teachers must decide what is best for the child.

The point is that we (researchers, parents, and teachers) should all be skeptical of "evidence" and should always question the accuracy of research. The National Standards Project listed its limitations, for example, by admitting the bias that comes along with deciding what articles to choose based on criteria it determined to be "generally agreed upon by scientists as sufficient for answering the question." Researchers also have to develop a standard for observer agreement. Finally, the National Standards Project did not look at whether the approaches they studied had been implemented in the real world or a naturalistic setting (Wilczynski & Pollack, 2009). Having children improve their behaviors in a highly controlled laboratory with researchers and assistants around to work with children one-on-one is very different than using an intervention in the real world where educators are never as well trained as the person designing the intervention and the peers and/or aides are not as well trained, as well chosen, or as well paid (or compensated) as in a laboratory study. The level of activity and noise is different in classroom settings. If a teacher can't get an evidence-based practice to work in her classroom, it might not be her fault; it might be simply impossible to get this specific strategy to work in the real world.

Problems With Language in Research Literature

When we talk about educating children with special needs, we also need to attend to the language we use, not only because the language we use sets the tone for the field, but because it can actually transform a field (Hutt & Schneider, 2012). The language in special education tends to be medically oriented in its vocabulary and language. The word "intervention" has become the catch phrase for all educational strategies, whether or not they are medical or even therapeutic in the traditional sense. If a person is helping a child with autism improve any skill, whether it is academic, vocation, linguistic, or social, somehow they are all called interventions. So, really, when we talk about an "intervention," we are usually talking about a specific educational technique, strategy, or pedagogical practice that educators are using with a child to help him or her improve in school or home. This is also true for the phrase "response to intervention" (RTI) which could just as easily have been called "response to a good instructional technique" and that would have cleared up a lot of confusion for general education teachers who do not use the word "intervention." An intervention is a specific way of presenting instruction, or a therapeutic technique (which is often educational in nature), for one child based on the needs of that child so that a teacher can move the child forward in his or her progress. Students are monitored to ensure they are responding adequately to an intervention designed to help them achieve at the level of their peers so they do not fall behind expected grade levels.

The history of special education language is complicated. We use some medical terms, in part, because some of our professional content comes from the fields of psychology; physical, occupational, and speech therapy; and medicine. In all of those fields, the goal is to diagnose people, design therapy, and/or prescribe cures. The underlying assumption is that there is a medical problem, a psychopathology, or another disorder that needs to be fixed. In education, the goal is often growth, with a sense that people need to learn; there is nothing wrong with students, they simply need to acquire knowledge, and usually we consider students normal from wherever they start their process. In special education, medical research informs our practice, and so our language has been influenced by medicine, both its language and its culture, and sometimes we get confused because the goals of the two fields are very different.

Many experts have suggested that as a "science," education, in general, has also tried to play catch up to hard sciences such as medicine in terms of creating a body of literature to drive improvements (Darling-Hammon, Bransford, & LePage, 2005), especially in addressing the teaching and learning of children with special needs. In doing so, the field has tried to prove its legitimacy with a particular nod to medical terminology and methods. Although increased rigor in research can move the field ahead and improve the delivery of education and services for children with special needs, forced medical terminology in educational research can be a source of confusion. Below, we have provided a paragraph from an article about an educational intervention that sounds like it was written by academics with backgrounds in medicine or psychology (Thomeer, 2012):

> Results of this study suggested that a CSBI adapted by school staff, parents, and researchers can be accepted, positively regarded, and implemented with high rates of **treatment integrity** in school settings. This finding is noteworthy, as the CSBI addressed both the **core clinical**

> **features** and individual needs of the children with HFASDs. It is also noteworthy that teacher ratings of acceptability (i.e., BIRS) were higher for teachers at the end of the **Phase II (compared with Phase I)**. This may suggest that experience with implementing the CSBI positively affects perceptions of the **treatment's acceptability.** At the end of Phase II, the descriptive feedback provided by parents and school staff during focus groups indicated that the **manualized instructional procedures, dosages, and content were feasible.** The only revision to the **protocol** involved a minor adjustment in the IDN feedback format used by teachers during the school day. (emphasis added)

Using this type of language presents two concerns. First, the material can be misleading, especially to parents, who think doctors are giving them medical advice. These researchers talk about treatment and even dosages, yet they are really talking about educational practices. Second, this language is not familiar to the teachers who would implement these programs and interventions. The abbreviation CSBI stands for the Comprehensive Summer Psychosocial Treatment program for children with high-functioning autism (Thomeer, 2012). In this article, the researchers discuss how focus-group participants identified five components of a summer camp that they believe should be included in camps for children with autism:

1. Social skills groups (SSGs): Each session was conducted using the nine-step instructional protocol of *Skillstreaming* (Goldstein, McGinnis, Sprafkin, Gershaw, & Klein, 1997). This protocol involves teaching, modeling, role-playing, performance feedback, and transfer of learning.
2. Therapeutic activities (TAs): The special/general education teacher, social worker, or school psychologist had target students work collaboratively with general education students in various activities. These cooperative activities required two or more students (but could involve an entire class) and were conducted to practice and reinforce skills learned in skills groups and expand the students' interests/activities.
3. Computer-based face and voice emotion recognition instruction: Included mind-reading computer instruction three times a week (Baron-Cohen, Golan, Wheelwright, & Hill, 2004).
4. An individual daily note (IDN): Included a behavioral reinforcement system used to reinforce skills and reduce behaviors. Performance was recorded on the sheet and sent home to parents.
5. Parent training (PT): Parents are provided with training on how to work with their children to assist in their social and educational development process.

A school that provides comprehensive intervention with the components listed above would probably help children with autism develop in many ways, but it is not "medical" and it is also not formally therapeutic in the way it is described in the various articles listed because none of the practices would require a registered psychologist or therapist to present them to children (Lopata et al., 2012; Thomeer, 2012).

Conclusion

What is important is that as the field of autism broadens and we learn more from researchers and practitioners, we—teachers, parents, and other researchers—must be critical consumers of all literature. We must be diligent in examining evidence with a discriminating eye toward cost, efficacy, and practicality, and we must be part of the conversation. It is important for teachers to use evidence-based practices, but it is also important for teachers to be educated about research and understand how experts determine how strategies are deemed evidence based.

References

Baron-Cohen, S., Golan, O., Wheelwright, S., & Hill, J. J. (2004). *Mind reading: The interactive guide to emotions.* London, UK: Jessica Kingsley Publishers.

Coe, R. (2002). It's effect size, Stupid: What effect size is and why it is important. Paper presented at the annual conference of the British Educational Research Association, University of Exeter, England.

Darling-Hammond, L., Bransford, J., & LePage, P. (2005). Introduction. In L. Darling-Hammond, J. Bransford, P. LePage, K. Hammerness, & H. Duffy (Eds.), *Preparing teachers for a changing world: What teachers should learn and be able to do* (pp. 1–39). San Francisco, CA: Jossey-Bass.

Dawson, G., Jones, E. J., Merkle, K., Venema, K., Lowy, R., Faja, S., Webb, S. J. (2012). Early behavioral intervention is associated with normalized brain activity in young children with autism. *Journal of American Academy of Child and Adolescent Psychiatry, 51*(11), 1150–1159.

Goldstein, A. P., McGinnis, E., Sprafkin, R. P., Gershaw, N. J., & Klein, P. (1997). *Skillstreaming the adolescent: New strategies and perspectives for teaching prosocial skills* (rev. ed.). Champaign, IL: Research Press.

Hutt, E. L., & Schneider, J. (2012, December 14). The rhetoric of reform. *Teachers College Record.* ID number: 16972. Retrieved from http://www.tcrecord.org.

Lopata, C., Thomeer, M., Volker, M. A., Lee, G., Smith, T. H., Smith, R. A., . . . Toomey, J. A. (2012). Feasibility and initial efficacy of a comprehensive school-based intervention for high-functioning autism spectrum disorders. *Psychology in the Schools, 49*(10), 963–974.

Odom, S., Collet-Klingenberg, L., Rogers, S., & Hatton, D. (2010). Evidence-based practices in interventions for children and youth with autism spectrum disorders. *Preventing School Failure, 54*(4), 275–282.

Reichow, B., & Wolery, M. (2009). Comprehensive synthesis of early intensive behavioral interventions for young children with autism based on the UCLA Young Autism Project Model. *Journal of Autism & Developmental Disorders, 39*(1), 23–41.

Rogers, S. J., Estes, A., Lord, C., Vismara, L., Winter, J., Fitzpatrick, A., . . . Dawson, G. (2012). Effects of a brief Early Start Denver Model (ESDM)-based parent intervention on toddlers at risk for autism spectrum disorders: A randomized controlled trial. *Journal of American Academy of Child Adolescent Psychiatry, 51*(10), 1052–1065.

Sparks, S. D. (2010). "What Works" broadens its Research Standards Clearinghouse moves past "gold standard." *Education Week, 30*(8), 1, 12.

Spaulding, L. S. (2009). Best practices and interventions in special education: How do we know what works? *Teaching Exceptional Children Plus, 5*(3). Retrieved from http://journals.cec.sped.org/tecplus/vol5/iss3/art2

Thomeer, M. L. (2012) Collaborative development and component trials of a comprehensive school-based intervention for children with HFSASDS. *Psychology in the Schools, 49*(10), 955–962.

Whitehurst, G. J. (2003). *Identifying and implementing educational practices supported by rigorous evidence: A user-friendly guide.* Washington, DC: U.S. Department of Education, Institute of Education Sciences, National Center for Educational Evaluation and Regional Assistance.

Wilczynski, S. M., & Pollack, E. G. (2009). *Autism-based practice and autism in the school.* Randolph, MA: National Autism Center.

Chapter Eight
Teaching Methods From Autism's Past

In the field of autism, it is common for people to develop instructional or behavioral interventions and then market them through packages or programs. Teachers are not only trained through university special education departments, but also by attending workshops, seminars, and conferences to learn about different models and methods such as the TEACCH Method, the Floortime model, Michelle Garcia Winner's social thinking, or the pivotal response method.

One of the most important challenges teachers face is evaluating novel approaches for children with autism. Over the past 20 to 30 years, both academics and practitioners who have been working in special education have been involved in evaluating various methods. Some of these strategies and products are what Dr. Laura Schreibman of the Autism Intervention Research Program at UC San Diego describes as "bogus" (American Psychological Association [APA], 2012). In a recent interview, Schreibman gave an example of one intervention she described as ineffective—facilitated communication. In this intervention, children with autism are "facilitated" by an adult who supports their hand or arm as they activate a keypad or other letter display. Through this method, children supposedly write text telling their parents things such as what they want for dinner or how they are feeling. Some are convinced that this approach works, even though experts, such as those in the National Autism Center's Standards Project, have concluded that this intervention has no evidence to support its effectiveness (Wilczynski & Pollack, 2009) and that intuitively it doesn't make sense.

Because children with high-level autism can improve so much over time, parents will do anything to help their children. Given our entrepreneurial culture, it is important to be extra careful where determining where money is spent. As discussed in Chapter 7, it is not always easy to determine whether an intervention is evidence based, so it is important to look for multiple criteria to determine efficacy.

What parents and teachers can do is to be critical consumers of research and theory. After interviewing the families who participated in our research, we were most impressed with their ongoing motivation and boundless energy to help their children find the resources they needed. These parents have worked hard to understand the nature of their children's challenges and to be informed consumers of services. Parents and teachers must ask questions, expect answers, understand instructional practices, and look for objective evidence of effectiveness.

Applied Behavior Analysis (ABA)

When the National Autism Center (Wilczynski & Pollack, 2009) published its results on what it determined was evidence based, many stakeholders expected it to look at specific programs. Instead, it looked more globally at "characteristics of groups of programs," such as whether a program was "naturalistic." The center determined that naturalistic programs are evidence based. For the most part, it didn't name specific programs but rather named evidence-based characteristics (see Chapter 7).

The one exception it made (in a way) was that it declared applied behavior analysis (ABA) to be evidence based, which gave all ABA programs the green flag to move ahead and start "treating," "intervening," and "teaching" children with autism. ABA, is not a specific treatment. According to Dillenburger & Keenan (2009), ABA is "the science on which a wide range of techniques are based that have been used to help people with a variety of behaviors and diagnoses, autism being one of them" (p. 193). ABA stands for behaviorism, the philosophy of science it is built upon; basic experimental analysis of behavior; and applied research, which is ABA. So Discrete Trial Training and Pivotal Response are two types of ABA.

Historians and psychologists claim that behaviorism emerged in the early twentieth century as a reaction to Freudian psychology, because Freud, and others like him, often made assumptions about people based on untested psychological methods (such as saying that someone is in "denial" or someone is "projecting"). The primary tenet of behaviorism, as expressed in the writings of J. B. Watson and B. F. Skinner, as well as many others, is that psychology should only concern itself with the observable behaviors of people and animals, not with unobservable events that take place in a person's mind. Behaviorists maintain that behaviors can be described scientifically without referring to internal physiological or psychological events or to hypothetical constructs such as thoughts, beliefs, and attitudes. In the field of autism, there are many different ABA methods. In this section, we discuss the following: (a) Lovaas, (b) discrete trial training (DTT), (c) pivotal response training (PVT), (d) incidental teaching (IT).

What Is Behaviorism?

In contrast to psychodynamic theorists (e.g., Freud), behaviorists study only observable behaviors. Their explanations of personality focus on learning. B. F. Skinner, Albert Bandura, and Walter Mischel all proposed important behaviorist theories. Skinner suggested that our responsibilities as adults, especially teachers, is to make educational choices and then to use whatever processes we have, including conditioning, to reach these goals (Ozmon & Craver, 1992).

Behaviorism is based on the idea that if children are rewarded for a behavior, they are more likely to repeat or continue a behavior. Eventually, over time, with enough practice, they acquire the skill. For example, a child who is rewarded whenever he looks at his teacher or when she calls his name may gradually learn to make eye contact on his own.

ABA includes the direct observation and measurement of behavior; it also uses positive reinforcement to promote skill acquisition and positive behavioral changes while reducing problematic behaviors.

Criticisms of Behaviorism

Behavioral methods in education have been criticized in the past (Gambrill, 2013). In special education in general, especially early childhood, a number of charges have been made against the behavioral perspective over the years. Many reflect differences in conceptual or philosophical perspective. Some may agree on the basic direction, but disagree on its relative value or importance, and some may have the wrong information. Johnston and Brinamen (2012), listed four criticisms that overlap in many ways, including, (a) behaviorism is a simple stimulus–response (S–R) approach, offering an overly mechanistic model of human behavior; (b) behaviorism offers a worldview that overemphasizes the external control of behavior, and thus is dehumanizing; (c) behaviorism is too complex and esoteric, without explicit links to problems or application; and (d) behaviorism is limited in its potential application and cannot address the range of "real-world" problems that confront fields such as early childhood special education. Another criticism often mentioned is that behavioral techniques rely too much on teacher-centered instruction and does not use the child's interests.

Malone (2003) argues that behaviorism has changed and that educators are more apt to be familiar with the older absolutist rendition of behaviorism, the familiar caricature of techniques aimed at changing "target" behaviors. This old behaviorism has the aura of animal training about it and portrays the child as a set of disconnected behaviors to be "modified" when necessary.

These two sets of educators lay out the most common criticisms, that behaviorism was dehumanizing because it resembled animal training as opposed to a more sophisticated form of teaching where children learn a more conceptual understanding of how the world works. The other criticism is that to study only those behaviors that we can observe is too limiting, that we cannot explore how people feel or what they think or why they think the way they do, and that this limits our understanding of the world.

Those who sing the praises of behavioral techniques, especially for children with autism will first say that it works for many children with autism better than other strategies and that is what is most important. Second, it is no longer teacher focused; many ABA techniques use student centered and context centered approaches. Others claim that it is actually humanizing because it helps children with autism communicate and live without behaviors that often get them ostracized and excluded from society. Finally, many behaviorists would argue that some educators who have negative feelings about behavioral methods are still under the impression that people use punishments, when all ABA providers are now trained to use positive behavior supports rather than any types of punishments. Rewards are used to motivate children, but the goal is ultimately to help children learn to be intrinsically motivated. Behaviorists believe that whenever children or adults engage in a behavior they are being rewarded, whether externally or internally.

Although behavioral researchers tout its effectiveness, ABA does not work for all children. Children diagnosed with ASD have varying symptoms and developmental disorders and no one therapy can possibly fit all children with autism. Intensive ABA has helped many children with ASD reach their full potential, but for many children with ASD the results of ABA have been disappointing.

Any type of ABA can be highly intensive for children with ASD; and it is more effective earlier in a child's life. Although ABA can benefit children at later ages, children who are older are more likely to resist this type of intervention and may become recalcitrant. Some proponents of ABA in the autism treatment debate recommend as much as 40 hours of therapy a week when children are young. However, ABA is too expensive for many parents to afford, costing as much as $70,000 per year.

ABA and the Autism Treatment Debate: It's About the Money

The question of who should pay for ABA for children diagnosed with ASD is central to the autism treatment debate. Health insurance companies argue that ABA is education, and therefore not medically necessary for the treatment of children with autism. The fact that many school districts have included ABA to varying extents bolsters the health insurers' argument. So does the fact that there is no specialized degree or certification required for practitioners of ABA as a treatment for ASD.

Others argue that ABA is a necessary treatment and should be covered by health insurance. Many states have passed health insurance reform laws that require health insurers to cover ABA as a medically necessary treatment for children with autism.

Whether people understand the new behaviorism or the old, whether the criticisms still make sense today or not, many parents sing the praises of ABA. That is especially true for parents who have young children with speech or communication problems or who have severe behavior problems. In our study, we found that about half of the children in our study were diagnosed after ABA would have been offered (as early intervention). Of those whose children had been diagnosed early, most of the working-class families had never heard of ABA. Those children who had received ABA were those diagnosed early from upper-income families. These are some of the comments from the families in our study who received ABA.

JANA: ABA—most useful, hands down.

STACY: I felt that ABA was great and helped us keep structure around the programs that we were doing with him and goals around it, and when we achieved those goals, go to new goals.

KIMBERLY: He made such progress quickly, they were organized, and I think there was a lot of mutual respect. They respected how I approached things, and I respected how they approached things. And we worked very creatively together; we put together a program that didn't look like a traditional ABA program.

Looking at Five ABA Methods

Lovaas

Ole Ivar Lovaas was a Norwegian-American psychologist at UCLA. He is considered to be one of the fathers of ABA, which was formerly called behavior modification. Through his development of the Lovaas technique, many give him credit for being the first researcher to provide evidence that the behavior of children with autism can be modified through teaching. Today his technique is called early intensive behavior intervention (EIBI) or the Lovaas model of ABA. Many researchers have described Lovaas's techniques as being effective in reducing inappropriate behaviors and enhancing communication, learning, and social behaviors based on 30 years of studies (for example see Reichow & Wolery, 2009, for a recent synthesis of research on EIBI).

The Lovaas method begins with intensive, one-on-one treatment for children with autism under the age of 4, preferably as young as 2 years. It is recommended that a person work with the child in his or her home for 30 to 40 hours per week for 2 to 3 years. Instruction should gradually progress from one-on-one to small group and, finally, to large group instruction. A one-on-one, or "shadow," aide is used in school settings to assist the child as needed; however, the goal is for the child to eventually function in the general classroom environment with little or no support. Although what ABA people used to call aversives (unpleasant stimuli or events) and punishment were once a part of the Lovaas method, these have now been eliminated (Smith & Lovaas, 1998). In the past, aversives used to consist of things such as taking children out of the class and into time-out when they did not respond to what they were supposed to do within 10 minutes. Then, they would be taken back to their seats. The timer would start again. The teacher would be expected to make sure this process was kept consistent. If the student did what he or she was asked, the child would get a reward; if not, the child would be escorted out of the room. Physical punishment and other aversives were used in the original studies but were quickly eliminated from the program.

Prompts and rewards are slowly phased out as the child learns the skill so that the child is able to generalize performance and positive behaviors for use outside the tutoring sessions. To reduce undesirable behaviors, such as aggressiveness, self-stimulatory actions, and tantrums, teachers try to ignore them while teaching more appropriate responses. With the Lovaas method, practitioners believe that to discipline or stop these behaviors is not only ineffective, but that it can actually encourage them. Children on the autism spectrum often respond to frustration, anger, and forcefulness from caregivers by repeating the actions that create such emotive responses. They tend to view them as more stimulation, which can be a positive reward for them.

In the Lovaas method, children are first taught readiness by learning to sit still and respond appropriately. Other beginning skills include early language, nonverbal and verbal imitation, and appropriate play with toys. In more advanced stages, children learn skills that are measured across various settings to help ensure that they can generalize and apply them to other environments, such as home and school. Skills might include learning the calendar, show and tell, listening and joining in conversation, asking questions and then repeating the answers to others, learning by observation, and basic techniques for improving social interaction.

Children are taught through the use of prompts. Prompts include helping the child by guiding his or her hand, gesturing the proper response, and providing verbal prompts. With each correct response, positive reinforcement is used to encourage the appropriate behaviors. Reinforcements, or positive rewards, are tailored according to each child's preferences. They can include a small break with a favorite toy, book, or snack, as well as social rewards, such as verbal praise, tickles, hugs, and physical reinforcement.

What constitutes ABA is still a bit confusing, however, and it is becoming even more confusing as funding sources are providing more money for behavioral therapy and not for other types of therapies. For example, according to the Lovaas Center website (2011), the following is the Lovaas plan for the first 3 years of treatment:

> During the first year, the primary instructional method during this time is individual discrete trial training (see entry) in the child's home. In the second year, children spend increasing amounts of time having

supervised playdates with typically developing peers (to provide opportunities for peer tutoring and increase social skills), enter general education preschools (to facilitate adjustment to school), and participate in Incidental Teaching in addition to Discrete Trial Training. During the third and final year, the focus is on gradually reducing individual instruction and increasing inclusion into classroom settings (either in general education if the children can function effectively in that setting, or in special education if the children continue to require specialized support services).

According to this plan, in the second year children have supervised integrated play dates, which many educators would not consider ABA, let alone part of the Lovaas method. Incidental teaching is considered a form of ABA, but it is surprising to see it listed as part of a Lovaas treatment plan.

On the other hand, ABA is the application of behaviorism. The main belief of early behaviorists was that psychologists should only be working to change observable behaviors that could be measured. And beyond that, the only way to make changes to people's behavior was by changing the reinforcement for that behavior, so interventions that change behavior through reinforcement should all be able to call themselves ABA.

Discrete Trial Training

Discrete trial training (DTT) is a one-on-one instructional approach used to teach skills in a planned, controlled, and systematic manner. The professionals who use DTT tell us that it is used when a learner needs to learn a skill best taught in small repeated steps. Each trial, or teaching opportunity, has a definite beginning and end, thus the descriptor "discrete trial." The DTT method makes use of antecedents and consequences, and they are carefully planned and implemented. Positive praise and specific rewards are used to reinforce desired skills or behaviors. Data collection is an important part of DTT and supports decision making by providing teachers and practitioners with information about beginning skill level, progress and challenges, skill acquisition and maintenance, and generalization of learned skills or behaviors (Bogin, 2008).

According to Anderson, Taras, and Cannon (1996), DTT has four distinct parts: (a) the trainer's presentation, (b) the child's response to the instruction, (c) the teacher's reaction or response, and (d) a short pause between the response and the next instruction (between interval trials).

DTT is an offshoot of the Lovaas method. For example, the UCLA Young Autism Project (aka Lovaas method) is one treatment program mainly for preschool aged children with autism. It uses discrete trials as its main instructional method and follows a fairly set instructional program beginning with early receptive language and ending with programs focused on achieving skills in self-help and community and school situations. Not all programs using DTT follow the same program sequences or curriculum as the UCLA program.

What distinguishes DTT programs is the intensity and duration of the training and the primary role of the discrete-trial method of instruction. DTT programs generally involve several hours of direct one-on-one instruction every day over many months or years. Though the basic model for DTT appears relatively straightforward, according to people who use the method applying the model effectively is not so straightforward. This is because the people who develop these models have a lot of ideas about the way autistic children learn and how they should be taught, and the steps they have developed over the years are meant to take advantage of these specific beliefs in order to help the child reach his or her full potential. For example, people who administer DTT believe a trainer should only ask a child once for a response and the child should be taught to respond quickly to instructions. Many parents of high-functioning children have been told their children have processing delays that cause their children to be slow to respond.

DTT behaviorists believe that most children can be taught to respond quickly with a simple prompt and fading technique because their delays are more likely related to an attention and compliance issue rather than a processing delay. In their view, asking the child once and making sure he or she responds within a few seconds is important. The people who train others how to use DTT have lots of rules that go along with their philosophy. Many people who have developed specific interventions are concerned that people will not "do them right." This is the reason they are so picky about making sure people are "trained appropriately" before they use their methods. So, simply handing out books describing the steps is not good enough for most of them; they want people to be trained in a way so they can implement the programs with fidelity.

One parent considered it important that through ABA she was able to better understand what her child could or could not do:

JANA: You couldn't figure out what did he know, what did he not know, what could you teach him if he wasn't compliant, if he wasn't attending and complying? So that was huge, so they [ABA professionals] did a lot of funky stuff with him just around getting that compliance.

Bogin (2008) explains how DTT meets the evidence-based practice criteria within the early childhood and elementary age groups for promoting the development of communication/language, adaptive behavior, cognitive/academic skills, and social and play skills and for reducing interfering behaviors. Various researchers have conducted studies looking at the effectiveness of DTT (Cohen, Amerine-Dickens, & Smith, 2006; McEachin, Smith, & Lovaas, 1993; Lovaas, 1987). In terms of age-appropriate treatment, DTT can be used to teach students from early childhood through elementary school at all ability levels. Because DTT is intensive and repetitive nature, there is more evidence for using

DTT with younger children (i.e., 2 to 9 years of age). What skills are most appropriate for DTT to address? DTT has been shown to have positive effects on children's academic, cognitive, communication/language, social, and behavioral skills. DTT can also be used to teach attending, imitation, and symbolic-play skills. What is the most appropriate setting for DTT? It can be taught in home, school, or community settings. Because discrete trials are often carried out in an intensive and repetitive fashion, quiet areas with limited distractions are often used (Bogin, 2008).

Pivotal Response Training (PRT)

Lynn and Robert Koegel at the University of California, Santa Barbara developed pivotal response training, or PRT (Koegel, Koegel, Harrower, & Carter, 1999). PRT is a behavioral intervention model based on the principles of ABA. It was originally called the natural language paradigm (NLP). PRT is described by the Koegels as being both comprehensive, as listed by the National Research Council (2001) of the National Academy of Sciences, and empirically supported, as recognized by both the National Professional Development Center (Odom, Collet-Klingenberg, Rogers, & Hatton, 2010) and the National Standards Project (Wilczynski & Pollack, 2009). PRT is considered a naturalistic intervention model.

Specific research-based procedures, including child choice, task variation, interspersing maintenance and acquisition tasks, rewarding attempts, and the use of direct natural reinforcements, are incorporated to make the intervention extremely powerful and efficient. The goal of PRT is to move the child with ASD towards a more typical developmental trajectory through individualized intervention objectives based on the child's needs.

PRT targets each core area of development and focuses on increasing motivation for learning in children with ASD. PRT is implemented in the child's natural environments (e.g., home, community, and school) and emphasizes parent education so that family members are agents of intervention and that learning can be embedded across daily routines.

According to the National Professional Development Center's report of evidence-based practices, the motivational techniques inside PRT's teaching framework can lead to the development of verbal communication as the primary mode of communication in 85%–90% of children with autism who begin intervention before the age of 5 (NPDC, 2007). By analyzing a number of research studies (Horner, Carr, Halle, McGee, Odom, & Wolery, 2005; Nathan & Gorman, 2002; Odom, Brantlinger, Gersten, Horner, Thompson, & Harris, 2004; Rogers & Vismara, 2008), the NPDC identified some positive outcomes for those using PRT, including the increased use of social initiations, less social avoidance, more toy play, and less stereotypic language (Odom et al., 2010).

The Koegel's and their colleagues state that PRT uses naturalistic environments and that attempts at a target behavior are rewarded with a natural reinforcement (e.g., if a child attempts a request for a stuffed animal, the child receives the animal, not a piece of candy or other unrelated reinforcement) (Koegel, Koegel, Harrower, & Carter, 1999).

In a critical review, Delprato (2001) demonstrated that PRT is more effective than DTT.

One of the major differences between PRT and DTT is that DTT breaks a skill into smaller parts and then practitioners teach each subpart one at a time. PRT focuses on strategies that motivate the child to complete an entire task, and when the child completes the entire task, the child is naturally reinforced to continue, improving the child's responsiveness. DTT is more structured and often uses flash cards and drill-type activities, whereas PRT uses activities found in the child's everyday environment with task variation. In addition to following the child's lead, PRT uses reinforcements directly related to the task in most cases. DTT uses a reinforcement not necessarily related to the task (such as food).

The Koegel's have spent a lot of time developing PRT programs and materials. People interested in PRT can attend live workshops or learn about the program through online modules. See www.koegelautism.com/about-pivotal-response-training.html for more information about PRT.

Incidental Teaching

Incidental teaching (IT) is an ABA strategy that was first described by Hart and Risley (1982) in their work with economically disadvantaged children. Incidental teaching, as used by Hart and Risley, was designed to increase the amount and complexity of the language used in the children they worked with, and to increase generalization and spontaneous use of language. They described the steps of IT as follows: (a) arrange the environment to contain items of interest for the child, (b) wait for the child to initiate an interaction about an item of interest, (c) ask for more elaborate language or approximations to speech, and (d) provide the object for which the child initiated contact (Fenske, Krantz, & McClannahan, 2001). For example, a teacher may put educational materials for a particular child who doesn't speak up and ask for things up on a shelf where he has to ask for help. When he asks for help, the teacher may prompt him to provide a more sophisticated question, such as "Will you help me get my materials off the top shelf?" instead of "Please help me." IT has been a strategy of interest to educators working with children with autism for some time because it seems like a positive way to address some of the problems with generalization and lack of spontaneity and initiation often seen in children with autism who have been primarily exposed to very structured, adult-directed teaching in other ABA programs, (McGee, Morrier, and Daly, 1999).

IT is unique in its focus on child-directed teaching, in other words, following the child's lead regarding interests with naturally occurring daily activities. This is particularly useful with children with autism, who often tend to exhibit difficulty maintaining interest in teacher- or parent-led activities. Most parents and teachers are very accustomed to teaching children many different skills throughout the day in the natural environment. For example, parents may point to pictures in a book and ask the child to label the pictures. Teachers ask children to make requests and choices in the classroom. These are all teaching opportunities. IT involves being intentional and planning for those "teachable moments" as if the child initiates them. Almost any situation throughout the day can be made into a "teachable moment." Daily routines that can be used for teaching include: snacks, playtime, field trips, videos, recess, and academic tasks. Here are the procedures as described by Fenske, Krantz, and McClannahan (2001):

1. Arrange the environment to contain items of interest for the child.
2. Wait for the child to initiate an interaction about an item of interest.
3. Ask for more elaborate language or approximations to speech.
4. Provide the object for which the child initiated.

Once the child responds appropriately, it is important to confirm the child's response by reacting to the request, giving praise, or expanding a phrase (this is the natural consequence or reinforcement). Also, data should be collected whenever possible to assess present levels of ability, ongoing progress, and necessary changes. Once initial levels of responses are achieved, prompting can be used to gain more elaborate responses. Researchers found that the naturalistic strategies of both PRT and IT were more effective at helping children to learn specific skills than the more clinical DTT (Delprato, 2001; Ingersoll, 2010).

As mentioned earlier, although ABA programs are considered successful by the research world, and also by some of the parents in our study, some still criticize ABA-based programs because they do not provide relationship-based programs that help children develop social relationships with adults or other children, which brings us to the DIR model and Floortime therapy.

The Developmental, Individual Differences, Relationship-Based (DIR) Model/Floortime

Floortime therapy derives from the Developmental, Individual-differences, Relationship-based (DIR) model developed by child psychiatrist Stanley Greenspan. Its premise is that adults can help children expand their circles of communication by meeting them at their developmental level and building on their strengths (Greenspan, Wieder, & Simmons, 1998). Greenspan developed his DIR model as therapy for children with a variety of developmental delays and issues and in a more practical sense, he called DIR "Floortime" (Wieder & Greenspan, 2003). This model represents a Floorplay approach for parents and caregivers. Floortime encourages parents to literally engage children at their level—by getting on the floor to play. Families can combine it with other behavioral therapies or use it as an alternative approach. Therapists and parents engage children through activities each individual child enjoys. Parents and caregivers enter the child's games and follow the child's lead. In turn, therapists teach parents how to direct their children into increasingly complex interactions. This process of "opening and closing circles of communication" is a central tenet of the Floortime approach.

Wieder and Greenspan (2003) explain that the DIR model doesn't just relate to development, individual, and relationship. The D stands for the *developmental* level of emotional and intellectual functioning, which determines the child's *individual* (I) way of reacting to and comprehending movement, sound, sight, and other sensations and formulates learning *relationships* (R) that affect basic interactions at home in school and in different therapies geared to the child's profile. Behavioral methods do not focus on the relationship between adult and child, or between the child with autism and his or her peers, to be social. In the DIR model, interactions that allow for sharing of emotions between the child and parent, teachers, or peers move the child up the developmental ladder.

Floortime is more than just following the child and commenting on what he or she is doing; it is the active process of interacting in a continuous and fast-paced manner with the child in all ways, including sensory-motor, preverbal, problem solving, symbolic play, and abstract conversations. The goal is to strengthen each of those developmental capacities, which together form the foundation for higher-order thinking and skill development. Wieder and Greenspan (2003) explain "that some children have language and some limited interests, but lack the interactive capacities for mutual attention, relationships, and the back and forth affect gesturing necessary to expand feelings and themes. These gaps derail development of symbolic and emotional abilities" (p. 427).

In 2003, Greenspan and Wieder studied Joey, a child on the autism spectrum who spent 3 years engaging in Floortime with his father. Over that time, Joey enjoyed six daily Floortime sessions. He continuously improved, and Greenspan and Wieder concluded that Floortime helped Joey progress. In 2007, independent researchers conducted a pilot study that showed the benefit of Floortime for children with autism (Solomon, Necheles, Ferch, & Bruckman, 2007). More recent studies by new researchers (e.g., Pajareya & Nopmaneejumruslers, 2011), have also demonstrated the value of Floortime.

Ideally, Floortime takes place in a calm environment. This can be at home or in a professional setting. Formal sessions range from 2 to 5 hours a day, although 5 hours seems excessive. They include training for parents and caregivers as well as interaction with the child. Therapists encourage families to use Floortime principles in their daily lives.

TEACCH

TEACCH is the acronym for Training and Education of Autistic and Related Communication Handicapped Children. It is an approach to teaching children with autism that was developed at the University of North Carolina by Dr. Eric

Schopler in 1972. It is one of the older and more establish educational teaching models for children with autism, and it was originally developed for children with more severe challenges. The main TEACCH website developed for their home base in North Carolina (TEACCH, 2013) seeks to dispel certain myths about TEACCH, such as the belief that TEACCH is only useful for children with intellectual disabilities or those in contained classrooms; it also refutes the belief that the TEACCH method isolates children and adults.

According to the Autism Speaks website (2013), "TEACCH is based on a respect for the culture of autism" as a way of thinking about the characteristic patterns of thinking and patterned behavior seen in individuals with ASD. TEACCH uses an intervention called structured teaching that is based on understanding the learning characteristics of individuals with autism and the use of visual supports to promote meaning and independence.

The TEACCH model is one of the most unique models of instruction in existence, in that in this instructional model the developers focused on changing the environment, as well as the instruction. A typical TEACCH classroom has separate stations and well-defined areas for tasks such as individual work, group activities and play, cooking, or self-care. Teachers use pictures, or "visual supports," to help communicate schedules to help students transition between activities. These areas or stations are often highly organized so that children can access materials independently and complete tasks on their own. Materials may be stored in bins or in cubbies or cupboards where individuals can access these materials. Below is a picture of a TEACCH workstation (Figure 8.1). The

Figure 8.1 Picture of a TEACCH workstation.

Photo provided by University of North Carolina TEACCH Autism Program with permission.

workstation is organized with bins and labeled, there are many visual supports around the station and the child is in an area where he can work by himself without distraction.

A student may sit at a workstation and complete activities such as matching pictures or letters or finishing a worksheet, use augmentative communication boards for answering questions or requesting items from the teacher. The use of visual supports can help relieve frustration for nonverbal children. In addition, it can foster the recall of words for those who are starting to speak.

Teachers and aides use visual supports to organize the physical and social environment. The aim is to help the student more easily predict and understand daily activities and respond in appropriate ways. Visual supports likewise help the student approach specific tasks in a step-by-step manner. See www.autismspeaks.org/what-autism/treatment/training-and-education-autistic-and-related-communication-handicapped-children for more on TEACCH.

The Ziggurat Model

The Ziggurat model was developed by Ruth Aspy and Barry G. Grossman. This model is not an instructional strategy, rather it is a framework into which the strategies are plugged in (Smith Myles, Grossman, Aspy, Henry, & Bixler, 2007). The framework helps to make sure that critical areas are not left unaddressed. The developers of the Ziggurat model believed that the reason why so many interventions fail and why so many children have unnecessary meltdowns is because critical areas are left unaddressed. The Ziggurat model has been used to develop an entire program of instruction with assessments as part of their model. Once teachers have learned the model, they can choose the strategies appropriate for the individual and plug them in at the appropriate level. A ziggurat, which looks like a stair-stepped pyramid, is used as a symbol for the model. The levels of the ziggurat represent different areas of intervention for individuals on the autism spectrum. Figure 8.2 is a picture of this Ziggurat and the types of supports that are needed at each level.

The Ziggurat model has five tiers corresponding to the essential areas required in the development of a child's program plan: (a) sensory and biological, (b) reinforcement, (c) structure and visual/tactile supports, (d) task demands, and (e) skills to teach. Aspy and Grossman claim that the Ziggurat model is simple to use but is also comprehensive and thorough. They developed this framework because they believed that although it was easy to find information describing specific interventions, it was difficult to find information on how to develop an intervention plan. So they designed this model to simplify a complex process. They designed this for both parents and professionals and expected the Ziggurat model to be a useful guide in developing more thorough and effective interventions. Although the Ziggurat Model is designed to address the needs of all individuals with ASD, they say that their book on the Ziggurat model was written explicitly for those who are higher

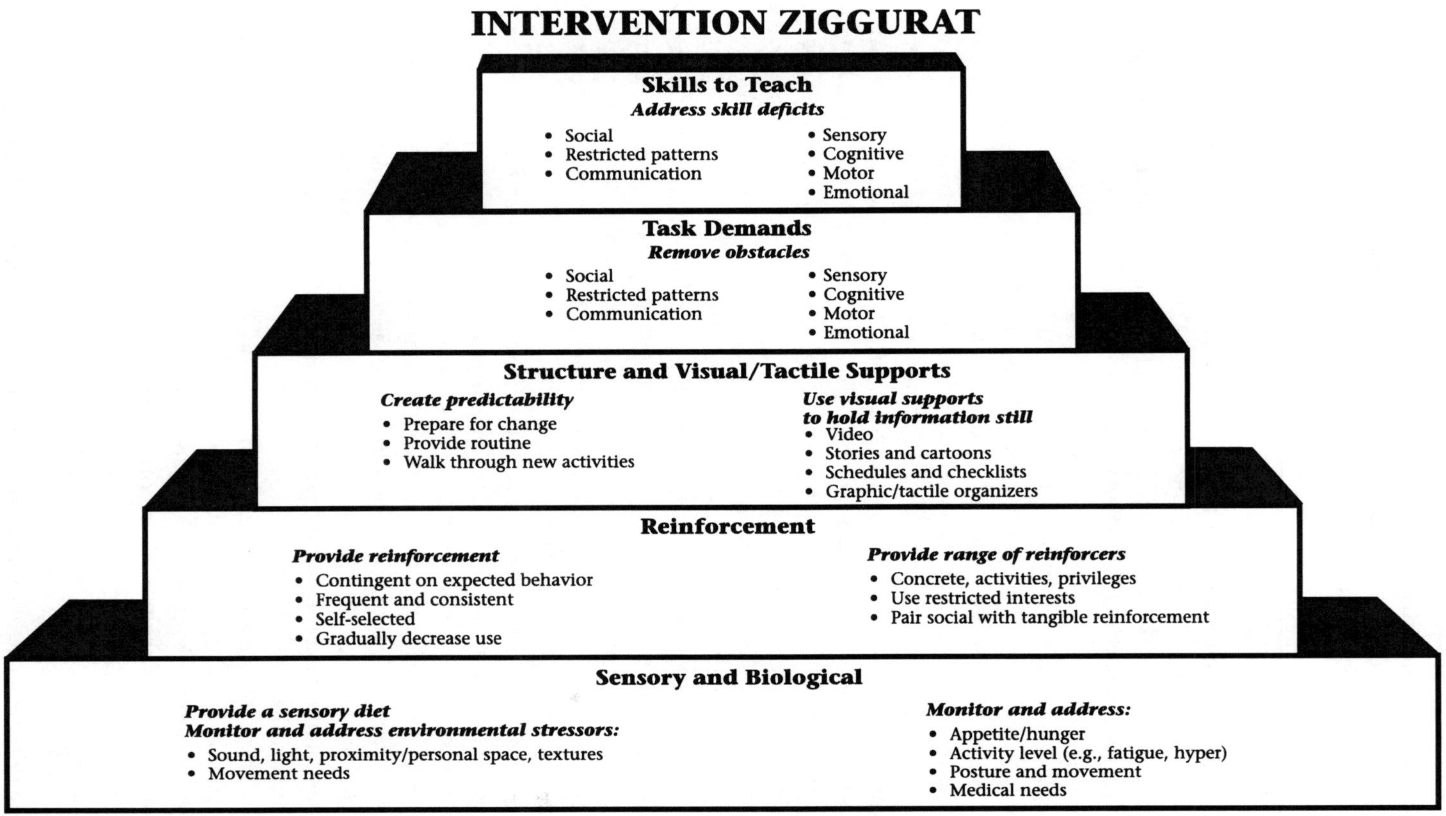

Figure 8.2 The Ziggurat Model.

From Aspy, R., & Grossman, B. G. (2011). The Ziggurat Model. Shawnee Mission, KS: AAPC Publishing; www.aapcpublishing.net; used with permission.

functioning. Their book includes assessment tools, case scenarios, and many interventions (instruction strategies) for higher-functioning children. Some parts of the book offer especially useful tools and assessments for teachers to use in their classrooms.

SCERTS

The SCERTS model was developed by a team of clinicians and researchers, including Prizant, Wetherby, Rubin, Rydell, and Laurent (2003). SCERTS, which is pronounced like "certs," stands for social communication, emotional regulation and transactional support. The creators of SCERTS also developed a framework for helping parents and professionals make decisions about what is best for children with autism. According to Prizant and colleagues (2003), the SCERTS model is based on research that has determined that educational programming should focus on developing spontaneous, functional communication and secure, trusting relationships with children and adults (social communication) and enhancing the ability to maintain a well-regulated emotional state for learning and interacting (emotional regulation) and supporting children, their families, and professionals to maximize positive social experiences across home, school, and community settings (transactional support). The TS—transactional support—stands for all the ways the child is supported in each program. For example, is the program responsive to the child's needs? When the child gets upset, what plan is in place to calm the child and make him or her feel accepted and successful? SCERTS is a collaborative model that helps families, educators, and therapists work cooperatively as a team, in a coordinated manner, to maximize progress in supporting a child. The model emphasizes including parents as partners and tapping into the parents' expertise to help them meet the child's needs.

This model doesn't talk about how children need to overcome deficits, but rather discusses how to help children to overcome challenges—challenges that seem to be imposed on them by society as opposed to their disability. SCERTS therapists provide a lot of supports, both to families and to children, including not only learning support, but also emotional support. The developers want children to see adults as a sense of comfort instead of a source of anxiety, and they admit that professionals can sometimes cause families and children more anxiety than they relieve.

They also talk about the need for professionals to provide support to each other and they emphasize the need for professionals to develop community and to provide both professional and emotional support and for leaders to develop a positive culture of support among colleagues.

Conclusion

In this chapter, we have discussed a few instructional models that provide strategies or frameworks for interventions that have been working for a number of families more than 10 years in the autism field. We started with more structured ABA programs and ended with less structured, more collaborative programs, showing how different types of programs are available to meet the needs of diverse children. Later we will talk about new strategies, for example, the Early Start Denver Model (ESDM), which is a behavioral program developed from research from the MIND Institute at the University of California. In later chapters, we will add more ideas about how teachers can help children with autism reach their full potential and be better integrated into the general education program.

References

American Psychological Association (APA). (2012). Individualized treatments are future of autism therapies, according to psychologist. Retrieved from http://www.apa.org/news/press/releases/2012/04/autism-therapies.aspx

Anderson, S. R., Taras, M., & Cannon, B. O. (1996). Teaching new skills to young children with autism. In C. Maurice (Ed.), *Behavioral intervention for young children with autism* (pp. 181–193). Austin, TX: Pro-Ed.

Aspy, R., & Grossman, B. G. (2011). The Ziggurat Model. Shawnee Mission, KS: AAPC Publishing.

Autism Speaks. (2013). Training and Education of Autistic and Related Communication Handicapped Children (TEACCH). Retrieved from http://www.autismspeaks.org/what-autism/treatment/training-and-education-autistic-and-related-communication-handicapped-children.

Bogin, J. (2008). *Overview of discrete trial training.* Sacramento, CA: National Professional Development Center on Autism Spectrum Disorders, MIND Institute, The University of California at Davis Medical School.

Cohen, H., Amerine-Dickens, M., & Smith, T. (2006). Early intensive behavioral treatment: Replication UCLA model in a community setting. *Journal of Developmental & Behavioral Pediatrics, 27,* 145–155.

Delprato, D. J. (2001). Comparisons of discrete-trial and normalized behavioral language intervention for young children with autism. *Journal of Autism and Developmental Disorders, 31*(3), 315–325.

Dillenburger, K., & Keenan, M. (2009). None of the As in ABA stand for autism: Dispelling the myths. *Journal of Intellectual & Developmental Disability., 34*(2), 193–195.

Fenske, E. C., Krantz, P. J., & McClannahan, L. E. (2001). Incidental teaching: A not-discrete-trial teaching procedure. Making a difference: Behavioral intervention for autism, 75–82.

Gambrill, E. (2013). Birds of a feather: Applied behavior analysis and quality of life. *Research on Social Work Practice, 23*(121), 121–140.

Greenspan, S. I., Wieder, S., & Simons, R. (1998). *The child with special needs: Encouraging intellectual and emotional growth.* New York: Perseus Books.

Hart, B., & Risley, T. R. (1982). *How to use incidental teaching for elaborating language.* Austin, TX: Pro-Ed.

Horner, R., Carr, E., Halle, J., McGee, G., Odom, S., & Wolery, M. (2005). The use of single subject research to identify evidence-based practice in special education. *Exceptional Children, 71,* 165–180.

Ingersoll, B. (2010). Teaching social communication: A comparison of naturalistic behavioral and developmental, social pragmatic approaches for children with autism spectrum disorders. *Journal of Positive Behavior Interventions, 12,* 13–43.

Johnston, K., & Brinamen, C. (2012). Integrating and adapting infant mental health principles in the training of consultants to childcare. *Infant Mental Health Journal, 33*(3), 226–233.

Koegel, L. K., Koegel, R. L., Harrower, J. K., & Carter, C. M. (1999). Pivotal response intervention I: Overview of approach. *Research and Practice for Persons with Severe Disabilities, 24*(3), 174–185.

Lord, C. & McGee, J. P. (Eds.) (2001). Educating children with autism. Committee on Educational Interventions for Children With Autism, Division of Behavioral and Social Sciences and Education. Washington, DC: National Academies Press.

Lovaas, O. I. (1987). Behavioral treatment and normal educational and intellectual functioning in young autistic children. *Journal of Consulting and Clinical Psychology, 55*, 3–9.

Lovaas Center. (2011). Welcome to the Lovaas Center. Lovaas ABA treatment for autism. Retrieved from http://www.thelovaascenter.org/index.php?pname=aba%20 treatment

Malone, J. C. (2003). Advances in behaviorism: It's not what it used to be. *Journal of Behavioral Education, 12*(2), 85–89.

McEachin, J. J., Smith, T., & Lovaas, O. I. (1993). Long-term outcomes for children with autism who received early intensive behavioral treatment. *American Journal on Mental Retardation, 97*(4), 359–372.

McGee, G. G., Morrier, M. J., & Daly, T. (1999). An incidental teaching approach to early intervention for toddlers with autism. *Journal of the Association for Persons With Severe Handicaps, 24*(3), 133–146.

Nathan, P., & Gorman, J. M. (2002). *A guide to treatments that work.* New York: Oxford University Press.

National Research Council. (2001). *Educating children with autism.* Committee on Educational Interventions for Children With Autism, Division of Behavioral and Social Sciences and Education. Washington, DC: National Academies Press.

NPDC - National Professional Development Center on Autism Spectrum Disorders (2007). Evidence-Based Practice: Pivotal Response Training (PRT). Taken from http://autismpdc.fpg.unc.edu/content/pivotal-response-training. August 2013.

Odom, S. L., Brantlinger, E., Gersten, R., Horner, R. D., Thompson, B., & Harris, K. (2004). *Quality indicators for research in special education and guidelines for evidence-based practices: Executive summary.* Arlington, VA: Council for Exceptional Children Division for Research.

Odom, S., Collet-Klingenberg, L., Rogers, S., & Hatton, D. (2010). Evidence-based practices in interventions for children and youth with autism spectrum disorders. *Preventing School Failure, 54*(4), 275–282.

Ozmon, H. A., & Craver, S. M. (1992). *Philosophical foundations of education* (5th ed.). Englewood Cliffs, NJ: Prentice Hall.

Pajareya, K., & Nopmaneejumruslers, K. (2011). A pilot randomized controlled trial of DIR/Floortime™ parent training intervention for preschool children with autistic spectrum disorders. *Autism, 15*(5), 563–577.

Prizant, B. M., Wetherby, A., Rubin, E., Rydell, P., & Laurent, A. (2003). THE SCERTS Model: A family-centered, transactional approach to enhancing communication and socioemotional abilities of young children with ASD. *Infants and Young Children, 16*, 296–316.

Reichow, B., & Wolery, M. (2009). Comprehensive synthesis of early intensive behavioral interventions for young children with autism based on the UCLA Young Autism Project model. *Journal of Autism and Developmental Disorder, 39*, 23–41.

Rogers, S. J., & Vismara, L. A. (2008). Evidence-based comprehensive treatments for early autism. *Journal of Clinical Child and Adolescent Psychology, 37*(1), 8–38.

Smith, T., & Lovaas, O. I. (1998). Intensive and early behavioral intervention with autism: The UCL A young autism project. *Infants and Young Children, 10*(3), 67–78.

Smith Myles, B., Grossman, B. C., Aspy, R., Henry, S. A., & Bixler, A. (2007). Planning a comprehensive program for students with autism spectrum disorders using evidence-based practices. *Education and Training in Developmental Disabilities, 42*(4), 398–409.

Solomon, R., Necheles, J., Ferch, C., & Bruckman, D. (2007). Evaluation of a parent training program for young children with autism: The PLAY Project Home Consulting Program. *Autism, 11*, 205–224.

TEACCH. (2013). *Teach approach: Common myths and misunderstandings about the TEACCH approach.* University of North Carolina at Chapel Hill School of Medicine. Retrieved from http://teacch.com/about-us/what-is-teacch.

Wieder, S., & Greenspan, S. I. (2003). Climbing the symbolic ladder in the DIR model through floor time/interactive play. *Autism, 7*(4), 425–435.

Wilczynski, S. M., & Pollack, E. G. (2009). *Autism-based practice and autism in the school.* Randolph, MA: National Autism Center.

Chapter Nine
Diagnoses, Early Intervention, and Preschool

Currently, we don't have a medical test that can diagnose autism. The etiology and pathology of autism are still relatively unknown because the wide clinical diversity between individual children with autism makes identifying common biomarkers difficult. Although research on gene factors and biomarkers is ongoing, diagnosis is based on symptomatology and performed by specially trained physicians and psychologists who administer autism-specific behavioral evaluations. Usually parents are the first to notice that their child is not responding to his or her name, not making eye contact, and not playing with toys in typical ways. Research suggests that parents of children with autism notice a developmental problem before their child's first birthday (Kozlowski, Matson, Horovitz, Worley, & Neal, 2011). Concerns about vision and hearing were more often reported in the first year, and then differences in social, communication, and fine motor skills were evident from 6 months of age. The average age of the children diagnosed in our study was 6 years old, although eight of the children were younger than age 6 when they were diagnosed. In two of the families, the children were not diagnosed until their late teens.

One of the parents whose child was diagnosed later thought the reason may have been because her child appeared so "good and sweet" that nobody really thought about him as having a problem. Although many teachers saw that perhaps he was different, because they liked him and he didn't really have any maladaptive behaviors, the school personnel continued to work with him in a way that suggested they knew that he needed some extra support, but not that he might have any serious problems:

ANA: And then when the weirdness started coming out in maybe fourth or fifth grade, the principal was very accepting, because Alberto wasn't a troublemaker. He just said, "Oh, well, your son tends to hide in the

> corner, (he didn't want to be with other kids or he'd hide in a chair), he hides under the desk," so he suggested seeing the school counselor, so Alberto started seeing the school counselor and she adored Alberto, and they built this relationship, and she even gave him a card at the end of the school year, "Oh, sorry I'm not gonna see you next year," and the principal was saying he likes to fidget. So he gave Alberto one of those fidget toys. He was just a good kid. Alberto would go to the office sometimes, and he and the principal would talk about Celtic music together.

Another child, who wasn't diagnosed until he was in elementary school, was first diagnosed with Tourette's and sensory integration problems. However, for most of the other parents, the reason they were concerned and decided to have their children examined and eventually diagnosed was because their children were not talking as much as they believed they should be talking. Most thought their children were either delayed in language or were losing words once they passed a certain age (around 2 years). Some other children demonstrated erratic behavior; for example, a few children often ran away from caregivers, and a few were even kicked out of preschool for this behavior. Preschool personnel were afraid these children might run off when they weren't looking and they would lose a child or a child would get hurt.

Diagnostic Overview: Autism, High-Functioning Autism, and Asperger's Syndrome

Asperger's syndrome was only officially recognized in the *DSM-IV* for the first time in 1994. And, as we mentioned in Chapter 1, in the *DSM-5*, professionals are planning to combine Asperger's and high-functioning autism into one category. The hope is that the broad classification will make it easier for service providers, education systems, and policy makers to provide necessary services. Pinto-Martin et al. (2008) sought to determine which screening strategies were most effective for early diagnosis. Many pediatricians were using a general developmental assessment for all of their patients and only tested specifically for autism after a child showed developmental delays on the general assessment. However, pediatricians using only the general developmental screening tool—the Parents' Evaluation of Developmental Status (PEDS) (Glascoe, 2003)—did not initially identify the majority of children who later tested positive on the Modified Checklist for Autism in Toddlers (M-CHAT), an ASD-specific assessment. Pinto-Martin et al. screened 152 children between the ages of 18 and 30 months using both the PEDS and M-CHAT tools at well-child visits with pediatricians. The researchers found that 16 of the 22 children (73%) who tested positive for ASD on the M-CHAT did not show any developmental concerns on the PEDS. These findings suggest that the two tools assess different areas of developmental concerns and support the American Academy of Pediatrics recommendations that, in addition to regular developmental screening, children need to be systematically screened starting at 18 months of age using an ASD-specific tool (Johnson & Meyers, 2007).

How important it is to have a child get early intervention is not completely clear in the research. However, a number of studies have concluded that children make greater gains when they enter a program at a younger age. It is important to keep in mind that most of the empirical support for the difference in gains is comparing children younger than 4 or 5 years to children older than that age. The preschool years are still considered "early" when it comes to early intervention (Corsello, 2005). Harris and Handleman (2000) found that IQ level and being younger at intake were both predictors of being placed in general education by age 6, and being older at diagnosis was closely related to having a placement in special education. Of course, in 2000, special education was thought of more as a place, or a placement, for children; now, professionals like to think of special education as a set of services. There is other, more recent evidence that early intervention helps children. Recently, a study was completed looking at the Denver Early Start Program; two important results of that study suggested that, first, the younger the child is at the initiation of the intervention, even among 1-year-old children, the more developmental gain and symptom reduction occurs over the short term. This provides strong empirical support both for the goal of beginning early intervention as soon as possible, and for the importance of identifying young children at risk for ASD as early as possible. The second finding was that the more intense the intervention (more hours) the greater the development gains (Rogers et al., 2012).

On the other hand, Kasari, Gulsrud, Freeman, Paparella, and Hellemann (2012) followed children for five years out of preschool and tested for theory of mind and executive function, and found only a small amount of evidence that children who received early intervention performed better than peers who started later, and the difference was slight. Finally, in a recent longitudinal study, researchers followed preschool children for seven years and found the variables that predicted what outcomes the child might have in the long run included initial receptive language skills, IQ and adaptive behavior (Magiati, Moss, Yates, Charman, & Howlin, 2011).

Diagnostic Assessments

The American Academy of Pediatrics (AAP) recommends that all children be screened for autism by their family pediatrician twice, first by the age of 18 months and again at 24 months. The AAP also recommends that treatment be started when an autism diagnosis is suspected rather than waiting for a formal diagnosis.. When autism is suspected, a pediatrician usually refers parents/caregivers to specially trained physicians or psychologists to administer autism-specific behavioral evaluations. For example, the M-CHAT is a list of informative questions about the child. A typical diagnostic evaluation involves a multidisciplinary team of doctors, including a pediatrician, psychologist, speech and language pathologist, and an occupational therapist. Genetic testing may be recommended, as well as screening for related medical issues and comorbid conditions, such as Attention Deficit Hyperactive Disorder and sleep difficulties. This type of comprehensive examination helps parents understand as much as possible about their child's strengths and needs (Autism Speaks, 2013).

To qualify for special education under the label of autism in the United States, families must have their children assessed in one of a number of ways. They can have them assessed privately through hospitals or clinics or through a psychologist, speech therapist, or doctor. Professionals will give parents behavioral questionnaires about their child and administer a number of tests or checklists to the child;, the child's age and circumstances, determine qualification for services under the autism diagnosis. Here are parents' recollections of the process:

DAWN: We went to a multidisciplinary clinic through UCSF and they said, "high-functioning autism," and then asked us what diagnosis we wanted.

JAMES: Our son had trouble following verbal directions and wasn't as attentive as his homecare providers thought typical kids would be, so she actually called that to the attention of the agency that was running this homecare program and they called us in and we had this big meeting where they told us about all the concerns they had. We weren't convinced initially, we thought maybe he just wasn't getting along with the woman's daughter, but they kind of encouraged us to get an assessment, so actually, the local school district in Fairfax County did an assessment for us and they diagnosed him with speech and language delays and said that he had characteristics of autism, and they put their money where their mouth was and put him in a special preschool program.

In other words, parents/caregivers may be given a choice regarding how they address their child's challenges, because children who are autistic may also qualify for services under speech delays, intellectual challenge (mental retardation), or developmental delay. In some states, different diagnoses, including those for children who qualify under low incidence categories (more severe disabilities) can provide families with more supportive options.

The Individualized Educational Program (IEP) team is the group of people who decide what is best for the child in terms of having access to the general education curriculum, and what resources the child needs according to his or her assessed strengths and challenges. Some of the different instruments that have been used to assess autism in children include checklists, diagnostic interview protocols, direct observation tools, and surveillance scales. Parents, along with teachers and psychologists, fill them out. Some that are used to "diagnose" autism are listed in Table 9.1.

Table 9.1 Examples of Diagnostic Assessments

Diagnostic Instrument	*References*	*Comments*
The Autism Diagnostic Interview-Revised (ADI-R)	Le Couteur et al. (1989); Lord, Rutter, & Le Couteur (1994)	The ADI-R is a semi-structured, investigator-based interview for caregivers of children and adults for whom autism or PDD is a possible diagnosis. Originally developed as a research diagnostic instrument, the ADI-R has been modified to be appropriate for a broader age range of children than the original.
The Childhood Autism Rating Scale (CARS)	Schopler, Reichler, & Rochen-Renner (1988)	CARS is the strongest; best documented, and most widely used clinical rating scale for behaviors associated with autism. Most of the information about CARS is from studies of autistic children who are in the mild to moderate range. The evidence that CARS accurately identifies children with autism is stronger than evidence that it discriminates between matched children with other disorders.
The Modified Checklist of Autism in Toddlers (M-CHAT)	Autism Speaks (see http://www.autismspeaks.org/what-autism/diagnosis/screen-your-child) Robins, Fein, & Barton (1999)	The M-CHAT is a tool for screening children between 16 and 30 months to assess their risk for ASD. Robins, Fein, and Barton (1999) developed the instrument. The M-CHAT's primary goal is to detect as many cases of ASD as possible. Therefore, there is a high false-positive rate, meaning that many children who score at risk for ASD will not be diagnosed with it. Available at: www2.gsu.edu/~psydlr/DianaLRobins/Official_M-CHAT_Website_files/M-CHATInterviewREV.pdf.
Pervasive Developmental Disorder Screening Test-II (PDDST-II)	Siegel (1998); Volkmar, Chawarska, & Klin (2005)	The PDDST-II is a clinical screening tool for pervasive developmental disorders (PDD) or autism spectrum disorders (ASD) designed for use by nonspecialist clinicians. It was designed to differentiate children as young as 18 months who may be at risk for autism from those at risk for other exceptionalities, such as language disorders or cognitive impairments (Volkmar, Chawarska, & Klin, 2005)
The Autism Behavior Checklist (ABC)	Krug, Arick, & Almond (1980)	The ABC is one component of the Autism Screening Instrument for Educational Planning (ASIEP; Krug et al., 1980) and the only one that has been evaluated psychometrically. It contains 57 items in five areas: sensory, relating, body and object use, language and social interaction, and self-help. Developers intended it to be completed by teachers as an initial step in educational planning. No special training is required.

(*Continued*)

Table 9.1 Continued

Diagnostic Instrument	*References*	*Comments*
The Gilliam Autism Rating Scale (GARS)	Gilliam (1995)	The GARS is a parent-completed surveillance questionnaire designed to indicate the probability that a child has autism. It is intended for individuals between 3 and 22 years of age. The questionnaire consists of 56 items across four subscales: Social Interaction, Communication, Stereotyped Behaviors, and Developmental Disturbances. The first three subscales listed are based on a child's current behavior, and the final scale is based on a child's developmental history. Each item is rated on a four-point scale, from "Never Observed" to "Frequently Observed."
The Autism Diagnostic Observation Schedule-Generic (ADOS-G)	DiLavore, Lord, & Rutter (1995); Lord et al. (2000); Lord et al. (1989)	The ADOS is a standardized protocol for the observation of social and communicative behavior of children for whom a diagnosis of autism or ASD is in question. They are scored in the context of a diagnostic algorithm for autism. The rationale is that context can have very significant effects on social-communicative behaviors. Consequently, it is important to standardize contexts as well as judgments in any diagnostic observation of these behaviors.
The Vineland Adaptive Behavior Scales (VABS)	Sparrow, Balla, & Cicchetti (1984)	The VABS are considered to be the most widely used instrument to assess adaptive behavior (Klin et al., 1997). The scales measure adaptive development in the areas of socialization, daily living skills, motor skills, and communication (including written communication).
Asperger's Syndrome (and High-Functioning Autism) Diagnostic Interview(ASDI)	Gillberg, Gillberg, Rastam, & Wentz (2001)	The interview is based on Gillberg's diagnostic criteria for Asperger's disorder and includes 20 items that operationalize six criteria (Social, Interests, Routines, Verbal and Speech, Communication, and Motor).

Although there is no one behavioral or communications test that can detect autism, several screening instruments have been developed that are now being used in diagnosing autism. For example, sometimes parents and teachers may be on the same page when it comes to a rating scale, and sometimes they are not. If a child acts very different at home than he or she does at school, the parents may have very different scores than those generated by the teacher. This can happen because a child feels more comfortable at home. Autistic children tend to not have social anxiety at home, and they are not being made to do a lot of different tasks that they may not want to do. They are not being embarrassed at home (which they may feel at school). They get more attention at home.

Lord and Corsello (2005) suggest that the autism community needs a valid and reliable instrument that would diagnose a child with autism in a way that provides an accurate picture of what his or her autism looks like and also a tool that might accurately help professionals follow the child's developmental changes. Teachers track progress now in different ways for different areas of development and for different children given the diversity of goals for children with autism.

Red Flags for Autism

Easter Seals, the Autism Society of America, and Autism Speaks, three large nonprofit organizations within the autism community, have all developed lists of the early signs or red flags that parents and caregivers should look out for. Table 9.2 gives red flags across these three non-profit organizations.

One of the most common red flags parents report is that they suspect their child is deaf. Because their child no longer responds to his or her name, and doesn't look at them when they speak, they often think there may be a hearing issue. In fact, the lack of response or eye contact can point to ASD. Other early signs include not pointing to things in the environment (most children begin to point at around 10 months), not speaking (children usually have single words by 15 months), and not showing interest in other children (children usually want to play with peers even as toddlers). Table 9.3 lists red flags across age groups.

Joint Attention, Play, and Therapy

Two interventions that professionals often use with young children are joint attention and play interventions. Joint attention interventions can be used with very young children and occur when two people, for example, a young child and her mother, share attention and focus on an interesting object or event in their environment. A second, more sophisticated form of joint attention involves gaze alternation, which means the child looks at the object, then back at the adult (as if to check in with the mother), and then back at

Table 9.2 Signs of Autism in Young Children as Listed by Three Autism Organizations

Easter Seals' 15 Signs of Autism	*Autism Society of America*	*Autism Speaks*
1. May avoid eye contact. 2. May prefer to be alone. 3. Echoes words or phrases. 4. Difficulty interacting with others. 5. Spins objects or self. 6. Insistence on sameness. 7. Inappropriate attachments to objects. 8. Inappropriate laughing or giggling. 9. May not want cuddling. 10. Difficulty in expressing needs; may use gestures. 11. Inappropriate response or no response to sound. 12. No real fear of dangers. 13. Apparent insensitivity to pain. 14. Sustained unusual or repetitive play. 15. Uneven physical or verbal skills.	1. Does not babble or coo by 12 months. 2. Does not gesture (point, wave, grasp) by 12 months. 3. Does not say single words by 16 months. 4. Does not say two-word phrases on his or her own by 24 months. 5. Has any loss of any language or social skill at any age.	1. No big smiles or other warm, joyful expressions by 6 months or thereafter. 2. No back-and-forth sharing of sounds, smiles, or other facial expressions by 9 months. 3. No babbling by 12 months. 4. No back-and-forth gestures such as pointing, showing, reaching, or waving by 12 months. 5. No words by 16 months. 6. No meaningful, two-word phrases (not including imitating or repeating) by 24 months. 7. Any loss of speech, babbling, or social skills at any age.

Adapted from lists made by: Taken from the Web sites of Autism Speaks (http://www.autismspeaks.org), Easter Seals (http://www.easterseals.com) and the Autism Society of America (http://www.autism-society.org). July 2013.

the object. A third type of joint attention involves looking at an object and pointing at it in some way and then directing another person to look at the object and then both people focusing attention to the object. The idea behind joint attention is simply to teach the child to be social in early stages of development. Children engage in joint attention to interact with another person about an object or event in their environment. This is the way young children are conveying a message (Jones, Carr, & Feeley, 2006; Mundy & Crowson, 1997).

Play Interventions

Play is essential to development because it contributes to the cognitive, physical, social, and emotional well-being of young children. One of the characteristics of autism is the inability to play or engage in imaginative activities. For

Table 9.3 Red Flags by Developmental Milestones

Red flags to look for by 6 months:	
Doesn't make eye contact. Doesn't smile or make other warm, joyful expressions. Doesn't babble or coo. Doesn't react when you play peek-a-boo or seem to enjoy face-to-face play. Doesn't repeat sounds you make. Doesn't like to be hugged and cuddled.	A child with high-functioning autism may not show any of these signs, because their symptoms have not yet developed, or they do not yet have autism.
Red flags to look for by 14 months:	
Doesn't say single words. No longer says words or sentences. Doesn't respond to his own name. Doesn't wave hello or point to things he wants. Seems unnaturally attached to one toy or object. Seems unaware of others. Is either overly sensitive or not at all sensitive to sound, smell, light, or touch. Rocks, spins and/or flaps hands or twirls fingers. Appears to be deaf. Likes routines and rituals and strongly resists change.	A child with high-functioning autism may only demonstrate one of these signs (e.g., seems deaf or resists change).
Red flags to look for by 2 years:	
Doesn't combine two words to communicate with others. Doesn't follow simple instructions. Doesn't recognize names of familiar people and objects. Seems obsessed with a few activities or interests. Doesn't speak or socialize anymore. Seems uncoordinated.	A child with high-level autism may demonstrate these types of behaviors, but not until they are older.

(*Continued*)

Table 9.3 Continued

Red flags to look for by 3 to 5 years	
Still isn't speaking. Speaks in a flat, emotionless tone, or has a high-pitched or sing-song voice. Repeats the same word over and over, or "parrots" what he hears (echolalia). Has violent or uncontrollable tantrum. Hurts himself (i.e., head banging, hair pulling, arm biting). Seems afraid of harmless objects. Doesn't fear danger or pain. Seems oblivious to extreme cold. Plays alone all the time, ignoring other children. Seems overly focused on one activity with little interest in anything else. Uses toys to line up or put in his mouth instead of for pretend play. Has unusual moods or emotional reactions (such as laughing or crying at unusual times or showing no emotion when you would typically expect one). Doesn't have separation anxiety when you leave or over reacts to separation. Has unusual eating habits (is a picky eater and rejects new foods). Has unusual sleep habits or patterns. Has repetitive behaviors (like hand flapping, tapping fingers, obsessively lining up toys, or turning lights on and off).	Children with high- and low-level autism become much more similar at about this time in their development. With intervention, children with higher functioning autism often start improving faster as they receive intervention.

example, a child might continually spin a wheel on his dump truck in order to get stimulation instead of using it to pretend he is building a dam. Children with autism tend to play in ways where they repeat the same routine over and over again.

Why is it important to learn to play? Some research has suggested that play for a young child is helpful for building theory of mind and executive function skills. To test this theory, McAlister and Peterson (2006) assessed the theory of mind and executive functioning abilities of 124 typically developing preschool children aged 3 to 5 years in relation to whether they had a child-aged sibling (i.e., a child aged 1 to 12 years) at home with whom to play and converse. On a theory of mind battery that included tests of false belief, appearance-reality (AR), and pretend representation, children who had at least one child-aged sibling scored significantly higher than both only children and those whose only siblings were infants or adults. The numbers of child-aged siblings in preschoolers' families positively predicted their scores on both a theory of mind test (four tasks) and an executive functioning test (two tasks), and these associations remained significant. Results revealed that language ability, executive functioning skill, and having a child-aged sibling made individual differences in theory of mind.

For children with autism, it may be even more important for them to play with other children than it is for typically developing children because many of them do not engage in pretend or symbolic play at all. Many do not have friends, and all of them need to learn and practice social skills. Many of the parents of the children who were in our study, whose children were diagnosed as young children, had a program set up for their children with play dates:

KIMBERLY: I started pulling any person I knew who had a child in and forcing them to come over for play dates with my son.

SAMATHA: For me, the really important thing was play dates. And that helped keep the attention and the pressure on. Y'know you have to have a couple play dates every single week, week in and week out, and I think that's part of what was helpful to him in terms of helping him being socialized as he is now.

JANA: The peers that came over, (for play dates) they were picked from his class, and they transferred some of the stuff they'd learned to class—how they dealt with Steven. They (saw) him in a different way and that helped to show the other kids how to see this person in a different way. This person isn't retarded; they just need to be more direct and explicit. So it was a little bit better at school.

Mildred Parten (1932) conducted one of the classic studies about how play develops over time in the late 1920s at the Institute of Child Development in Minnesota. She closely observed children between the ages of 2 and 5 years old and categorized their play into six types:

1. **Unoccupied play:** The child is relatively stationary and appears to be performing random movements with no apparent purpose. A relatively infrequent style of play.
2. **Solitary play:** The child is completely engrossed in playing and does not seem to notice other children. Most often seen in children between 2 and 3 years old.
3. **Onlooker play:** Child takes an interest in other children's play but does not join in. May ask questions or just talk to other children, but the main activity is simply to watch.
4. **Parallel play:** The child mimics other children's play but doesn't actively engage with them. For example, they may play with the same toys side by side.
5. **Associative play:** Children are now more interested in each other than the toys they are using. This is the first category that involves strong social interaction between the children while they play.
6. **Cooperative play:** Some organization enters children's play; for example, the playing has some goal and children often adopt roles and act as a group.

Parten (1932) collected data by systematically sampling the children's behavior. She observed them for prearranged 1-minute periods, which were varied systematically. It is important to note that the first four categories of play don't involve much interaction with others, whereas the last two do. Although the children shifted between the types of play, what Parten noticed was that as they grew up, children participated less in the first four types and more in the last two—those that involved greater interaction.

Unlike Jean Piaget, who saw children's play in primarily cognitive developmental terms, Parten (1932) emphasized that learning to play involved learning how to relate to others. Children's play all along the spectrum will need to be taught, monitored, and facilitated for best effect.

Kasari and her colleagues (2012) are now conducting research on play and autism. In one study, they examined the cognitive and language outcomes of 58 children with ASD over a 5-year period after receiving targeted early interventions focused on joint attention and play skills. The researchers found that focusing on joint attention and play skills in comprehensive treatment models is important for long-term spoken language outcomes. In fact, they found three specific outcomes. First, children who could demonstrate simple combination play at 3 to 4 years old were able to use functional spoken language as opposed to children who played with objects indiscriminately, such as mouthing or banging, or with simple discriminations of pushing a pop-up toy. Second, children who showed more functional play types at baseline obtained better cognitive scores. Third, spoken vocabulary was predicted by a wider set of factors than cognitive outcomes. Thus, beginning intervention at an earlier age, initiating more joint attention, demonstrating higher play levels, and receiving the experimental interventions yielded greater spoken vocabulary scores at the 5-year follow-up.

Therapy for Young Children

A lot of young children will be going through different types of therapies before they start school; parents are looking for what works with these children, but they are also eager to get their children services when they are young and can benefit from early intervention. Children make a lot of progress when they are young, and they have a lot of energy, so going to therapy is fine, and if most of the sessions are fun and playful, children will do well. For some time, therapies were too much like therapy, and therapists learned quickly that a lot of young children started *not liking therapy*, or at least not liking too much therapy. Some of the therapies they were getting included speech, occupational, art, fine and/or gross motor (physical) therapy, and also sensory-integration therapies. These therapists use brushes, swings, balls, and other specially designed therapeutic or recreational equipment, and they work on vestibular, proprioceptive, auditory, and tactile inputs.

Many children will also have behavioral therapy, and that tires children out. However, behavioral therapy is much more play based than it used to be. Sometimes we look at people's "behavior therapy" and we think "hmmm, interesting take on ABA." Children with autism also have speech therapy and work with speech language pathologists (SLPs). SLPs specialize in treating language problems and speech disorders. They are a key part of the autism treatment team. With early screening and detection of people at risk, speech therapists often lead the way in helping with the diagnosis of autism and in making referrals to other specialists. Once autism is diagnosed, speech therapists assess the best ways to improve communication and enhance a person's quality of life. Throughout therapy, the SLP also works closely with the family, school, and other professionals. If someone with autism is nonverbal or has major trouble with speech, the speech therapist may introduce alternatives to speech.

And, finally, the children will have play dates, and other types of therapies, such as music therapy, counseling, karate (for muscle coordination), social skills classes, or drama or film groups. It is important for teachers to advise parents to make sure that the child is not getting too worn out and that these therapies are not too much for the child such that he or she seems too tired during the day to socialize and have fun at school.

The child will also have a pediatrician, and the parent may want to discuss options with a doctor or with an advocate of some type. So it is important to know the local resources and where to send parents so they can get the resources they need, especially when their children are young. When their children get a bit older, parents often know where to go for advice. The following are some comments from our parents about some of the therapies their children had when they were young:

DONNA: As soon as school started, I knew there were issues. And I think probably at around 6, he was diagnosed with Tourette's and sensory integration. It at least got him into occupational therapy.

LENA: No, we tried it for a while, music therapy. I think it was somewhat helpful, but not enough that we were motivated. Something where he was really motivated to keep doing it? Nothing. And he had a therapist that he saw once every other week. And I think the one-to-one therapy wasn't all that useful for him either.

SAMATHA: We've done, I feel like everything, under the sun. We did tons of play dates, we did Michelle Garcia-Winner for a couple years.

TAMRA: We were running around to therapists, he started with play therapy when he was around 3 or 4 and he graduated to behavioral therapy and he is only seeing a doctor now once a month. We tried everything. We even tried psychiatrists, tried medications, that was not good.

Different therapies work for different children and one key aspect of whether a therapy works is whether the child likes the therapist. Sometimes parents might need to try a few different therapists, because not all are the same or have the same skill sets.

Support for Parents After Diagnosis

Different parents find out about their child's autism in different ways. Keep in mind that when a child is diagnosed and the age of a child will have a great effect on the parents' perspective on their children's diagnoses. For example, many parents have children who seemed perfectly healthy and happy and then one day, when the child was around 2 years old, they notice their children starting to change, and they find out later their child has autism. It is a shock and takes a while to process. For parents whose children have been diagnosed for many years, their children have mostly grown up, and the family has gotten to know their child as the person they have started to become, and when they realize that their child is happy, their perspective is completely different. The best support for parents of young children is to help them to meet other parents of children with autism. Professionals are helpful, but it is not the same as someone who shares your concerns, your challenges, and your goals.

One of the challenges to setting up support groups for parents of children with high-functioning autism and low-functioning autism together, as well as parents who have children who are 5 versus 15, is that these parents often don't have the same problems in common. So, it is more difficult to make a connection. Also, parents have different stress levels and pressures. Parents of very low-functioning children can be a bit envious of parents with high-functioning children. For example, we once heard parents in a group actually talking about this very topic, with one parent of a child with more severe challenges admitting that it was hard not to be jealous because sometimes all she can think is, "If only . . . If only . . . If only I could talk to my child, the way parents of high-level children with autism do, I'd be happy." In contrast, it is sometimes a myth that parents of higher-level children with autism don't deal with serious problems. In turn, they sometimes feel stifled in parent groups where they feel like they have little right to complain or express frustration.

An additional source of stress for parents with a newly diagnosed child is wondering if a child will ultimately be higher or lower functioning, because when children are younger the symptoms are fairly similar. It is only as they develop that parents learn whether their child will become higher functioning over time (Corsello, 2005). This can be difficult for parents of children who are not developing as quickly as other children. When children with high-level autism are older, they have different problems, such as severe anxiety. So, although parents' concerns aren't the same, or arguably as stressful as parents of children with more severe challenges, these parents still need support. Below we share comments demonstrating some of the difficulties and challenges parents in our study had to deal with when their children were younger:

TAMRA: He went through this stage when he was say 2½, poop smearing and all this other mess, but by the time he was 4, that stuff was behind us. We had a lot of tantrums with him, even at home, but nothing that we couldn't manage. We had tantrums with him all the time. He just was prone to them a lot, and as he's grown it's just not so much anymore. He still has issues and things like that.

KIMBERLY: Even with an aide, I had to come in, he'd have a meltdown at school, he'd fallen apart. I came in probably 2 to 3 times a week sometimes for months and I never felt like I could leave him at school.

TINA: When she was young, she couldn't talk. So she would just cry and start hitting her head. She kicked me a lot, kicked the doors. She used to bite herself. Very little flapping, but she liked to spin.

SAMATHA: He's definitely a kid who prefers doing the same thing again and again. And doesn't care if he goes to a new place. He's always been who he is.

LENA: When he got into a regular preschool where there were 15 kids per teacher, or teacher's aide. Then he started to have problems. He got kicked out of two preschools because he was not able to cooperate. He would run away. If the door was open, even if it was somehow not opened, he got over stimulated like there's lots of bright colors, posters on the walls, and he got over stimulated; he'd get too excited, he'd run out of the room, or he'd lock himself in the bathroom, and he'd run away. He had some idiosyncratic behaviors like he would not sit in the circle for circle time. He would sit outside the circle, but not in the circle.

LENA: I don't know how many parents with Asperger's have kids who run and hide, but I could be looking at something, and look back, and he's gone. And I can't tell you how many times I'd be going up and down the aisles calling, "Ash, Ash!" 'cuz he'd be hiding somewhere. Like if somebody teased him (verbal teasing), he might make it physical; he might, if he gets upset, shove the kid or something like that, or scream, or yell and cry. And he did that beyond the age that other kids had stopped crying. So some kids were really leery or were afraid of him or just, y'know, he's weird and avoid him. I mean the school literally begged me to take him to a psychiatrist to evaluate him for ADD when he was 6. Y'know, so I did, I really was kind of reluctant about meds and they said, "Please, put him on meds." And I did, and it was night and day. And they said it's just a miracle. So the hyperactivity was as much a problem, maybe more at first, than the Asperger's issues.

JANINE: I can remember going to people's houses when we were in play groups, and their stuff would be out, they would have a tower of CDs [out in the living room], and then I'd say, "How can you do that?" 'Because Jake would tear it apart immediately and then she would say, "Oh we're just consistent. We just tell her [not to touch] and we're very consistent about it. And, I thought ok, I'm obviously a bad parent. And, then I came home and I thought about it and I thought, we are consistent, He still does it!

Later Diagnosis

If children are not diagnosed until they are older, they most likely have higher-level autism that was not diagnosed earlier because they did not exhibit "red flag" behavior and they hit most of their developmental milestones. One longitudinal study showed that it was higher-functioning children on the spectrum who made good progress over time, and that included those who started after kindergarten (Szatmari, Bryson, Boyle, Streiner & Duku 2003). One child in our study was diagnosed somewhere between the ages of 7 and 9 and, according to his mother, he has turned around completely through the teen years. Landa, Holman, and Garett-Mayer (2007) suggest that ASD may appear after a period of nonautistic development, and though some have suggested that parents remember incorrectly, it is not due to recall bias. Thus, the researchers propose a continuum of impairment, where children reach the threshold for diagnosis at different times in the first 3 years of life.

Helping Parents Be Social

When professionals set up play dates, they create opportunities for families to get to know other families who have children with and without autism. For parents of children with autism, getting to know other families can be difficult. The parents may be young and going through a transition period trying to understand what it means to have a child with a disability. They may be grieving or frantically trying to understand and find help for their child. In turn, the child may be demonstrating serious behavior problems. Parents are learning how to work with their child and many, especially those who don't have any other children, may not know how to interact with other parents, or may not feel comfortable interacting with other parents when they are trying to learn how to parent a child with special needs. Some may be too shy to engage with other parents. Some may be extremely thankful for any help another parent is willing to give. Some may not want to deal with their friends until they can understand their situation and feel prepared to explain their child's disability and answer all the questions their friends and family will be asking of them. Play dates with typical peers need to be planned out and prepared. Parents who have children newly diagnosed will not always understand what might happen in Play dates.

On the other side, some parents of typically developing children are apprehensive about being around children with disabilities. They just don't know what to expect or are concerned that there is more to know with regard to caregiving. Sometimes they simply don't want to say the wrong thing (like accidently insult the parents in some way). Sometimes the children don't want to play with children with disabilities. Sometimes the children will get together with typically developing children and then not know how to facilitate play and one child will go into one room and the other in another room. It is important to never tell parents just go set up Play dates or just go get kids together outside of school without understanding the complexity of what you are asking parents to do.

References

Autism Speaks. (2013). Training and Education of Autistic and Related Communication Handicapped Children (TEACCH). Retrieved from http://www.autismspeaks.org/what-autism/treatment/training-and-education-autistic-and-related-communication-handicapped-children.

Corsello, C. M. (2005). Early intervention in autism. *Infants and Young Children, 18*(2), 74–85.

DiLavore, P. C., Lord, C., & Rutter, M. (1995). The prelinguistic autism diagnostic observation schedule. *Journal of Autism and Developmental Disorders, 25,* 355–379.

Gillberg, C., Gillberg, C., Rastam, M., & Wentz, E. (2001). The Asperger syndrome (and high-functioning autism) diagnostic interview (ASDI): A preliminary study of a new structured clinical interview. *Autism, 5*(1), 57–66.

Gilliam, J. E. (1995). *Gilliam Autism Rating Scale (GARS).* Austin, TX: Pro-Ed.

Glascoe, F. P. (2003). Parents' evaluation of developmental status: How well do parents' concerns identify children with behavioral and emotional problems. *Clinical Pediatrics (Phila), 42,* 133–138.

Harris, S. L., & Handleman, J. S. (2000). Age and IQ at intake as predictors of placement for young children with autism: A four- to six-year follow-up. *Journal of Autism* and *Developmental Disorders, 30,* 137–142.

Johnson, C. P., & Meyers, S. M. (2007). Identification and evaluation of children with autism spectrum disorders. *Pediatrics, 120*, 1183–1215.

Jones, E. A., Carr, E. G., & Feeley, K. M. (2006). Multiple effects of joint attention intervention for children with autism. *Behavior Modification, 30*(6), 782–834.

Kasari, C., Gulsrud, A., Freeman, S., Paparella, T., & Hellemann, G. (2012). Longitudinal follow-up of children with autism receiving targeted interventions on joint attention and play. *Journal of American Academy of Child Adolescent Psychiatry, 51*(5), 487–495.

Klin, A., Carter, A., Volkmar, F. R., Cohen, D. J., Marans, W. D., & Sparrow, S. (1997). Developmentally based assessments. In D. J. Cohen & F. R. Volkmar (Eds.), *Handbook of autism and pervasive developmental disorders* (2nd ed., pp. 411–447). New York: Wiley.

Kozlowski, A. M., Matson, J. L., Horovitz, M., Worley, J. A., & Neal, D. (2011). Parents' first concerns of their child's development in toddlers with autism spectrum disorders. *Developmental Neurorehabilitation, 14*, 72–78.

Krug, D. A., Arick, J. R., & Almond, P. J. (1980). Behavior checklist for identifying severely handicapped individuals with high levels of autistic behavior. *Journal of Child Psychology and Psychiatry and Allied Disciplines, 21*(3), 221–229.

Landa, R. J., Holman, K. C., & Garett-Mayer, E. (2007). Social and communication development in toddlers with early and later diagnosis of autism spectrum disorders. *JAMA Psychiatry, 64*(7), 853–864.

Le Couteur, A., Rutter, M., Lord, C., Rios, P., Robertson, S., Holdgrafer, M., & McLennan, J. (1989). Autism diagnostic interview: A standardized investigator-based instrument. *Journal of Autism and Developmental Disorders, 19*, 363–387.

Lord, C., & Corsello, C. (2005). Diagnostic instruments in autistic spectrum disorders. In F. Volkmar, R. Paul, A. Klin, & D. Cohen (Eds.), *Handbook of autism and pervasive developmental disorders, Vol. Two: Assessment, interventions, and policy* (pp. 730–771). Hoboken, NJ: Wiley.

Lord, C., Risi, S., Lambrecht, L., Cook, E. H., Jr., Leventhal, B. L., DiLavore, P. C., Rutter, M. (2000). The Autism Diagnostic Observation Schedule-Generic: A standard measure of social and communication deficits associated with the spectrum of autism. *Journal of Autism and Developmental Disorders, 30*(3), 205–223.

Lord, C., Rutter, M., Goode, S., Heemsbergen, J., Jordan, H., Mawhood, L., & Schopler, E. (1989). Autism Diagnostic Observation Schedule: A standardized observation of communicative and social behavior. *Journal of Autism and Developmental Disorders, 19*, 185–212.

Lord C, Rutter M, Le Couteur A. (1994). Autism Diagnostic Interview-Revised: a revised version of a diagnostic interview for caregivers of individuals with possible pervasive developmental disorders. Journal of Autism and Developmental Disorders, 24(5). 659–85.

Magiati, I., Moss, J., Yates, R., Charman, T., & Howlin, P. (2011). Is the Autism Treatment Evaluation Checklist a useful tool for monitoring progress in children with autism spectrum disorders? *Journal of Intellectual Disability Research, 55*(3), 302–312.

McAlister, A., & Peterson, C. C. (2006). Mental playmates: Siblings, executive functioning and theory of mind. *British Journal of Developmental Psychology, 24*, 733–751.

Mundy, P., & Crowson, M. (1997). Joint attention and early social communication: Implications for research on intervention with autism. *Journal of Autism and Developmental Disorders, 27*(6), 653–676.

Parten, M. (1932). Social participation among preschool children. *Journal of Abnormal and Social Psychology, 28*(3), 136–147.

Pinto-Martin, J. A., Young, L. M., Mandell, D. S., Poghosyan, L., Giarelli, E., & Levy S. E. (2008). Screening strategies for autism spectrum disorders in pediatric primary care. *Journal of Developmental and Behavioral Pediatrics, 29*(5), 345–350.

Robins, D. L., Fein, D., & Barton, M. L. (1999). Modified Checklist for Autism in Toddlers (M-CHAT) follow-up interview. Autism Speaks. Retrieved from http://www2.gsu.edu/~psydlr/DianaLRobins/Official_M-CHAT_Website_files/M-CHATInterviewREV.pdf

Rogers, S. J., Estes, A., Lord, C., Vismara, L., Winter, J., Fitzpatrick, A., . . . Dawson, G. (2012). Effects of a brief early start Denver Model (ESDM)–based parent intervention on toddlers at risk for autism spectrum disorders: A randomized controlled trial. *Journal of the American Academy of Child & Adolescent Psychiatry, 51*(10), 1052–1065.

Schopler, E., Reichler, R., & Rochen-Renner, B. (1988). *The Childhood Autism Rating Scale (CARS).* Los Angeles, CA: Western Psychological Services.

Siegel, B. (1998, June 15–17). Early screening and diagnosis in autism spectrum disorders: The Pervasive Developmental Disorders Screening Test (PDDST). Paper presented at the NIH State of the Science in Autism. Screening and Diagnosis Working Conference, Bethesda, MD.

Sparrow, S. S., Balla, D. A., & Cicchetti, D. V. (1984). *Vineland adaptive behavior scales* (Survey Edition). Circle Pines, MN: American Guidance Service.

Szatmari, P., Bryson, S. E., Boyle, M. H., Streiner, D. L., & Duku, E. (2003). Predictors of outcome among high functioning children with autism and Asperger syndrome. *Journal of Child Psychology & Psychiatry & Allied Disciplines, 44*(4), 520–528.

Volkmar, F., Chawarska, K., & Klin, A. (2005). Autism in Infancy and Early Childhood. Annual. Review of Psychology, 2005, (56) 315–336.

Chapter Ten
Elementary School

Most of the children in our study had more trouble with social issues in late elementary and middle school than at any other time during their K–12 school career. This was also the time that many of the children started having trouble with schoolwork. Some had fairly serious behaviors as young children before they started kindergarten, but once they moved beyond those behaviors they slowly started to improve in most areas. In about third or fourth grade the work started getting harder and other children started becoming more aware of their differences, and these children started having to deal with social rejection, more difficult schoolwork, and more homework.

In high school, parents became savvier, better able to work the system, and more knowledgeable about what their children needed. In the earlier grades, not only were parents struggling to understand what might help their children, but the schools were also struggling to understand these children, especially 15 years ago. Over the last 10 years, there has been quite a bit of improvement in the amount of information provided for both teachers and parents about the needs of children with autism.

Another problem has been the lack of out-of-school resources for children with autism. Some community organizations have been working to provide out-of-school resources for children with high-level autism, but the process has been slow and funding scarce.

Thus, even if children are fairly social, around third or fourth grade they start becoming more self-aware, and they want to start hiding their challenges so that other children do not know how much they lag behind in schoolwork. Some children might become angry and aggressive, whereas others become more anxious, which can be exacerbated by hormonal changes.

Some children with autism will assertively push other children away, rather than waiting for other children to push them away. They might start acting mean, swear at other children or teachers, or stomp out of the room. If they lack impulse control, they may hit another child either on purpose or by accident in a ball game. For example, if a child with autism accidently hits someone when throwing a ball while playing, the child might start laughing, probably because he is nervous. This might be a sign of a micro-aggression toward a rejecting peers who the child doesn't understand. It could simply be a reaction. The entire social situation might come across as confusing to him, because just the other day he saw another boy accidentally hit another kid in the face with a ball and everyone laughed, but somehow for him the situation is different. To other kids, he might come across like a bully, in part because he acts odd, and that scares them. They cannot predict how he might act in various situations. For many people, trust and friendship are about being able to predict how another person is going to act in diverse situations. To help children make friends, you have to help them develop trust.

When typically developing children become fearful of children on the spectrum, this makes the problem worse. Generally, these types of children on the spectrum (i.e., those who are more aggressive) are not in the majority, but they are the children teachers remember, because they are the ones that they have the most trouble working with.

These children need to express frustration and anger. Without the verbal skills to express these emotions, they resort to aggressive or odd and unpredictable behaviors, forcing us to guess how to respond, and that makes us uncomfortable. In young children in particular, anger, hitting, and biting can occur if they do not know how to cope with intense frustration and angry feelings and they are confronted with an unfamiliar situation (Myles & Southwick, 2005).

By the time children get into about fourth grade, it is obvious to their peers, and to themselves, that something is definitely different about them. If they once had typically developing friends, for some of them those friends will drop away, not necessarily because children are mean, but rather because the children have chosen other friends that they are more compatible with. Children start feeling more stress in the upper elementary grades. Here are some comments from teenagers from our study:

ASH: All the teachers are pretty awesome, but I guess there's stress with like friends and stuff like that I guess, kind of being accepted.

GABRIELA: Sometimes they listen, sometimes they don't. If they are in trouble, you can't talk to them, and then they shout out at me! Whenever people are rude to me, then I get frustrated in class and the teachers tell me to, "Watch my attitude!"

Development in the Elementary Years

In preschool, parents want educators to prepare their children for school. If their children have behavior problems that will make it difficult for their children to function in school, they want preschool teachers to decrease those maladaptive behaviors and increase positive behaviors. Preschool parents want their children to learn to communicate, to learn language, to learn their letters and their numbers. They recognize that children with autism take longer to learn certain types of information; for example, many still have problems tying shoes, opening bottles, pouring milk, and getting dressed in elementary school. These types of activities require fine and gross motor coordination. The child's development is splintered, and it is easy to see how they can accomplish some tasks quite well and others not nearly as well.

Children in junior high school are the ones who become particularly cliquish, hanging out with just those kids who they believe are "the right kids." In many cases, older children are being taught that it is wrong to pick on or exclude children with disabilities. Children in the upper elementary grades are often too young to understand the moral implications of exclusion, but old enough to understand the embarrassment of being with children who are different, so that is why these problems often come up in fourth, fifth, and sixth grades, because they are both too young to understand inclusion and old enough to want to be like everyone else.

Relationships With Adults

As teacher-educators, both of us have heard general education teachers tell us proudly, "We don't treat children with autism any differently in our classes than anyone else. We treat them just like our other children." Although we understand the sentiment, and we recognize why teachers believe this is a good strategy, special education teachers know that sooner or later they will likely have trouble with children with ASD if they stick to this particular philosophy. In reality, treating children the same is not necessarily treating children equally or appropriately. This is one of the reasons children with disabilities have Individualized Education Programs (IEPs) that ensure that their programs are individualized. A teacher must spend time accommodating specific children and thinking about what each child needs to be successful in his or her classroom.

Although children with autism have a lot of trouble connecting with peers, many connect well with adults; teachers should recognize this as strength. They look to adults to protect them from the outside world and to understand their needs. They need them to understand and address some of their odd quirks:

EMILY: He has a complete fear/phobia of butterflies and moths for some reason. When he was 2 or 3, a moth flew in his face, so he's very afraid. So typically, they go to these camping sites where they have these restrooms, and he's like, "The moths are in there," and so it freaks him out. He's not a fan of the outdoor stuff. He did go to the Academy of Sciences, and he was so anxious because he knew he was going to have to go into that rain forest and he knew there were butterflies, and it really

> freaked him out, and he talked about it for a week, but he went. And one of the counselors there held him—had his arm around him, and he came home and he said, "I did it, I did it, I got through and Nick helped me!"

For many children with autism, fears become obsessive, so if a child is talking about one topic, it could be out of a fear that needs to be addressed. Most often, however, obsessive fascinations and interests are topic areas that children with autism pursue with unconditional totality. A few years ago one of the authors of this book was observing children during recess; a typically developing 5-year-old child approached an adult and asked him to guess what she had in her pocket. The adult said, "What?" She pulled out a big marble and told him she found a marble on her way to school. He told her that was a very pretty marble. She smiled and skipped away, content with her big shiny marble.

A bit later, another child approached the same adult. This child, who was also about 5 years old, had autism. He asked this aide if he had seen the latest Disney movie, the aide told him that yes he had seen that movie because his daughter wanted to see it. The boy then asked how old his daughter was and he answered 4 years old. The boy quickly switched back to talking about the movie and started asking him about what he thought of the movie. Did he like it? What was his favorite character? When did he go? What theater did he go to? Did his daughter like it? Did he know who directed the film? Did he know who produced the film? Did he know how many films Disney had made over the years? Did he know that Disney made the first animated movie? Did he know that Disneyland was in Anaheim, California, and not in Los Angeles? The adult knew most of what the boy was asking and answered him when he could and let the boy shout out the answers when he couldn't. Although it was more or less a question–answer conversation between a 5-year-old child with autism and an adult, it was certainly a longer conversation than the adult's earlier conversation. After a few minutes the aide told the boy that he should go play with the other children. At that cue, the boy sadly shuffled off toward the playground and started climbing on the jungle gym by himself until the bell rang signaling the end of recess.

Two things were evident from observing this interaction. First, the boy with autism obviously had some type of special interest or obsession with Disney movies or Disneyland and knew a lot, probably a lot more than he mentioned in his movie-related mini-grilling. Second, he had a connection to this adult because he felt that he could talk to him about his special interest. When he mentioned Disney and Anaheim and animated movies, obviously this adult knew exactly what he was talking about. If he had tried to talk to another 5 year old about this topic, the child would have gotten fed up fast with him prattling on about Disney movies.

In elementary school, it is important that children with autism have connections to caring adults because it is very difficult for them to connect with other children. They can be taught in social skills classes to engage with their peers and to talk about more appropriate topics, but at that age it is difficult for them to actually put their skills into practice. When children with autism talk, work with, or think about their special topics, it is an obsession. A parent in our study had this comment about her son's interest in special topics:

ELIZABETH: He's obsessed with things, and I didn't think too much of it; his obsession was with strange things. Like when he was little he liked wind chimes. And so I remember taking him for walks to look at all the wind chimes in the neighborhood because he was obsessed with them.

I: And did his obsessive interests change later on?

ELIZABETH: Yes, it was trains.

I: Yeah, that's a real typical one too.

ELIZABETH: And he still, to this day, he won't admit it. He really likes trains still.

I: How old is he now?

ELIZABETH: He's 16, but when you mention trains, he gets kind of excited.

TAMRA: He was basically getting close to being ready for kindergarten. That's the kind of kid he was, except for the fact that he would babble SpongeBob stuff. Like anything he'd hear about SpongeBob, he'd talked about that.

According to the research, people with ASD may develop obsessions for several reasons. Obsessions may provide structure, order, and predictability and help people cope with the uncertainties of daily life. When social interactions are difficult, a child with autism might use his special interests as a way to start conversations. Additionally, obsessions may help children with autism to relax and feel happy; they can get a lot of enjoyment from learning about a particular subject or gathering together items of interest. One young person with Asperger's explained how he felt about his obsessions on a website: "My mind was constantly whirring with thoughts, worries, and concerns. The time spent with my obsession was the only time in which I had a clear mind—it gave me that much sought-after relaxation" (The National Autistic Society, 2013).

One of the teenagers in our study said this:

LINDA: Special interest, this is my hypothesis—it is a comfort thing. It comes down to comfort. That is why I talk about my novel. Sometimes I talk about it too much and I worry that I am making references out of nowhere, but it is because if I am in a situation where I am with unfamiliar people, and I will grasp onto something that I am familiar with for comfort.

Some teachers use a child's fascination/obsession as a reward for good behavior. This usually works as long as it is not used as punishment and taken away when the child has failed, otherwise a tantrum could ensue. If a child is constantly asking or talking about his obsession, the child might not only frustrate other children, but also other adults. Some adults will put boundaries around how much they are willing to engage in these conversations and say, for example, "We can have a 10-minute conversation at the end of the day about (for example) Disney movies, but we need to focus on other school work until that time."

It is also important to remember that typically developing children will treat children with disabilities better or worse depending on how they see that teacher treat those children. If a child frustrates a teacher, and other children know it, they are much more likely to bully that child (Cassady, 2011). If the teacher likes and respects a child, children in a class are more likely to like and respect that same child. Sometimes children with autism are difficult to like, but it is important that a teacher find positive attributes in that child and emphasize those qualities. More important, when teachers have negative attitudes toward inclusion and are unwilling to have students with disabilities in their classrooms, they may (unintentionally) forgo the necessary supports that could create a beneficial learning environment for the students, and this just causes more problems for the child and the teacher (Cassady, 2011).

Strengths

It almost seems like a cliché to say that teachers should use a child's strengths when teaching. However, using the talents of children with autism is not only important; it could be the key to their success. Focusing on their strengths is more than just helpful for children with autism. It is a way to refocus one's thinking about children with autism.

If educators constantly think about how to remediate deficits or cure autism, they may be overlooking important information. If we change our mindset and start thinking about how we can help these children adapt to the changes they are experiencing, to embrace, rather than fight, the changes, to help their brains develop, rather than stop the process, to go forward, rather than backward, to seek out what is positive and learn from those developments, rather than constantly looking for what these children are missing, perhaps we might find answers that have alluded us.

A number of parents in our study told us that their children had gifts:

DAWN: I mean he can build a very complex 2,000-piece Lego set in 3 hours. He's totally spatial. He's totally spatial, and memory . . . spatial skills and memory are his spikes . . . intelligent spikes.

EMILY: He plays piano, he did, I can't say that he does anymore. Of course he plays beautifully, like unbelievable, without feeling, but he plays the notes accurately. He was playing Chopin 5 years ago. He loves patterns. He won't listen to music, but he can play music, and he can create music. He has perfect pitch, absolutely perfect pitch. You can play three notes on a piano, and he can tell you which three without looking. And he's always right.

ALONZO: He enjoys drawing, he can draw what's on the Bay Bridge or whenever they went outdoors, he would draw, painting drawings about the things that he saw.

These abilities tend to come and go over time:

TAMRA: I haven't noticed him being as good at that anymore. He did when he was younger, he said that was a passing thing when he was really, really on top of it, but as it becomes Algebra and it's becoming more challenging, he's not having the gift anymore as much. Before, it would drive his teachers crazy. Other kids would have to add by hand, he would never do that, he would do it in his head.

So on one side of the spectrum of high-functioning children with autism you have children who come across as incredibly smart, and sometimes these children have savant-like splinter skills. On the other side of the spectrum, you have high-level children with autism who struggle in school, in much the same way as children with learning disabilities and/or ADHD. What is interesting is that research tells us that these savant-like splinter skills and learning problems are often found in the same child. Children with savant-like splinter skills are more likely to have been diagnosed with high-functioning autism rather than with Asperger's, who are generally considered (or used to be considered, before the new *DSM-5*) some of the smartest children on the spectrum. Many of the children who used to be labeled as high-level autism are the ones who have trouble with auditory processing and expressive language (Boddaert et al., 2004).

Research suggests that the abnormal cortical auditory processing observed in both children and adults with autism could be associated with inadequate behavioral responses to sounds and in language impairments characteristic of autism (Boddaert et al., 2004). Auditory processing is probably the most common delay, but many children with autism also have verbal processing or visual processing delays, which slows them down even more. What is important to remember is that it might take time for some children to understand and then to respond. Children with autism who have trouble in school also commonly have problems with handwriting and comprehension.

In elementary school, however, children with autism have strengths that shine through even more than they do in the higher grades. These children have more problematic behaviors, but they also have some amazing talents, and these talents are often not used to their fullest potential. According to the parents we interviewed, about 30% of the children in our study had really good memories for things they liked, and that was especially true in the lower grades:

JANA: It's a little hard for him to look at the board sometimes, or listen and write, but he remembers everything.

DAWN: He's good at math. He has an excellent memory. He has a, y'know, an off the charts memory.

JAMES: Another thing he's great at is remembering stuff like details and dates, I mean, I think as with many kids at least with high level autism, right, he's got a little bit of blinders on him, like he'll have a hard time, and this is one of his challenges in school. A hard time retaining things, he's not that interested in. He has an amazingly, magnetic mind for stuff that he wants to learn about.

TAMRA: His whole life, he's been like that (able to remember things). We almost hoped that he could channel it sometimes into other things because there's times when he doesn't channel that energy. But he does for some reason channel it with history.

A teacher should not hesitate to point out to other children the special abilities of a child with ASD in the lower grades. Although it may seem odd to emphasize a child's ability in spelling (for example) in first grade, if a child gets a reputation for doing really well in even one subject that will help her feel good about herself, especially if she has trouble later on as she faces other challenges.

If a child has a special talent, the teacher should capitalize on it. For example, if a teacher is working with the child who likes Disneyland, she could ask that child to write sentences using the spelling words that describe different aspects of the theme park. She can use Disneyland as a theme for teaching the different parts of speech. Let the child write stories about Disneyland. Let the child write a Disney movie script instead of a "story." Let the child figure out how much profit Walt Disney would make if he sold 10 tickets at $100.00 each and had to pay his employees $10.00 an hour for 40 hours a week. With these types of accommodations, the teacher would see the child flourish in the classroom and become strong and independent and on the path to future success. One parent commented:

JAMES: I think one thing I would do, if you're sort of going for inclusive classrooms with kids with autism is try to highlight their special skills. And I think that has really helped Reese.

Academic Supports

Concentration is another complicated issue. One thing a teacher should know is that if you yell across a room to a child with autism, you might as well yell across the city, because it is unlikely that the child will understand you or focus on what you are saying. When talking with a child with autism, whether the child is 3, 8, 12, or 16, it is important to make a connection with that child so that he or she is focused on what you are saying. Oftentimes children with autism are in their own heads and will block out other stimuli around them.

Some elementary children with autism can go into their room and concentrate on the computer for hours, going over the same webpage or short video clip on a particular topic 25 times. Unfortunately, however, in class the same children can't pay attention for 10 minutes. The reason is simple, if they are interested, they can talk about it for 6 months; if the content they are learning holds no interest for them, it is hard for the children to keep their heads off the desk:

I: Do you feel like you have a good memory?

DANIEL: When I want to use it. If I don't wanna use it, I don't remember things.

RAYNE: It's like, and whenever they tell us take notes, copy this off the board, it's like, bored, not doing it. And they don't realize it, but taking notes, it just goes through one ear and out the other. If we do more hands on stuff and more creative stuff, it sticks in, which is what I've noticed a lot.

CHRIS: I got so bored to the point where I literally drove myself to madness.

How do you keep a kid from getting bored? This takes a multipronged solution. It is always important to first try to connect whatever you are doing with what they are interested in. For example, if a child is interested in trains, and you are teaching about the history of the United States, we suggest that you allow the child to view the history of the United States through the eyes of a train conductor or a train designer or to let the child map the spread of the railways in the United States through the years. Universal design for learning (Rose & Meyer, 2002) reminds us that we should think about how we present information, how students respond or demonstrate their knowledge and skills, and how we need to engage students. Teachers can reach out to children with autism through the use of the creative arts, technology, multimedia, and collaborative groups.

Group Work and Peer Teaching

Most children love to do group work or cooperative learning. It has been shown to be effective as a teaching strategy for everyone (Johnson & Johnson, 1989). It is so much more fun than sitting down and having information poured into you by a teacher. It also has a lot of research evidence to suggest that it works. Johnson and Johnson (1989) discovered that cooperative learning has many positive outcomes. Their research shows that cooperative learning improves students' efforts to achieve. They work harder, achievement levels go up, material is remembered longer, and higher-level reasoning is used more. It provides not just external motivation, but also intrinsic motivation (Bertucci, Johnson, Johnson, & Conte, 2012; Johnson & Johnson, 1989). With group work, a child works with friends, and the teacher has more time to work one-on-one with other children or with particular groups.

Unfortunately, there are some drawbacks. Most teachers know the criticisms. First, not all students do all the work; some children hang around and simply watch the work being done, especially if they are passive or isolated. Second, many teachers set up collaborative work so the children will have fun, but they put less work into making sure the children are learning. Third, sometimes the child with autism (unless the child is assertive) will get stuck doing something that is not as thoughtful, like cutting or coloring, while the others write or do research; this is something the children often decide together. Fourth, children with autism will get frustrated if other children do not give them time to think, and this may cause them to act out. Children with autism do not like being put into situations where other children can easily see their academic challenges and rush them into finishing something they want to think about. These children often have their own sense of time. They don't like to rush, and they don't like to wait. It is important to give them "a heads up" when moving to another activity. Sometimes they also resent getting "help." They want to do it themselves and they want to take the time to finish on their own. When someone helps them, it reminds them that others are faster so these children can respond negatively to typically developing children trying to help them. So, putting a child with autism in a situation where they are always the one helped and typically developing children as the helpers can be problematic. It is important to allow children with autism to demonstrate their strengths.

If you set up cooperative groups, make sure that all of the children are in compatible groups; never just tell children (as a whole class) to get into groups. There will always be a few children left out, and before you continue with the lesson, you will have to dry some tears, not only for the child with autism, but for other children who also feel like outcasts. In this situation, you will be surprised how much time it takes for you to not only talk to the children who were turned away, but also to the children who were being exclusionary. This will take your time, and you will not be able to teach content.

The solution is to set up your groups and make sure everyone has an assignment. Teach children how you want them to interact in groups. Make sure everyone has a role to play and that the child with autism's role is just as important and challenging as everyone else's. Make sure they know they will be in class all period so they should take their time and think about what they are doing. If some children need more to do, have them take notes or do some additional tasks in the group, answer questions, or add a more challenging piece to the assignment for those who need more stimulation. The teacher should be thinking about how to differentiate so that all children are challenged. Don't make it obvious that one person is struggling or another child is excelling beyond the rest of the class. Make sure all children get public, positive reinforcement for effort and development beyond their own current level of thinking and achievement.

Many teachers ask about peer tutoring. Should teachers bring in peers to tutor young children? Should they bring in older children without autism to work with younger children with autism? Should they bring in older children with high-functioning autism to work with young children with or without autism? The answer is yes most of the time, but remember not all children can work with other children.

One example of a peer-assisted learning program that works according to research is the PALS program (Fuchs et al., 2001). Peer-Assisted Learning Strategies for reading (PALS-R or PALS) is an effective model to improve the reading skills of children with and without disabilities in the general education classroom. PALS, which was modeled after ClassWide Peer Tutoring (CWPT), is an approach to teaching children important reading skills. It complements the existing reading curriculum by providing research-validated learning strategies through peer-mediated instruction (i.e., peer pairing, peer tutoring). In the PALS approach, teachers pair a high-performing reader with a low-performing one in order to complete activities designed to promote the development of reading skills. PALS incorporates the following components: (a) highly structured activities that have been demonstrated to improve students' learning, (b) reciprocal peer tutoring (i.e., during the session, each student in the pair serves as a coach and as a reader), (c) the use of scripted prompts, (d) frequent verbal interaction and feedback between the coach and reader, and (e) a competitive game format. The teacher ranks the students based on their reading achievement level, divides the list in half, and pairs the highest-performing student with the lowest-performing student. This process is repeated until all of the students have been paired. Students in grades 2 through 6 usually remain in their assigned pairs for 3 or 4 weeks, after which time the teacher will need to reassign partners. Reports from instructors indicate that switching partners at regular intervals is among the most effective methods of keeping students enthusiastic about PALS and of improving behavior. Of course, this changing of partners has the added advantage of allowing students to work with a wider variety of their peers. Teachers should also be aware that, at times, circumstances might necessitate adjustments to their initial pairings. Before teachers can successfully implement any strategy in their classrooms, they first must ensure that their students are adequately trained. The training for PALS consists of twelve 35-minute sessions that are typically held 3 days a week for 4 weeks. Through them, teachers gradually introduce their students to each of the strategy's three activities, allowing them more opportunities to discretely practice partner reading with retell, paragraph shrinking, and prediction relay before all three are combined into one session (Fuchs et al., 2001).

Cooperative groups can be a great way for kids to learn, but they need to be structured appropriately for all children. You don't want children with autism to work in groups where the children are impatient or rude. Children with autism want to have time to think about things; it frustrates them when typical kids do not want to give them time to think. They also don't like doing something very easy, such as pasting pictures on a poster, while the rest of the group figures out the story. They usually understand more than they can articulate, so they may appear less intelligent than they are, but they like to learn and they like to be challenged, even if they sometimes seem like they don't want to work.

Visual Supports and Social Stories

In elementary school, it is easy to overlook simple solutions like writing down instructions for assignments on the board or on a child's desk. Visual supports can be used in a variety of ways in many settings: school, home, work, and community. Kluth and Darmody-Latham (2003) suggest using graphic organizers, flowcharts, and Venn diagrams in addition to verbal instructions for students with autism. Teachers sometimes complain that children with autism constantly need directions to be repeated. By writing instructions on the board or on an overhead where children can glance back up to the next step in the directions, teachers will find that they will spend less time moving from desk to desk explaining the directions, and children will be learning how to follow directions independently.

When children are younger and unable to read or more severely challenged, a teacher will use picture symbols or picture directions, or actual pictures as part of their visual supports. As they get older, high-level children with autism can use written directions. Figure 10.1 is an example of simple picture directions.

Children with autism tend to ask a lot of questions. The more visual supports a teacher uses, such as calendars or schedules, named cubbies, and labeled drawers and stations, the less likely the children will be asking questions and the more independent the children will be in the classroom. Allowing young children to be independent, decide what they need, and get materials on their own, is just one way to start helping children build executive functioning skills for when they get older.

Social stories were developed in the 1990s to improve the social skills of people with ASD and other disabilities (Gray & Garand, 1993). A social story is an individualized short story that breaks down a challenging social situation into understandable steps by omitting irrelevant information and by being highly descriptive to help an individual with an ASD understand the situation. It includes answers to questions such as who, what, when, where, and why in social situations through the use of visuals and written text. Social stories are used to teach particular social skills, such as identifying important cues in a given situation; taking another's point of view; understanding rules,

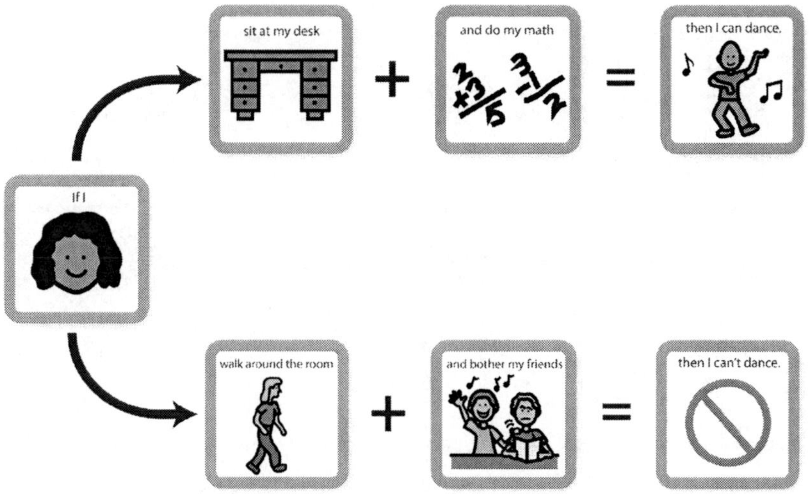

Figure 10.1 Simple picture symbol directions developed from Mayer-Johnson symbols. The Picture Communication Symbols ©1981–2013 by DynaVox Mayer-Johnson LLC. All Rights Reserved Worldwide. Used with permission.

routines, situations, upcoming events, or abstract concepts; and understanding expectations.

Social stories describe social situations in some detail—highlighting relevant cues and offering examples of appropriate responding—and are aimed at helping children with autism to adjust to changes in routine, to adapt their own behavior based on the social and physical cues of a situation, or to learn specific social skills or behaviors. They are individualized and typically are quite short, perhaps including pictures or other visual aids. Sentence types used in constructing social stories include descriptive, directive, perspective, affirmative, control, and cooperative (Gray & Garand, 1993). Figure 10.2 is an example of a short social story using Mayor Johnson Picture Symbols, which are also used for augmentative and alternative communication boards and devices for children with more severe challenges.

Social stories can also be developed primarily with words or with regular pictures. Students are encouraged to develop these stories. Many are also premade and available in books or on the Internet, and in fact some are animated in various ways online or can be created by teachers or children with animation software such as XTRA NORMAL, which can be accessed free online.

Usually people present social stories as written text. Other formats have been tried with younger children and people with intellectual disabilities, including using picture symbols and computer-based presentations. The goal of a social story is to reveal accurate social information in a clear and reassuring manner that is easily understood by the individual with ASD.

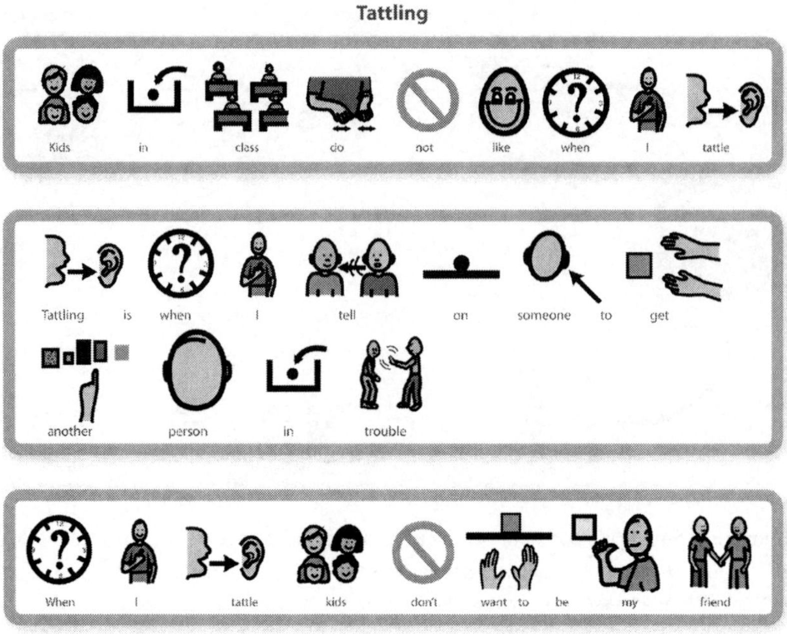

Figure 10.2 The Picture Communication Symbols ©1981–2013 by DynaVox Mayer-Johnson LLC. All Rights Reserved Worldwide. Used with permission.

The National Autism Center calls social stories an "emerging" intervention, which means that it has some research behind it but not enough for the center to describe it as clearly evidence based. Research reviews of the use of social stories have found the effects to be mixed (Ali & Frederickson, 2006; Reynhout & Carter, 2006; Kokina & Kern, 2010; Nichols, Hupp, Jewell, & Zeigler, 2005; Test, Richter, Knight, & Spooner, 2011; Sansosti, Powell-Smith, & Kincaid, 2004). Researchers have admitted that it has been difficult to collect data on social stories, because sometimes the intervention is not being used as it is intended and many of the children are involved in other interventions while also using social stories. These types of problems distort the results of a study.

Although "social stories" have had mixed results, the National Professional Development Center and the National Standards Project claim that story narratives (NPDC) and story-based intervention packages (NSP) are evidence-based practices and social social stories fit under those categories.

Children with autism want to feel secure and in control, so it is important that they know where they are, what they are doing, how to do what they need to do, and why they are doing whatever it is they are doing. Using visual schedules, calendars, and directions will help them feel in control and grounded.

Literacy

Anaphoric Expressions

In the chapter on cognition, we learned that children with autism were better at completing nonverbal tasks. Activities that are language intensive may be more difficult for them to understand and complete. For example, here is a paragraph that a child with autism might have trouble understanding:

> In January, the "Burj" skyscraper opened its doors in Dubai, a city in the Middle East. The tower is 2,717 feet high, and is the world's tallest building. People are already planning trips to see the edifice.

In this sentence, the author uses *skyscraper, building,* and *edifice* all to mean the same thing. These are called anaphoric expressions, and they are difficult for a child with autism to understand. This is also true when a child with autism must read a story that makes use of a lot of pronouns. For example,

> Sandy and Sally went to the store, but when they got there, Sally wanted candy, but she felt a bit guilty because it is bad for her teeth. Sandy, instead bought an apple, and told Sally that she thought that she should also buy an apple instead of candy and that would make her feel better.

In this paragraph, the child with autism would have to follow along with the passage and understand which pronoun is being used for which girl at any given time. This might also confuse the child.

Learning to Use the Computer

Children with autism also have the ability to focus for long periods of time on things they are interested in, so allowing them to research those topics, for example, on the computer, will help teachers have more time with other children. For that reason, children should be taught how to use a computer and to type in the lower grades, especially if they have dysgraphia. It is helpful if they are taught how to do appropriate research early, and they should be taught to use a computer as a tool so they can use it to create better products. Children with autism spend a lot of time on the Internet looking up their favorite topics. In addition, they spend a lot of time just looking up information; they should be taught at a young age what types of evidence to look for on the Internet; that is, to know what types of sources are reliable, how to search reliable sources, and how to access those sources using the computer. They should also learn to keyboard as early as possible. This is a way for teachers to use a child with autism's strength. Later on, higher-level children with autism need to take notes in classes in junior high and high school. To prepare them for taking notes, teach them how to type fast on the computer in the lower grades, because it is hard to take notes on a computer if you can't type very fast. It is easier to write notes out by hand, but teens with dysgraphia oftentimes are unable to read their own handwriting.

Having them learn to create art on the computer might also help them as they get older. Many children with autism are good with computers, but they do not have very good fine motor skills, so they can't draw. Instead of asking them to draw pictures, have them create pictures on the computer. Children with autism like computers, but most of them learn relatively few computer skills as young children; mostly they learn to browse the Internet and play games. Children should be taught to use the computer as a tool as soon as they are capable of keyboarding.

Reciprocal Teaching

Children with high-level autism are often in and out of general and special education during their school career. They have special needs and yet general education is where they belong, There, they are challenged with curriculum and pedagogy, they can interact socially with all of their peers, and it is the least restrictive environment for them. Combining strategies that are used in general education and those used in special education is logical. Whalon and Hart (2011b) combined general education and special education strategies when they used question-generation strategy instruction and reciprocal teaching (Palinscar & Brown, 1984). Reciprocal teaching is a type of multimethod comprehension strategy that includes question generation. Following reciprocal teaching, children with reading comprehension difficulties have increased performance on reading comprehension measures, improved ability to discuss text with others (Lipson & Wixson, 2009), and enhanced clarity and quality of their questions to better reflect main ideas (Palincsar & Brown, 1984). When careful scaffolding (i.e., instructional supports faded over time) was used, children as young as first grade improved their dialogue and became more independent in their conversations about text; this reduced the need for teacher scaffolding over time (Palincsar, 1986). Additionally, generating questions places students in the active role of initiator (Rosenshine, Meister, & Chapman, 1996). Increasing initiations is an important instructional goal for children with ASD (Earles-Vollrath, Cook, Robins & Ben-Arieh, 2008). These children tend to initiate comments or questions for the purpose of seeking additional information infrequently (Freeden & Koegel, 2006).

Question-generation strategy instruction teaches students directly how to generate and respond to questions about text. Generating questions helps students identify the main ideas or gist as well as salient details from text and assists with comprehension monitoring (RAND, 2002; Rosenshine et al., 1996). Question generation improves students' ability to make connections, respond to comprehension questions, and produce quality retells (RAND, 2002). The entire process of the instruction is detailed, but it is easier to understand with an example. In the following example, the authors (Whalon & Hart, 2011b, p. 198) demonstrate how a teacher is showing the children how to generate questions using a reciprocal approach:

> Mrs. Clearly explains that there are two kinds of questions, (a) in the book and (b) in my head.
>
> **In the Book**
>
> Fran the Fact Finder
>
> Sid the Summarizer
>
> **In My Head**
>
> Izzy the Inference Maker
>
> Connie the Connection Maker
>
> Mrs. Clearly reads "Arthur's Teacher Moves In," and models a question, "Who is moving in?" She waits for one of the students to answer, and replies, "Good, Arthur's teacher is moving in. How did you know the answer?"
>
> After students respond, Mrs. Clearly elaborates, "The answer is right there in the title. Which character asks questions that are right there in the book?" Mrs. Clearly directs the students back to the question cards, rereading while pointing to the text on the cue card, "It says here that Fran the Fact Finder asks questions about things we can find right in our book. Where did we find the answer to, 'Who's moving in?'" One student says, "On the cover of the book." Mrs. Clearly confirms.
>
> After introducing the strategy, Mrs. Clearly begins reading the story aloud and modeling question generation. She models by first restating what was read, "I just learned that it is the weekend. Arthur's teacher's, Mr. Ratburn's, roof collapsed from the snow. Arthur's mother told him that his teacher has nowhere to stay." Mrs. Clearly identifies the type of question she plans to generate, "I'll ask an Izzy the Inference Maker question." Mrs. Clearly explains, "It says here [pointing to a script] that Izzy asks questions that are not in the book but that we can guess from what the author says. I want to know, where do you think Mr. Ratburn will stay?"

Obviously Mr. Ratburn is going to stay at Arthur's house, and anyone who knows these stories knows that Arthur (who is a very odd-looking young aardvark) is not going to be very happy about that. So, the children need to make the inference and also start learning how to ask questions about making inferences. Both skills are very challenging for children with autism, but these are very important skills to learn. Also note in this scenario that the teacher seems to be asking all of the children, and they seem to be answering together. In other scenarios, a teacher might ask the child with autism to try to get him engaged even when it is clear that the child does not know. In this case, the teacher's heart is in the right place, she wants to make sure the child stays with the group, rather than space off in his own world, but this is not a good strategy in this case. For example, in a recent study researchers observed a fifth-grade teacher trying to use this strategy (Whalon & Hart, 2011a, p. 251):

> In what appeared to be an attempt to redirect Brad to the group, the teacher inquired about his favorite character. Brad replied, "I would choose the fox." At this point, the students began giggling because the story was not about a fox but about a young boy and his sled dog. Brad told his peers, "Shut it."
>
> Despite the supports provided by the teacher, and Brad's attempts to monitor his own comprehension, his difficulty continued and began to distance him from his peers. For example, when Brad's teacher asked, "Who is searchlight?" Brad did his best to answer based on the question clues provided within the question, "A person who searches lights." Peers laughed and he said, "Stop laughing." The teacher commented, "I think he had a good answer, but it is not what a searchlight is in this story."

The teacher is really trying to be kind and to help Brad. Throughout the instruction, the child wasn't paying attention, he was looking up at the ceiling and picking at his clothes and lying on the floor (they were in a circle). This was a clear communication from the child—"I don't want to be here. Leave me alone."—and it was probably not a good place for him to be. He was failing and the other children in the room were laughing at him. For typical children who commonly make mistakes, this might seem like nothing, this happens all the time, they run outside and play and forget about their "wrong" answers and move on, but for children with autism, this is not something they forget. These are the types of issues they have to deal with multiple times a day, every day, and these are experiences they don't forget; they probably push them down into their subconscious as they sink more and more into themselves and away from everyone else. It is possible that Brad may have been able to answer those questions, but he was so socially anxious that he couldn't focus enough to answer correctly. If a teachers calls out a child with autism to answer questions in front of his classmates, for the sake of his social issues, he needs to be successful. One parent in our study commented:

DAWN: Don't ask them too many questions out loud uh, don't single them out with their peers, never condemn their work in front of their peers. Expect their peers to just be uh respectful at a minimum. Gracious, if possible.

Recess

Just recently a teacher asked us if she should allow a child with autism to take a break at recess. She explained that the child seemed tired and a bit overwhelmed by all the other children and seemed to really want to spend some time alone at school, so she let the child stay in at recess. What frustrated her was that the child had really come far with his reading and yet every time she met with his parents all they cared about was what she was doing with him at recess. Our answer to her was that she should try to work with the child at recess. Why? Because he needs to practice interacting with peers in a social setting. His biggest challenges are social, so you don't want to give him a break during the time when he can practice social skills, you should find a time during the day when he is doing really well and give him a break then. Giving him a break during recess is like taking a child with reading problems and giving her a break during reading time. One of our parents said this:

ELIZABETH: I don't know if he is that unusual, he's a pretty good kid. I like the fact now that he has friends. For a long time, he didn't. It's the social part that's really hard, wanting your child to have friends.

Part of her IEP should include someone helping her work on social skills during recess. Children with autism spend time by themselves at home. It is better to give children with autism short breaks during the day when they get overwhelmed or frustrated then to let them spend time indoors during recess. However, you might have the child play with other children in a more secluded quiet area, if they don't like a lot of noise and feel overwhelmed with children running and making noise.

During recess, a child should be taught to ask other children to play and interact in games, but also how to observe other children to see how they talk to each other and play with each other, what they do and how they interact, what are the rules for the games and why we have rules. In elementary school, the goal is to help a child learn about how to make friends, to play and to socialize; these things do not happen overnight, they happen over time. Part of the reason to take children out to a playground is to teach them about what their peers are doing during social time. There is nothing parents dislike more than their child with autism pacing around, talking to themselves just outside the school yard while other children are playing. These children are lonely and isolated and this makes them look very odd to those around them.

References

Ali, S., & Frederickson, N. (2006). Investigating the evidence base of social stories. *Educational Psychology in Practice, 22,* 355–377.

Bertucci, A., Johnson, D. W., Johnson, R. T., & Conte, S. (2012). Influence of group processing on achievement and perception of social and academic support in elementary inexperienced cooperative learning groups. *Journal of Educational Research, 105*, 329–335.

Boddaert, N., Chabane, N., Belin, P., Bourgeois, M., Royer, V., Barthelemy, C., . . . Zilbovicius, M. (2004). Perception of complex sounds in autism: Abnormal auditory cortical processing in children. *American Journal of Psychiatry, 161*, 2117–2120.

Cassady, J. M. (2011). Teachers' attitudes toward the inclusion of students with autism and emotional behavioral disorder. *Electronic Journal for Inclusive Education, 2*(7), 1–23.

Earles-Vollrath, T. L., Cook, K. T., Robins, L., & Ben-Arieh, J. (2008). Instructional strategies to facilitate successful learning outcomes for students with autism spectrum disorders. In R. L. Simpson & B. S. Myles (Eds.), *Educating children and youth with autism: Strategies for effective practice* (2nd ed., pp. 222–243). Austin, TX: PRO-ED.

Fredeen, R. M., & Koegel, R. L. (2006). The pivotal role of initiations in habilitation. In R. L. Koegel & L. K. Koegel (Eds.), *Pivotal response treatments for autism: Communication, social, and academic development* (pp. 165–186). Baltimore, MD: Paul Brooks.

Fuchs, D., Fuchs, L., Thompson, A., Svenson, E., Yen, L., Al Otaiba, S., . . . Saenz, L. (2001). Peer-assisted learning strategies in reading: Extensions for kindergarten, first grade, and high school. *Remedial and Special Education, 22*(1), 15–21.

Gray, C. A., & Garand, J. D. (1993). Social stories: Improving responses of students with autism with accurate social information. *Focus on Autistic Behavior, 8*(1), 1–10.

Johnson, D. W., & Johnson, R. T. (1989). *Cooperation and competition. Theory and research.* Edina, MN: Interaction.

Kluth, P., & Darmody-Latham, J. (2003). Beyond sight words: Literacy opportunities for students with autism. *Reading Teacher, 56*, 532–535.

Kokina, A., & Kern, L. (2010). Social story interventions for students with autism spectrum disorders: A meta-analyis. *Journal of Autism and Developmental Disorders, 40*, 812–826.

Lipson, M. Y., & Wixson, K. K. (2009). *Assessment and instruction of reading and writing difficulties: An interactive approach* (4th ed.). Boston, MA: Pearson.

Myles, B. S., & Southwick, J. (2005). *Asperger syndrome and difficult moments.* Overland Park, KS: AAPC.

The National Autistic Society. (2013). Obsessions, repetitive behaviors, and routines. Retrieved from http://www.autism.org.uk/living-with-autism/understanding-behaviour/obsessions-repetitive-behaviours-and-routines.aspx

Nichols, S. L., Hupp, S. D. A., Jewell, J. D., & Zeigler, C. S. (2005). Review of social story interventions for children diagnosed with autism spectrum disorders. *Journal for Evidence-Based Practices for Schools, 6*(1), 90–120.

Palincsar, A. S. (1986). The role of dialogue in providing scaffolded instruction. *Educational Psychologist, 21*, 73–98.

Palincsar, A. S., & Brown, A. L. (1984). Reciprocal teaching of comprehension-fostering and comprehension-monitoring activities. *Cognition and Instruction, 2*, 117–175.

RAND. (2002). *Reading for understanding: Toward an R&D program in reading comprehension.* Santa Monica, CA: Author.

Reynhout, G., & Carter, M. (2006). Social stories for children with disabilities. *Journal of Autism and Developmental Disorders, 36*, 445–469.

Rose, D., & Meyer, A. (2002). *Teaching every student in the digital age: Universal design for learning.* Alexandria, VA: Association for Supervision and Curriculum Development.

Rosenshine, B., Meister, C., & Chapman, S. (1996). Teaching students to generate questions: A review of the intervention studies. *Review of Educational Research, 66*(2), 181–211.

Sansosti, F. J., Powell-Smith, K. A., & Kincaid, D. (2004). A research synthesis of social story interventions for children with autism spectrum disorders. *Focus on Autism and Other Develeopmental Disabilities, 19*(4), 194–204.

Test, D. W., Richter, S., Knight, V., & Spooner, F. (2011). A comprehensive review and meta-analysis of the social stories literature. *Focus Autism Other Developmental Disabilities, 26*(49), 49–62.

Whalon, K., & Hart, J. E. (2011a). Children with autism spectrum disorder and literacy instruction: An exploratory study of elementary inclusive settings. *Remedial & Special Education, 32*(3), 243–255.

Whalon, K., & Hart, J. E. (2011b). Adapting an evidence-based reading comprehension strategy for learners with autism spectrum disorder. *Intervention in School & Clinic, 46*(4), 195–203.

Chapter Eleven
Middle School

Making the transition to middle school is the first big change for children in school. By the time children get into fourth and fifth grade, most of them are finally comfortable with their setting and have learned to adapt to their school environment and now people want to uproot them and move them to a new setting. It often takes a family some time to find the "right" elementary school, and now they have to look for a middle school, and everyone fears middle school. Changing schools at this time seems like a nightmare to have to go through. This is a difficult time in a child's life, when their bodies are changing and they are going through hormonal changes. In addition, many suffer from anxiety and depression. Many middle school students may also be afraid of high school because of rumors being spread that high school is harder and has more homework.

Therefore, it is important to help make these transitions as seamless as possible for children. A teacher should allow for children in fifth grade to visit the middle schools, and middle school teachers should take these children on tours so they get to know the middle school teachers and students. They should also let their middle school students in eighth grade take time off of school to visit high schools to do the same.

Having a group of kids who can show these new students around and answer questions would help to welcome these new students with autism into the school. The new students should have the chance to meet their guidance counselors, the principal, and the special education or resource room teachers. The school should also make general education teachers available to show that everyone in the school welcomes inclusion. The school schedule should also be explained, and, if at all possible, the child should have the chance to shadow another student. This all should happen in whatever grade comes before middle school or high school.

At the start of middle school, the children with autism should have the option to have a homeroom together with other autistic youths so they can meet and get to know each other and be able to connect when they need to do so. This homeroom should also have a small "get together" room as part of the program, where these children can come in at lunch or on breaks, as part of the social skills class, or if they need to touch base or cool down or take a rest. These children should have a "space of their own" if possible. The middle school will no doubt have a number of elementary schools that feed into this centralized middle school.

The school should have someone who is in charge of helping children become involved in clubs, plays, music, sports, and other types of social clubs outside of school. This doesn't mean just handing them a map. It means working with them on getting involved and talking to them about how they are involved and how they can get more involved and how they can make friends in these groups.

A parent support group is helpful for parents of these children, because if the goal is to get these children together and help them develop friendships, the parents need to be able to make connections.

Support should be set up for academics, perhaps allowing for children to start off by breaking the day up into four periods as opposed to seven periods and allowing aides to follow certain children (in groups) out into general education. A resource room should be offered at the end of the day to allow students to organize their work and perhaps complete their homework before they go home.

Finally, if at all possible, it is helpful to children on the spectrum if they can keep the same homeroom teacher (and perhaps more) who not only understands children with autism but can also work with them on social skills and executive functioning. If the same homeroom teacher can stay with them and follow their development over the years while they are in the school, then the children will know at least one adult who will track their progress all the way through school and who will get to know them and their families well. In large public middle schools and high schools, it is important to have some type of structured program for children on the spectrum and a person who is in charge of these children; otherwise, these young teenagers will most likely flounder. One parent was asked why she chose a private school when her son went into middle school, and this is what she said:

EMILY: I already know he can be academically superior, so I didn't care about that. I wanted him in a place where he was safe and not getting lunch thrown at him. What solidified my decision? When I see kids coming in fifth and sixth grade who have PTSD from the school they were in, and I see the parents faces at the meetings; they have been down trod; they have been beaten down to the point of now we're gonna try this. We didn't bother with funding. I couldn't deal with it. We just decided to privately pay and do what we could. We asked for family help, whatever it took. I did not want him going back to a public school because at the end of the day, he's happy and he goes to school.

The following is a child's view of learning about a new school:

LINDA: My first day of shadowing (in a private school for kids with autism and LD), I learned more in one day than I had in like a week or a month (in public school) because they taught how I understood and they were so nice. They really understood.

Public schools can be set up to encourage children with autism, but they need the structure and the supports in place. Another one of the teenagers had this to say about his middle school experience.

REESE: Yeah, junior high, like a lot more teachers began to understand what autism was and stuff. And, I started to enjoy a little bit more. I think more kids started to become more mature and stuff, and not act quite as mean. So, yeah, I think in Jr. High, it's kind of like when it started to get a little bit better.

This boy had always been in public schools, so he was able to get what he needed in middle school.

Academic Supports

In middle school, homework becomes very important, and students are expected to become more independent and to finish homework and to keep their work and projects organized. For children who have organizational issues, homework problems become very pronounced in middle school. Some children/teens with autism practically refuse to do homework. For their parents, every night is a battle. These teenagers believe that when they get home, their "home time" is their time and doing more schoolwork at home is not going to happen. Children on the spectrum can be incredibly stubborn. It is our belief that homework is not worth destroying a family's home life, causing a mental health crisis, or triggering divorce. We suggest that teachers work with parents to resolve this issue peaceably. We found that the teenagers who spoke to us had quite a lot to say about homework:

RAYNE: I like teachers who know that homework affects the child's mental health, then you like that person, cuz' in my opinion it does affect it. More homework means more likely to get stressed, which stress leads to self-abuse or suicide.

I: OK, what about homework, do you have any feelings about homework?

MASON: I really despise it. I know we have to practice things, but really, it's just like a blank page full of empty promises. I wish they could give us homework that's more specialized with our environment. Like for social studies, they should say, "What do you think the future will look like?" Or math, you could write your own problem based on (real life). Like one complaint when I was taking algebra was when we were learning really complicated equations, most of the students asked when were you gonna use this in life. And that's when the teacher was kind of a little stopped. She didn't know what to say because you don't really use it in life unless you're gonna become a mathematician.

If the child will complete homework with help and learn how to independently organize the material, this is an important piece of the puzzle. If the child is feeling confident, learning the material, and can do the work herself, the child is on a good path through middle school. In classes, it might also be helpful to make sure that children with autism are seated at the front of the room, especially those who want to be left alone.

Children need to be taught to become self-advocates. They should be going to teachers themselves and setting up appointments. Even if they need an aide to go with them in case they need help, they should try to talk to the teachers themselves, ask questions, and tell them about their autism and what accommodations they need as part of their disability. In high school, they should be doing this by themselves. They don't necessarily need to be talking about these things with other children, but in school they need to start learning to become self-advocates and explain some of their differences. They will need to do that in high school, college, and most likely as part of their jobs. They need to start getting comfortable with this difficult topic. One suggestion for preparing them for this is to give them some examples of teenagers on the spectrum who have published stories about themselves (e.g., Lees, 2013, Heiman, 2010, Moss, 2011).

In middle school, try to make sure that children get caught up in their academics. Many of them have matured past their behavior problems. They may still not be socially where they want to be, but they have matured to a place where they can try to catch up academically, and many of the families in our study worked on academics in middle school to prepare the children for high school:

LIDIA: This year's been hard for her without her IEP; and she felt pretty good about herself, but this year, she's feeling she's not good enough. Or maybe she's not smart enough. And it's like, Oh, yes you are, don't worry, it's how things are being presented or how you're not able to show what's there. So we're working on it because it has to be fixed before we go to high school because she's gonna need more to succeed.

One final suggestion is get to know the children with autism. For middle school teachers, it is important to spend some time talking with them. Find out how many of them are open about their autism and what they know about their disability. Ask them what they need as far as support in your class. Autism should not be a taboo topic. Children want teachers to know them for who they are and to accept them for who they are. For those who are open, it would be helpful for them to get some reinforcement, especially at this young age, that teachers appreciate their openness and willingness to discuss their disability.

Tools for Organization

Binder reminders, daily planners, calendars, daily homework notes to parents, color-coded notebooks, task organizers, and visual-based management systems are all strategies a teacher can use to help children with autism stay organized. If these types of planning materials are used on the computer, both children and parents need to learn how to use the computer programs so they know how to access the materials easily.

Children with autism, like children with learning disabilities, do better if they keep track of what is required and do not get overwhelmed and fall behind. Children with autism tend to shut down when they feel overwhelmed. Children with learning disabilities will give up. Children with autism often want to please the teacher, so allowing some time after school to make sure these children know what they are supposed to do and are confident they know how to do what has been assigned as homework will help them feel less anxious.

Arts-Based Teaching

This may seem a bit counterintuitive, given that children with autism may appear shy, but some children with autism are very good at public speaking in elementary school. Some of these children can mimic voices, almost exactly, and they get their skills from some of their echolalia.

These children especially like talking about their special interests, and sometimes become very knowledgeable. But they can also talk about other topics. Some can memorize dialogues and speeches, which can help them. Some are shy to talk to individuals but are not shy on a stage. This is because shyness on stage is a learned behavior. This is where their lack of social awareness is a strength that teachers can use to their advantage. Many have creative ideas and are not afraid to talk about their ideas, even if they seem far-fetched, and, as a lot of artists will tell you, thinking outside the box is important in the world of creative arts. Typically developing children can be timid about their ideas, especially as they get older and feel embarrassed in front of their peers to act, sing, dance, or speak out in public. This is where some typically developing children can learn from children with autism; because this is the time when a person needs to ignore social norms and be free to entertain.

Physical Education

Physical education (PE) often poses more challenges than are necessary for children with autism. First, these children are always mainstreamed in PE, even if they are in special education. Second, starting in middle or junior high school, preteens usually have to change clothes. Third, they have to change clothes, take a shower, and then get into and out of PE in time for this class and the next. Also, most of the children also keep clothes in their lockers and are expected to keep these clothes safe, use a combination lock, and take them home over the weekend to get them clean and then bring them back on Monday. And, finally, because some children with autism are not extraordinarily coordinated, most are not considered athletic stars in PE. So, for all those reasons, PE is not always the favorite class of children with autism, even though it is often an outdoor activity. This type of class causes anxiety in children with autism.

The best idea is to have an aide go with the new sixth graders, at least for a while, until they get the routine of the PE class down and feel comfortable moving in and out of the locker room with ease. In addition, most PE programs know better nowadays then to let students "pick teams." If schools are going to use physical education as classes for appropriate mainstreaming and inclusion, they need to stop having children pick teams and drop the dodge ball games.

How Social Knowledge is Tied to Academics

As children with ASD get older and enter middle school, some have more problems with academics. Even among those who do well in academics, most must work harder and harder. For those who struggle, they start struggling even more. It is important for teachers to recognize that social delays will affect children's academic achievement. Obviously, children work hard at trying to overcome their challenges in social, communication, and repetitive behaviors during school hours; this tires them out and affects their ability to concentrate and to do homework. More specifically, social challenges often cause children trouble with reading comprehension, especially stories that use complex social contexts and interactions and multiple time lines to present moral messages regarding the social, political, and moral inadequacies of our society. On the other hand, a well-written book like this taught well might allow a child to be transported into another country or another time; given enough background and context a child with autism can learn about culture and social systems from those books. That is what children with high-level autism need to be taught about our social systems and cultural context because they do not pick it up naturally in the way that other children pick it up from the environment.

But there are other ways that social delays also affect academic achievement, children with autism often do not develop the same vocabulary as typically developing children about common things people learn from watching TV or having family conversations. This is because these children are often focused on certain objects or interests and are oblivious to other things around them. For example, just recently, a teenager with autism was listening to a rap song about a thrift store. Although the song was humorous, there was also an underlying message that people shouldn't be judged for being poor and that to buy secondhand clothes from a thrift store is not something to be ashamed of, in part because a lot of people do it. Many teenagers think this song is funny and clever; the child with autism who was listening didn't understand it at all. The reason was because that child didn't even know what a thrift store was, and this wasn't because he had never been to a thrift store, it was because he had never paid attention to thrift stores when he visited them with his family so he didn't know these stores were any different than any other stores, or where the "stuff" in the store came from or why anyone would care about where or why people bought clothes or furniture. He didn't understand why new clothes are often perceived to be better than secondhand clothes or why someone would be embarrassed to wear certain clothes and not others. He didn't understand the song at all because the song presented vocabulary as well as social and cultural information that made no sense to him. Rarely would adults have to explain what a thrift store was to a typically developing teenager who was 15 years old.

Language can also cause problems for children with ASD even as they get older. Some children may not understand metaphors or slang. If you tell some children with ASD that you want to kill two birds with one stone, they may actually think you hate birds and have some serious rock-throwing talent. Many children with autism have problems with metaphors and modern expressions. They need things stated clearly. The following is a story told by one of our interviewees about an incident with her child when he got confused because something was not expressed in a straightforward manner, but the teacher expected the student to understand what he meant:

JANA: I don't want Steven to go to PE because his clavicle is healing. So they say, "You have to come to PE for the lecture part, but you don't have to run track." The teacher is kind of a hard guy, and so Steven comes in with his note from me saying, "I don't want my son to participate because his clavicle is healing." And, I guess Steven came for the talking part, and then wasn't paying attention very well and was talking to his neighbors. And the guy looks at him and says, (this is reported to me) "Steven, if you're gonna come to PE, then you have to do it right," meaning don't talk while I'm addressing the group. And so, what did Steven do? He went along and did all of the PE class for that day and reinjured his arm.

These types of discussions and expressions confuse children on the spectrum when we don't provide specific direct explanations or directions.

Reading comprehension, social and cultural studies, as well as history, psychology, sociology, language, and vocabulary are all content areas that are affected by social delays, and conversely all content areas are affected by reading, social and cultural comprehension, psychology, sociology, language, and vocabulary. Beyond the fact that children with autism have more cognitive load and are constantly learning about social cues so they can survive in a highly social atmosphere, they also need to understand social content and aspects of our culture so they can achieve in school.

We also have to keep in mind that children with autism process information differently; for example, researchers have found that the way children with autism process faces is a bit different than their typical peers (Strauss et al., 2012). Strauss and colleagues (2012) found that children with autism were not able to distinguish pictures of young faces of men and women who were "nontraditional" as well as their typical developing peers could. Although they could recognize men versus women who had more traditionally male and female faces, when the faces were slightly less feminine or masculine, it was much harder for them to distinguish, even up until adulthood, when typically developing children could distinguish even nontraditional faces between the ages of 8 and 12. While children need to learn about the many explorers in history or the presidents of the United States, the fact that children with autism have a hard time processing faces can have a significant impact on children's ability to learn about important people who to them look the same. In each case, the children's social challenges we have talked about in this section can have a direct effect on their achievement in content areas, and much of that content starts in middle school.

Socializing in Middle School

In the middle school years, children go through a difficult transition from elementary school to middle school where they move from a school setting where they were with the same teacher all day long to a larger school setting where they have to move from one class to another about once an hour with only a few minutes in between. It is in the later elementary years when parents spend a lot of time deciding what educational placement is appropriate for the next leg of the child's instructional journey. Parents fear this change because children on the spectrum seem like they would be overwhelmed with the number of children, the loud noises, and the way the children have to rush from class to class, but none of the parents in this study mentioned problematic transitions (except one) from elementary to middle school or from middle school to high school. Anecdotally, with good supports, we have found that many children with autism are actually happier once they move up into different classes taught by different teachers because, although many children with ASD suffer from anxiety, many are also bored, and they are ready for a change by the time they transition and they want more intellectual stimulation.

We believe that the only way for teenagers to truly learn from the typical teen culture is for them to spend time with typically developing teens in places where these children authentically hang out with other teenagers. These kids need to be in clubs or sports teams or after school activities, but in places where children on the spectrum are welcomed by typically developing children who are interested in diversity. The best way to set up this type of activity is to have typically developing peers in these groups as buddies who provide friendship and protection to the teens with autism and then report what goes on in the groups. The peers are there to watch out for the teens with autism and to help them navigate the social scene and make sure they are not mistreated, teased, or bullied.

These typically developing children, once again, need to be trained on what constitutes bullying and how to confront bullies, especially girls who are bullied by boys who sexually harass girls and call it "joking."

In teen culture, a lot of teens joke and laugh and make fun of each other and themselves; children with autism can't always tell when this joking is being done in fun or to tease. This is something they need to learn, but having a "friend," a protector, someone who can report to a teacher or a social coach, is the best way for high-level teens to learn from peer culture. We suggest that typical peers be trained to be "social coaches" for children with autism.

For the most part, the teens had mixed social experiences in middle school. Some preteens and teens had very bad experiences. Here are some comments from three middle school students who were interviewed in our study:

I: How about junior high, how is junior high?
RAYNE: Oh, living hell.
I: Yeah, you don't like it?
RAYNE: No, I hate it!
I: And why is that?
RAYNE: Because, the "It" crowd. All these little cliques and it's just like, what is this?
I: They don't get your style?
RAYNE: No, they keep saying I'm emo, and asking me if I cut myself, and it's like, do you see any scars?
LIDIA: She doesn't really talk to anybody.
RAYNE: Just because I don't talk to you, doesn't mean I'm emo, it's 'cuz you're utterly stupid.
LINDA: Eighth grade, I have never been a fan of fitting in. You should just be happy, eighth grade, it started going downhill. I dropped out of middle school completely. My most vivid image of eighth grade was in English class, I went to the bathroom and cried for about 30 minutes and I came back to the classroom and nobody batted an eye. I was gone for a half hour and my eyes were ruined and nobody noticed. I talked about this in my senior speech. My OCD is connected to stress: it is all interconnected. My OCD was through the roof. My self-esteem was through the ground. In middle school you can't have super high self-esteem, I had suicidal thoughts, I was never seriously planning, but I had these ideas in my head.

CHRIS: I have to admit though, growing up because I had autism and stuff, um some kids, some stupid kids like have been mean to me and stuff and that's led me to not trust a lot of people. So, that's the only reason I'm afraid to go, I'm afraid of high school, well not afraid, I'm just nervous.

Some of the parents made these comments:

EMILY: I think probably, there was a period of time, and it's not good. It was maybe a junior high, seventh or eighth grade, probably coincides with puberty a little bit. He just got really angry when something wouldn't go his way. He's very rigid and sometimes his rigidity gets worse, and there were a few times, even in Tammy's class where he got mad and he would kick a desk over or throw a book. He threw a laptop last year and thank God, we are who we are. I was ready to go write a check, and they're like, "No, no, no." They gave an autistic a laptop, so I figured they know what they're in for.

ANA: We had connections through my work and stuff, so Alberto would hang out with him (a friend) all the time, and they got to know each other really well, so when they did go up to the big school, the middle school, his friend, Juan would have his back and say, "Well, don't pick on Alberto." So he'd stand for us, he'd stand up for Alberto all the time so they just basically left him alone and then he ended up being friends with some of the kids who were a year younger, which was interesting. So when he was a seventh grader he would hang out with some of the misfits from the sixth-grade class 'because his seventh-grade friend, Juan and maybe another boy were hanging out playing basketball or something and so he wouldn't socialize really with Juan anymore, except after school.

Other boys had mostly decent experiences, but no one had great experiences in middle school; it was definitely a tough time for most of the teens in the study:

MASON: Junior high was good starting seventh grade. Sixth grade, I was really not getting along with a lot of people. But during seventh, during the summer between seventh grade and sixth grade, I really started to learn more social skills. So then in seventh grade, I really started to get along with a lot more people.

Resisting the Changes

By the time children get into middle school there is a bit of resistance. Not only do children with autism have a hard time recognizing the difference between children with autism and themselves, they also have a hard time giving up things they love, even if these things seem odd to those on the outside of the autism world. Sometimes their interests or their quirks may seem odd and are certainly outside of the norm, but families have come to accept and accommodate for these differences and they no longer seem odd within the child's own household. For example, one of the teenagers who was interviewed is interested in cartoons, and especially a cartoon that would seem more for girls. This not only might look immature for his age, but a bit odd and girly. But, he is interested in different types of animation. He is especially interested in animated movies and likes to draw cartoon figures. He may even be interested in going into some type of career one day that involves animation. He is, however, clear that he does not tell typically developing friends from his school about his interest because he has been bullied for interests that fall outside what is normal for boys his age.

It is during middle school that children start getting frustrated with everyone telling them what to do and they start choosing to be alone rather than being with peers:

RAYNE: I would rather do bungee jumping with no bungee cord than be friends with the "it" crowd. Because, they're total jerks, they're sizing each other out, "Uh swagg, uhh, like totally," you guys are stupid, and they're dressed like they're in their 30s, and getting piercings at parks, wearing makeup that makes them look 40, and they're talking about booty tickling, and other stuff like that. OK, if only you had a slice of reality . . . what if I gave you the life of a person that you're acting like—3, 2, 1 herpes! Not only the teachers are stupid; but also a lot of students are stupid! My school is not what it used to be. According to my sister, it used to be fun and nice, and now it's a total home of the ghetto, home of the bad teachers.

Some of these kids convince their parents that they would rather be reading books, watching movies, playing on the computer, and engaging in other such activities rather than being around other people who are engaged in activities that they don't want to be involved in.

Unstructured Time

Unstructured time is when preteens/teens have the most difficult time getting along and interacting socially with typically developing children. This is why PE locker rooms, hallways, and lunchrooms can be so problematic. Children can also get into trouble at bus stops and during field trips. These are the times, when children are not being supervised, when children with autism get teased or bullied. Asking children in the school to be peer buddies and assigning well-mannered children whose parents care about citizenship is a good place to start. If the entire school knows these types of jobs are not only expected, but also required of everyone in the school, including children with disabilities, then children who are different don't feel so left out. And, in fact, it can be prestigious, because only those children/preteens who are well thought of, those considered honorable, should be allowed to be peer buddies. We believe the idea of bringing a sense of honor to schools would resonate with children, just as it often does with adults.

References

Heiman, H. (2010). *Running on dreams.* Overland Park, KS: AAPC Publishing.

Lees, G. (2013, January–February). Spreading the word. *Autism Bay Area Magazine,* 18–21.

Moss, H. (2011). *Middle school—The stuff nobody tells you about—A teenage girl with high-functioning autism shares her experiences.* Overland Park, KS: AAPC Publishing.

Strauss, M. S., Newell, L. C., Best, C. A., Hannigen, S. F., Zajac, H., Gastgeb, H., & Joyce L. (2012). The development of facial gender categorization in individuals with and without autism: The impact of typicality. *Journal Autism Developmental Disorders, 42,* 1847–1855.

Chapter Twelve
High School

For many of the teenagers and young adults who we interviewed for this book, high school had been their most positive educational experience thus far, and, for those beyond high school, college was also a positive experience, although the transition from high school was difficult. Most of the teenagers were doing well academically in high school, with only a couple of exceptions, and even those who were having trouble were passing, they were just not doing as well as they would have liked. However, all of them had to work very hard to keep up their grades, especially on homework.

According to statistics, only about 56% of students with autism finish high school (Wagner, Newman, Cameto, Levine, & Garza, 2006). For typically developing teenagers, about 70%–80% graduate from high school and for children with learning disabilities about 67% graduate (National Center for Learning Disabilities, 2013). It is important to work on high school completion rates for children with autism.

Nine of the children in our study were fully included in general education (or had been) in high school and/or middle school and were given some special education supports, such as access to a resource room class period, extra time for tests, computers for writing notes, and other similar resources, as needed. Eight children were in private schools specifically designed for children with high-level autism or Asperger's and/or learning disabilities. The others were in public school.

Nine of the children had very little trouble with academics in school, certainly no worse than typically developing children, and in most cases they did better. Many got As and Bs on the majority of their report cards. That is not to say that academics were easy for them; some had processing problems or attention deficits or concentration issues, but they were able to get past these challenges, study hard enough, and work with the schools so that they were able to maintain good grades.

Some of the wealthier families in this study hired tutors and sent their children to therapists; families with less money often took on the burden of reteaching some of the content to their children after they came home from school. One of the single mothers who we interviewed, Donna, said that she was now in the process of relearning algebra and geometry and teaching Mason because she was determined to get him through high school. From her description, this sounded like a difficult process, with a lot of arguing and frustration shared between the two of them. I asked her why she didn't ask the school for some help tutoring him. She said that Mason was stubborn about asking for help; he was often embarrassed to ask for help because it made him feel like he was stupid. He refused to tell anyone about his math problems. According to Donna, the only way the school would help Mason was if he was failing, and she was not really sure she was willing to let him fail.

Five of the children struggled at some time in their school careers (so far) with academics, but not because of cognitive deficits or even developmental delays, but because of anxiety or depression or some type of behavioral issue associated with their autism. Some had to be taken out of school and placed in other settings, sometimes more than once. Some of these children did well most of the time with the exception of some important time in their lives that moved them backward in their achievement trajectory. Sometimes the parents were appalled at the lack of understanding, flexibility, or sympathy when their children had these bad times in their lives:

MARIA: Finally we had to go to the principal and the dean of academics and in the end he did come around and pass Alberto, but I thought that it was uncalled for. He certainly didn't make the whole process any easier. You could just see the stress that Alberto was going through; he would have outbursts and just lash out, just be mad, "I'm sick of deadlines, I'm sick." It was his religion teacher who was really understanding and said, "Here, take the final home."

I: He spends 12 years doing pretty much everything that was asked of him, and he ends up having a bad year his last year. It's like chill people, chill!

MARIA: I know, two teachers who didn't want to give at all who just wouldn't give and that was like the hardest. That was a struggle all the way up to the very last day before graduation when he turned in the work. And there was a lot of interaction between his psychiatrist and the principal. It came down to that, because the principal didn't want to give me the time of day. His psychiatrist was the one that told us, "Well I've gotten to know the principal really well," because she talked to him and it took a doctor to convince him. Yeah, it took a doctor to tell the principal, "OK, this kid is not gonna make it, he's really depressed."

Three of the children from our study struggled, in part, because they had problems with reading or math or other academic challenges that mirrored those experienced by children with learning disabilities. Some of their parents thought their children might have had auditory processing problems or attention issues. Certainly many of these children complained about being bored with topic areas they were not interested in learning about at the time.

In high school, children with high-level autism become much more self-aware, which is really helpful to their growth and learning. As they get older and learn more about themselves and how they differ from other children, they can start regulating their behavior and learning how to fit in with other teenagers. They also can communicate better, so they start to learn how they might be able to talk to other children, ask questions, and carry on conversations:

I: How should teachers work with children with autism?

ASH: Well it kind of depends on how bad it is or how serious it is.

I: The autism?

ASH: For example, the character from that book with autism, you'd have to be very delicate with that character, he overreacts. You have to kind of figure out—like that character did not like to be touched, even if you kind of tapped him, he'd flip out and maybe punch you, something like that 'cuz he didn't like it. And it's more like a reflex. If it's like that, be very careful. But if you're told he has autism or Asperger's, but he seems normal, just try to treat him like a normal person.

REESE: I think in elementary school, I was in completely general education

I: Are you glad you were in general ed. then?

REESE: Some ways yes, some ways no. I'm glad 'cuz it helped me regulate myself in some ways, but in other ways I don't think it was always easy.

I: Did it help you that you stayed in the same town and knew these kids all along?

REESE: I do think it was helpful in some ways. I think it definitely helped so that I learned about being kind of more typical, like how to regulate myself in some ways.

In high school a lot of children find their niches. Children who like drama should join a drama club or try out for plays. Others might be artists or musicians. Many children with autism tend to show some talent in creative endeavors and enjoy creativity, whether it is in writing, art, music, theater, or video production. Others are good in things such as chess or other types of activities such as complex puzzles or video games. Some students might be athletes and try out for soccer or basketball.

Differences Between Girls and Boys

Many people claim there is a need for more research with girls and women with autism, and we agree. Our study provides some preliminary evidence that girls with autism are very different from boys with autism. There are some overlaps, but the greatest difference we noted was in their abilities to talk about how people think and feel. For example, girls were able to "guess" or make assumptions about other people's motivations that boys were either not willing or able to do. In fact, in some cases they went out of their way (not on purpose, but automatically) to talk about these issues in concrete ways, rather than make assumptions about how others felt. Here is Rayne making assumptions about her parents' feelings and motivations in a social situation:

I: Do you think that the homework is part of the reason that you and your dad have a hard time getting along?

RAYNE: That's only a small part. It's because I have an opinion now and I'm not a small little kid who will do whatever you say. I actually have the guts to talk back at him and he doesn't like it when I say my opinion and if it takes power away from him. So then he grounds me, and it's like, "Oh, know your place, blah, blah, blah." I'm like, "Shut up, OK, you are not top good dog, And mom's a lot nicer than dad because she actually understands unlike dad does . . . .

I: Is it because she understands your Asperger's and your autism?

RAYNE: Well she understands that I want a life.

I: Oh, so she understands you being a teenage girl too?

RAYNE: Yeah.

I: Is your dad just stricter and stuff?

RAYNE: Yes, he expects me to be perfect and like, "I'm not your little trophy to brag about . . "

And here is an example of Chris going out of his way to answer the question concretely, speaking only of actions:

I: What do you like about your best friend?

CHRIS: Um, basically, he shares a brain with me, he's in my grade and there's only four kids, and while the other two kids bicker at each other sometimes. One's definitely more mature than the other one. We just look at them; we just look at them both and say, "My God, this is stupid!" Like, to each other basically.

I: Why do you think teachers like you?

CHRIS: I make them laugh. I uh, I be friendly to them and uh, stuff like that.

When we asked Ash how he felt about being autistic, he talked about "it" and how it affected him, but not how he felt about it.

ASH: I don't really think much of it. It's just something on me. It doesn't really hinder me too much.

I: They might say they don't understand "Why."

REESE: Yeah, being honest, I think it was helpful for me because, I don't really understand why myself, but I don't think it's ever been easy for me to approach people like in a large crowd if they're with a bunch of their friends.

Parents often have trouble getting their daughters diagnosed because their symptoms don't manifest themselves in the same way that boys' do. Below Teresa tell us about her experience with her daughter's diagnoses:

TERESA: Linda is our daughter and is 17, she was diagnosed in middle school with Asperger's as most girls are never diagnosed unless they follow the typical boy Asperger's symptoms. They diagnosed her with everything under the sun and then it was after six specialists that it became a thought, it was with the help of Tony Attwood that helped me finally find a diagnosis. It was a real shock. But I am thankful for getting it right! They are both doing great and happy with who they are.

Thoughts on Behavior

What sometimes frustrates children with autism is this idea that teachers somehow don't believe they have a disability:

RHONDA: Because he doesn't look obviously autistic, [the teacher's] social radar is picking up that this kid is being defiant because they can't believe he really doesn't get it. So that's also part of what happened in high school. So that's memorable, you're feeling like you're in a world full of minefields where you can't see where the mines are. And you just know that every time you take a step out, you may step on one. No wonder they want to stay in their rooms, right?

Teachers often don't take into account that these students have something they must overcome. By the time these children are in high school, they are aware that they are different from other children.

Children with learning disabilities also bear this burden. Many teachers believe that children with learning disabilities are just lazy rather than truly disabled, and so they also tend to treat them with less empathy. The difference between children with autism and children with learning disabilities is that children with learning disabilities usually do not have significant social problems. Although children with learning disabilities can have anxiety or depression, it usually doesn't manifest itself in phobias or OCD, as it might in children with autism. On the other hand, some children with autism are very smart and do well in school and they can also hide their symptoms.

As has been mentioned before, one problem that children with high-level autism have as they get older is that teachers in the higher grades see these children as being fairly typical in appearance and behavior and are skeptical that they are autistic (or ever were), when in fact many of these children demonstrated fairly severe autistic behaviors when they were younger. This also happens because as teenagers these children refuse to talk as much as they did when they were younger (which is also typical for teenagers in general), so it is more difficult to get a sense for the typical challenges that autism poses. Some teachers think that perhaps the parents are either scamming the system or being hysterical, overly fearful of autism. Once again this makes the teachers (especially general education teachers) who don't understand less apt to provide accommodations.

Teachers don't always realize that some of these children have moved past their autistic behaviors in fairly significant ways from when they were young. Many of these children may seem typical from the outside, but inside many are still struggling with their disability. For example, many still suffer with significant anxiety or depression, especially if they don't have friends. One high school student in our study said this:

LINDA: Current challenges are stress management; it is getting better, and anxiety—generalized anxiety and my raging inferiority complex. We all have a distorted view! I have this problem; I feel this need to apologize. Sometimes people won't respond if they think it is not necessary for me to apologize. I even apologize for apologizing too much. And, then people will say stop, and I apologize for apologizing too much and it just snowballs.

Many of these children still have problems with schoolwork and need assistance and accommodation. Most still struggle with self-esteem issues acquired over the years from being rejected by peers and being told over and over in different ways that they needed to change to fit better into society. Just as typical children work to develop an identity, children with autism also need to understand who they are as they get older. They are smart enough to know they are different, and during high school they need to figure out exactly what that means. Many still fight against the idea that they are odd or mentally retarded in the traditional sense. They also have a hard time reading typical peers—their innuendos and their humor. They don't know when children are being funny and poking fun as a friend or being funny and being mean to make fun of them. They don't know who they can trust or when should they stand up for themselves if others seek to criticize who they are. Some work hard to regulate their behavior:

JANA: Steven doesn't have to process, but to regulate—it's too much, it's too much, it's too fast, it's too many. And then he goes away a lot. So he comes to the party, the big gathering, be all in and everything, and then in the next minute, you don't know where he is. And that's what he does.

High school teachers need to help children with autism develop their identity and learn to advocate for themselves, make judgments about other people's intentions, and communicate their feelings and their frustrations in appropriate ways.

Helping Teenagers Become Self-Advocates

- In a high school class, the students were reading the book *Of Mice and Men* by Hemingway, one of the students asked the teacher if Lenny was autistic and the teacher in the class replied that he could be. How should the child with autism in the class respond to that exchange?
- A student in high school told a general education teacher that he had autism before the semester began and the teacher said, "I don't know how to respond to that."
- A girl in high school told a teacher that some girls were picking on her in class and the teacher spoke to them, but now those girls are being nice to her on the surface, but saying mean things about her secretly in revenge, making things worse than they were before. Now what should she do?

In high school, all children need to navigate the rugged waters of the social world that can drown the optimism of the naive teen. Many people look back on their high school years as one of the most difficult times in their lives if their social problems were traumatic.

Teachers should remember that sometimes teens with autism will ask questions that other teenagers wish they could ask because our social norms may pressure children to keep quiet. The answers still elude many students, and not those only with autism.

Most high-functioning teens with autism would stay silent in the above scenarios because we still have not given them the permission to speak out and speak their minds. We are still focusing on telling them how they should be fitting in and acting like other typical children in accordance with our outdated and dysfunctional social norms, even though many of our typically developing children are not happy with the norms themselves.

Difference does bring a new perspective. For us to grow and change, we need to embrace these new perspectives. In our experience, the more children and teen-agers people are accepted for who they are, the more they accept the dominant culture.

Finding a Niche

It is important for children to find a niche at any age, but especially in high school this will allow them to make friends and learn social skills in an environment where they excel. In high school they are trying to figure out what they might want to do with the rest of their lives. They should start trying to find their niche in middle school, but not all middle schools have all the resources or opportunities that high schools might have. For example, Austin found out when he was in high school that he was good at Chinese, which is a difficult language. This is a niche that might help him find a career path:

KIMBERLY: His absolute favorite class is Mandarin. He likes the subject, he loves the teacher, but I think the other piece to it is that it's not a huge group of kids and they've been together in class now two years in a row. And they developed friendships in the class and it's a community feeling and he feels really comfortable, and I think he's also well accepted in that particular classroom situation.

For some children, sports can be a place where they make friends. A lot of children and teens with autism don't like sports because many are not very athletic. Others don't like the competition or they are too competitive. Some have a hard time understanding complicated rules that make no sense, especially when they are young, so they get angry and frustrated (e.g., a person can steal a ball away from another person in basketball). But sports can be a good outlet for some children. First, it helps all children stay healthy. Second, the exercise and outdoor activity can sometimes help children with disabilities: It can ward off depression or anxiety, and; it has been shown to improve children's ability to concentrate. Specifically, it can help children with ADHD (Lullo, & Van Puymbroeck, 2006). Helping children engage in sports in school can help them make friends and maintain their health:

JAMES: In middle school his PE was mainstream, and by the end of middle school, he discovered he really liked running and so he joined the cross-country team and made a bunch of friends in high school who are actually still having lunch with him, including a couple of typical kids.

ANA: She likes meeting people; she remembers their names. She's been in a childhood baseball since she was 7 years now. We joined, actually when she was, I guess first grade soccer. And then from there, I met the other parents, asked about catechism, they had a group at St. Veronica's, she got her first communion there and then she did her confirmation last year, but those are the same kids who are still on her baseball team. So she's known those kids.

Executive Functioning With Teenagers

Research suggests that children with autism have trouble with executive functioning (Verte, Geurts, Roeyers, Oosterlaan, & Sergeant, 2006). Executive functioning is a theorized cognitive system that controls and manages other cognitive processes. Executive functioning is a term used to describe the performance of many tasks that include thinking, acting, and solving problems. Whether a person has executive functioning skills determines whether he can live, work, and learn with an appropriate level of independence and competence for his age. Table 12.1 lists a number of skills associated with executive functioning.

Table 12.2 is a list of executive functions identified by Gioia, Isquith, Kenworthy, and Barton (2002). The executive functions represent diverse but related and overlapping skills. In order to understand a person, it is important to look at which executive skills are problematic for that person and to what degree.

The theory is that a person's executive function may be impaired by damage to the brain's prefrontal cortex (Damasio & Maurer, 1978). Problems with executive function have also been linked with Alzheimer's disease, strokes, and head injuries. Problems with executive function can run in families. They may become most apparent during a child's grade school years, when they interfere with the ability to start and complete schoolwork on time (Endedik, Denessen, & Hendriks, 2011). There are warning signs that a child may be having difficulty with executive functioning at a young age, including having trouble in planning school projects.

The good news is that the brain continues to develop well into adulthood (Chamberlain, 2009). A person's executive functions are shaped by physical changes as well as by ongoing experiences. Many believe that early attention to problems with executive functioning can help children outgrow and compensate for weaknesses.

Problems identified by individual tests can't predict how well adults or children will function in complex, real-world situations. Sometimes careful observation and trial teaching are more valuable ways of identifying and improving weak executive function.

It is important to start working on executive functioning skills as soon as possible. Parents should be encouraged to have their children do chores and to learn to do them independently. Over the years, teachers need to allow children to become more and more independent at organizing their schoolwork and remembering their homework assignments.

Executive function is about more than just organizing, however; it is about setting priorities. For example, it is as if you have someone at work who will complete a project for you next month when the deadline for the project is the end of the week. This person can't set priorities. Or, the person can't make a decision about what color to choose for the cover of the report although it doesn't really matter, but when the person does decide on a cover color it is bright orange, blinding everyone in the room.

As another example, a teenager might ask the teacher a question such as, "How much sunscreen should I use when I go outside on a sunny day?" as he heads out on a field trip. Without thinking, most of us would answer back, "When you go outside on a sunny day, you should cover yourself completely, wherever you are exposed. The sun can be dangerous to your skin." We are used to answering children's questions. We are used to protecting children, and this seems a reasonable question. However, if we stop to think, a child with

Table 12.1 Executive Functioning Challenges and Accommodations

Executive Functioning Challenges	*Suggestions for Accommodations*
• Planning and completing projects. • Understanding how long a project will take to complete. • Telling a story in the right sequence with important details and minimal irrelevant details. • Communicating details in an organized, sequential manner. • Initiating activities or tasks or generating ideas independently. • Retaining information while doing something else, such as remembering a phone number while dialing. • Estimating and visualizing outcomes. • Analyzing sights, sounds, and physical sensory information. • Perceiving and estimating time, distance, and force. • Anticipating consequences. • Evaluating possible outcomes of different problem-solving strategies. • Choosing actions based on the likelihood of positive outcomes. • Choosing the most appropriate action based on social expectations and norms. • Performing tasks necessary to carry out decisions.	• Give clear step-by-step instructions with visual aids. Children with executive functioning disorders may not make logical leaps to know what to do. Be as explicit as possible with instructions. Use visual models and hands-on activities when possible. Adjust your level of detail based on the student's success. • Use planners, organizers, computers, or timers. • Provide visual schedules and review frequently. • Pair written directions with spoken instructions and visual models whenever possible. • If possible, use a daily routine. • Create checklists and "to do" lists. • Use positive reinforcement to help kids stay on task. • Break long assignments into smaller tasks and assign mini-timelines for completion. If children become overwhelmed, share only a few at a time. • Use visual calendars or planners to keep track of long-term activities, assignments, and deadlines. • Teens may find time management planners or software helpful. • Organize the workspace, and minimize clutter on a weekly basis. Schedule time to clean and organize the workspace to improve work habits. • Consider having separate work areas with complete sets of supplies for different activities. This reduces time lost while searching around for materials. • Try to keep your strategies consistent across classrooms, at home, or in the workplace. People with executive functioning disorders are more likely to do well when their routines are similar in different settings. • Provide matrixes, grids, models, structures, forms, etc., to help children predict, decide, estimate, choose, plan, and anticipate outcomes.

Adapted from A. Logsdon. (2013). Executive functioning, understanding executive functioning disorders. Retrieved from: http://learningdisabilities.about.com/od/eh/a/executive_funct.htm.

Table 12.2 More Executive Functions and Definitions

More Executive Functions	*Definitions*
Inhibition	The ability to stop one's own behavior at the appropriate time, including stopping actions and thoughts. The flip side of inhibition is impulsivity.
Shift	The ability to move freely from one situation to another and think flexibly in order to respond appropriately to the situation.
Emotional control	The ability to modulate emotional responses by bringing rational thought to bear on feeling.
Initiation	The ability to begin a task or activity and to independently generate ideas, responses, or problem-solving strategies.
Working memory	The capacity to hold information in mind for the purpose of completing a task.
Planning	The ability to manage current and future-oriented task demands.
Organizing material	The ability to impose order on work, play, and storage spaces.
Self-monitoring	The ability to monitor one's own performance and to measure it against some standard of what is needed or expected.

high-level autism who is 13 years old should know (and more than likely does know) the answer to that question.

Why is he asking the question? There could be several answers to that. Perhaps he is just used to asking his parents to affirm everything he knows and he is getting confirmation. Perhaps he wants attention, but probably not in the same way that typical children want attention. He may want attention that reassures children on the spectrum that if there is a social issue that comes up, he knows the teacher will be there for him. Or, maybe it is just a habit, a habit that he has picked up over the years from his parents and his teachers automatically answering questions for a child who can answer his own questions when asked.

This child needs to start trusting his own judgment. Many children with autism can't make a decision. One way to handle this situation is to ask the question back:

> "If you were 20 years old and all alone in an apartment, and had to make your own decision, how would you answer that question?"

Tell the child that he needs to start preparing for adulthood as a teenager. This teenager not only needs to be ready for college or for work, he also needs to be independent and ready to make decisions about his life and his sunscreen usage.

Parents need to work with children to learn chores at home, but at school students should also learn to do chores and other "heavy work" that will help them learn certain skills. We should also let them help out in the school cafeteria or library; this gives them experience working for other people, following through with instructions and making decisions.

We've also heard of people taking pictures of workspaces and how they should look (for example) when a child cleans so that instead of making a list of what the child needs to do, the picture tells the child to make the room look like the one in the picture. Just telling the child to "clean this room" doesn't always get you the results you want, mostly because the child doesn't know what you want.

These are the types of situations where students learn executive functioning when they are young. Parents should be encouraged to get teenagers with Asperger's a job or some type of responsibility for helping others over the summer as they get older. Not only will it help with their social skills and executive functioning, it will help them to get some work experience and references that they can use in applying for jobs in the future.

Despite the fact that homework is important to many teachers, many students fail to take advantage of the long-term benefits of doing homework. Several executive skills, including cognitive flexibility, monitoring, and planning, are considered prerequisites for the completion of homework. It makes sense that homework difficulties may relate to executive function. In a recent study, researchers examined the extent to which differences in homework difficulties of 100 seventh and eighth grade students with, and 86 without, ASD related to their level of executive functioning (Endedik, Denessen, & Hendriks, 2011). Homework difficulties were examined with student and parent versions of the Homework Difficulties Questionnaire (HDQ), and executive functioning was examined with the Behavior Rating Inventory of Executive Functioning (BRIEF). In contrast to students with ASD, parents of students with ASD perceived their children to suffer from more homework problems than students without ASD. For both groups, the level of executive functioning was related to the degree of homework difficulty experienced.

For example, students who were often late or who had difficulty with new situations or who are unaware of their own strengths and weaknesses often had trouble with homework, such as misunderstanding homework assignments, being easily distracted, or handing in work past the due dates. Mainly the lack of planning skills, such as disorganization of materials and problems with determining the priorities of activities, seemed to contribute to the extent to which students experienced homework difficulties. No significant group differences were found between students with and without ASD in homework difficulties, but students with ASD reported lower levels of executive functioning. These findings are in line with previous studies, which found that students with ASD were impaired with respect to organization, self-monitoring (Ozonoff, 1998), planning, and flexibility (Ozonoff, Pennington, & Rogers, 1991).

Transition Planning

Transition planning, or creating the Individualized Transition Plan (ITP), is a step-by-step process to prepare a student for work, higher education, and adult living. The planning team creates a plan to help the student reach his or her life goals, based on what the student would like to do after graduation. Transition plans outline the necessary training, experiences, and educational services the students will receive during the remaining years of their school programs. This prepares them to be as productive and independent as possible as they enter adulthood.

Participants in transition planning are typically those who participate in IEP meetings, as well as additional school district staff and representatives of outside agencies (such as the teen's regional center case manager). Parents and the family have an important role in the transition planning process as well.

Parents know the teen or young adult and have a good idea of what works and what doesn't work for him or her. As the children get older, their right to self-determination becomes more important. The young person should have as much input and choice in the decision-making process as possible. For this reason, the ITP is considered to be "student centered." Even from the age of 14 the student can be invited to attend and participate in the meetings to provide input about his or her choices, preferences, and desires.

Although the transition plan itself may be legally mandated, the items included in the plan are not. To turn ideas into legally mandated objectives, the team must develop appropriate measurable goals and objectives from the "visioning" document into the IEP. If the parents, child, and school district have worked together to develop a solid transition plan, it should be relatively easy to use that plan to enhance the IEP. If, however, the team members are in disagreement or have a not-so-solid transition plan, the process can be much tougher.

What makes a transition plan solid? The plan should include a vision, objectives, and steps required to meet the objectives and fulfill the vision. If the team has identified and described clear, actionable steps, then those steps can become IEP goals themselves. The trick, of course, is to determine which steps to include at which point in the child's development.

When students with ASD plan to attend college, preparation begins while the student is still in high school (Hewitt, 2011). Unlike laws for K–12 education, laws surrounding higher education do not ensure individual success. Instead they remove barriers preventing an individual from accessing an education; education, itself, is not changed in any way. In addition to changes in available educational supports, students may have fewer available external services as well. If college is a goal, student supports during high school should include long-term learning that will allow for independent problem solving and self-advocacy when going to college. A plan should be in place for how the student can grow out of the system of services in high school with as little disruption as possible (Hewitt, 2011).

Transportation access should also be included in any transition plan. For some students, this includes driver's education. For others, it means learning to handle complex public transportation systems. During high school, students should also become familiar with the college they plan to attend (Hewitt, 2011). Students should visit campus as much as possible and meet with disability services to discuss individual strengths, needs, and plans. Engaging in these activities will make the transition from high school to college easier. The following is a checklist of steps for planning for college (Hewitt, 2011):

- Incorporate college as a goal into transition plan in the K–12 system.
- Be actively involved in transition planning.
- Create a plan for leaving services that will discontinue at adulthood.
- Consider long-term learning program for problem solving.
- Gain skills as a self-advocate.
- Research college programs.
- Get familiar with campus life and personnel.
- Understand the legal system for higher education.
- Meet with the disability services office at college.
- Understand individual strengths/needs/desires.
- Address potential problems early.

Life as an Adult

According to one research study, five variables had a major impact on whether teenagers with autism went on to college; these included: parental education, verbal skill, cognitive abilities (in that the children did not have intellectual disabilities), whether the child had graduated from high school, and whether the student participated in transition planning (Chiang, Cheung, Hickson, Xiang, & Tsai, 2012).

In our study, every child who was interviewed, except one, said they wanted to go to college. A couple of students said they might want to go to college or to work, but most of them mentioned college. Many of them had different ideas about how they planned to go to college, from attending 2-year colleges to arts colleges to expensive and prestigious private colleges, but almost all of them had some ideas:

GABRIELA: After I leave high school and graduate, probably wanna work at Whole Foods or go to college.

RAYNE: I just want to go to the Academy of Arts. I don't want to go to these crazy Yale or Stanford or anything like that. I want to do art. I just want to get out of there and be like, I'm doing art, I don't care if you want me to become a doctor or if my dad does because I have a feeling he doesn't want me as I am.

ASH: I wanna go to college. No, I see all these kids just saying, "Oh, I'm going to UCLA," and like, how do you know so much about it already? Most of time they all say just to be on the sports teams, and just like, y'know is kinda hard to do. I have no idea which college I'm going to, but yeah.

I: Where do you guys see yourself being in 10 years?

LANE: I don't know?

LINDA: Being an engineer?

LANE: Probably

LINDA: We have this group called the nerd squad. We are all really sciency.

I: Are you going to college too?

LINDA: In 10 years I see myself married, thinking about kids because that is a good age, stable age, good house, good job.

LANE: One of my biggest fears is living independently, paying the bills and all that.

LINDA: I am not sure what I want to study. Psychology, I think I understand psychology and also physical medicine. I am interested in anything in medicine. I want to make an impact on people.

Parent

JOAN: Dennis is very smart. He wants to be an engineer. He always has.

According to the Autism Society of America, in the United States 60% of the costs of care for children and adults with autism are in adult services (Autism Society of America, 2013). The cost of lifelong care can be reduced by two-thirds with early diagnosis and intervention. The Autism Society estimates that in 10 years the annual cost of adult care will be somewhere between $200 and $400 billion.

The unemployment rate for people with disabilities was 14%, compared with 9% for people without disabilities (Bureau of Labor Statistics, 2010). Additionally, during the same period, only 21% of all adults with disabilities participated in the labor force, as compared with 69% of the nondisabled population (Bureau of Labor Statistics, 2010).

The average per-pupil expenditure for educating a child with autism was estimated to be over $18,000 in the 1999–2000 school year, the most current information from the US (Government Accountability Office, 2005). This estimate was nearly three times the expenditure for a typical regular education student who did not receive special education services. However, it is still much less expensive than supporting an adult with autism completely for 60 years during his adult lifetime.

Although the public school system is responsible for providing services until the person with ASD reaches age 22, in severe cases a person with ASD will need full-time residential care for life. The hope is that adults with high-functioning autism or Asperger's will be able to work successfully in mainstream jobs.

Adults with severe ASD are capable of employment in sheltered workshops under the supervision of managers trained in working with persons with disabilities, and some moderate functioning adults gain employment and are monitored from supported employment programs where programs provide services to help individuals prepare for, look for, interview for, and maintain a job.

Compared to the general population, fewer adults with autism marry or have children or live in a metropolitan area. This trend is changing as more diagnosed adults are forming relationships with others on the autistic spectrum. This autistic culture, as it is being referred to, is based on an accepting belief that autism is a unique way of being and not a disorder to be cured. People with autism are often attracted to others with the condition because they share interests or obsessions and have compatible personality types. Perhaps most important, they understand each others' differences. Many people living with an ASD have expressed the importance of companionship in their lives similar to those without an ASD.

Some adults with autism or Asperger's are capable of independent living—either entirely on their own or semi-independently in their own home or apartment with assistance in solving serious problems. This assistance is provided either by the family, a professional agency, or another type of provider. For families who choose to have their adult child live at home, government funds are available to help the families. These programs include Supplemental Security Income (SSI), Social Security Disability Insurance (SSDI), and Medicaid waivers. Information about these programs can be found through the Social Security Administration (SSA). Supervised group living is also available for persons with disabilities. Professionals who help residents with basic needs, including meal preparation, housekeeping, and personal care, often work in these group homes. High-functioning adults may be able to live in a home or apartment where staff people visit a few times a week and provide advice and assistance.

In the past, a small percentage of high-level adults were able to work successfully in mainstream jobs, although frequently far below their actual level of skills and qualifications, with some exception, such as Temple Grandin, the noted veterinarian and author with autism who has served as an advocate for the rights of autistic adults (Grandin, 2011). It is hoped that in the future employers will take advantage of each individual's strengths and abilities.

Three employment possibilities are available for adults with autism: competitive, supported, or sheltered employment. Competitive employment is the most independent, with no offered support in the work environment. Individuals with Asperger's have been successful in the past in careers that require focus on details but have limited social interaction with colleagues, such as computer sciences.

Supported employment is a system of support that allows adults to have paid employment within the community, sometimes as part of a small crew or in a job specifically designed for the person or the group. In secure or sheltered employment, an individual is guaranteed a job in a facility-based setting. Individuals in secure settings generally also receive work skills and social skills training. The Internet has been a decent means of communication, because it is almost devoid of the nonverbal cues that people with ASD find hard to navigate. To locate employment opportunities, the adults begin by contacting agencies that may be able to help, such as state employment offices, social services that focus on disability and employment, mental health agencies, and disability-specific organizations such as the department of rehabilitation.

One problem that adults have had is getting a diagnosis for ASD as an adult. It can be hard to convince a doctor that a diagnosis is relevant and/or necessary. The main route for seeking a diagnosis as an adult is to see a doctor and ask for a referral to a psychiatrist or psychologist. When bringing up the topic with a primary physician it is important for a person to make sure that this is what the appointment is for, because this is an issue that needs everyone's full attention.

Many people with ASD have suffered from mental health problems and have been misdiagnosed as having mental health problems such as schizophrenia. A firm diagnosis of ASD can be a relief, because it allows them to learn about their condition and understand where and why they have difficulties. Others will also gain a better understanding, because it will be easier for them to empathize with the person once they learn there is a reason for his or her difficulties. It is also helpful to meet others within the community with ASD by learning about their experiences. Support is a good step in seeking treatment and relieving anxieties, helping to maintain a healthier lifestyle while dealing with this disorder.

References

Autism Society of America. (2013). About autism. Retrieved from http://www.autism-society.org.

Bureau of Labor Statistics. (2010). *Labor force statistics from the current population survey.* Washington, DC. Retrieved from http://www.bls.gov/cps/

Chamberlain, L. B. (2009). The amazing teen brain: What every child advocate needs to know. *Child Law Practice, 28*(2), 17–24.

Chiang, H., Cheung, Y. K., Hickson, L., Xiang, R., & Tsai, L. Y. (2012). Predictive factors of participation in postsecondary education for high school leavers with autism. *Journal of Autism and Developmental Disorders, 42,* 685–696.

Damasio, A. R., & Maurer, R. G. (1978). A neurological model for childhood autism. *Archives of Neurology, 35,* 777–786.

Endedik, H. M., Denessen, E.J.P.G., & Hendriks, A.W.C.J. (2011). Relationships between executive functioning and homework difficulties in students with and without autism spectrum disorder: An analysis of student- and parent-reports. *Learning and Individual Differences, 21*(6), 765–770

Gioia, G. A., Isquith, P. K., Kenworthy, L., & Barton, R. (2002). Profiles of everyday executive function in acquired and developmental disorders. *Child Neuropsychology, 8,* 121–137.

Government Accountability Office. (2005). *Report to the Chairman and Ranking Minority Member, Subcommittee on Human Rights and Wellness, Committee on Government Reform, House of Representatives. Special Education Children with Autism.* Washington DC. Retrieved from http://www.gao.gov/products/GAO-05-220

Grandin, T. (2011). *The way I see it. A personal look at autism and Asperger's* (2nd ed.). Arlington, TX: Future Horizons.

Hewitt, L. (2011). Perspectives on support needs of individuals with autism spectrum disorders: Transition to college. *Topics in Language Disorders, 31*(3), 273–285.

Logsdon, A. (2013). Executive functioning: Understanding executive functioning disorders. *About.com Learning Disabilities.* Retrieved from http://learningdisabilities.about.com/od/eh/a/executive_funct.htm

Lullo, C., & Van Puymbroeck, M. (2006). Research update: Sports for children with ADHD. *Parks & Recreation, 41*(12), 20–24.

National Center for Learning Disabilities. (2013). Learning disability fast facts. Retrieved from http://www.ncld.org/types-learning-disabilities/what-is-ld/learning-disability-fast-facts

Ozonoff, S. (1998). Assessment and remediation of executive dysfunction in autism and Asperger syndrome. In E. Schopler, G. B. Mesibov, & L. J. Kunce (Eds.), *Asperger syndrome or high-functioning autism?* (pp. 263–289). New York: Plenum Press.

Ozonoff, S., Pennington, B. F., & Rogers, S. J. (1991). Executive function deficits in high-functioning autistic individuals: Relationship to theory of mind. *Journal of Child Psychology and Psychiatry, 32*(7), 1081–1105.

Verte, S., Geurts, H. M., Roeyers, H., Oosterlaan, J., & Sergeant, J. A. (2006). Executive functioning in children with an autism spectrum disorder: Can we differentiate within the spectrum? *Journal of Autism and Developmental Disorders, 36*(3). doi: 10.1007/s10803–006–0074–5.

Wagner, M., Newman, L., Cameto, R., Levine, P., & Garza, N. (2006). *An overview of findings from wave 2 of the national longitudinal transition study-2 (NLTS2).* (NCSER 2006–3004). Menlo Park, CA: SRI International.

Chapter Thirteen
Teaching Strategies–NOS (Not Otherwise Specified)

Children with high-level autism are like very few children with special needs that have come before them. There are three types of children with special needs. There are children with developmental disabilities, maybe a traumatic brain injury or multiple disabilities, whose schoolwork often centers on helping them become more independent and self-reliant. These children want to work and live independently. They want to be able to communicate and to access resources. They want to travel and to access the community. When they grow up, they do not want to depend on other adults to take care of them. They want to live to their full potential, work, and socialize with friends and family.

Another group of children with disabilities are in general education and their goal is to achieve as well as children without disabilities. These children usually have no reason to talk about their challenges. Some of them may include children with learning disabilities or speech impairments; these children are smart and many only have challenges in certain subject areas. Most of these children do not have social problems or physical challenges. They don't use communication devices or wheelchairs.

The final group of students includes those who have visual or hearing impairments and perhaps other health impairments. These children are actually more like children with high-functioning autism than any of the others. They will most likely have to deal with their disabilities for the rest of their lives. They will need to learn to work around their disabilities. Many are smart and capable, and yet still their disabilities have caused them some delays in their academics. Many have trouble in school. Some have trouble with social skills because they do not have access to some of the same information (either visual or auditory) that typically developing children have as they grow up. Some have no trouble at all in academics, and even if they start out a bit behind, they easily catch up and do well in school. For children who are deaf or hard of hearing or visually impaired, many choose to go to special schools, because the teachers there understand their special needs, and teachers in regular schools are not adequately prepared to work with them. They also find a community at these schools where they are accepted for who they are and can communicate and socialize with others like them much more easily.

The point is that for children with high-level autism, we must recognize that this group of students represents a new type of child that we haven't worked with before. Adults with autism are now coming forward and saying they are autistic, but the autistic children in schools often feel as though teachers are looking at them as if they appeared yesterday from out of nowhere. They don't understand why teachers don't know who they are or why they exist. Why have these teachers never met a child with autism before? Why do they not know what autism is or how autistic children act? They do not understand why there are so few children like themselves.

There are adults who have high-level autism, but few of them reach out to children, because they are busy with their own concerns about how to relate to a diagnosis that for many of them is new and for some is still being questioned. And some feel very little connection to children who grew up very different from themselves, knowing about their autism as youngsters and having access to at least some services that they never had when they were young.

It is our suggestion that children need to learn more about who they are as people. Where do they fit in our world? We believe that children with autism should be doing more narrative work, reading books about other children with autism, and learning about their experiences so they don't feel like they are the only people in the world like them. For example, Davidson and Henderson (2010) recently analyzed writings of adults on the spectrum to better understand disclosure issues. They found that there were four different ways that people high on the spectrum represented themselves with regard to disclosure. They called these types "repertories." The four types were (a) the keeping safe repertoire, (b) the qualified deception repertoire, (c) the like/as resistance repertoire, and (d) the education repertoire. In each of these repertoires, different people had varied reasons for either disclosing or not disclosing their autism. With the keeping safe repertoire, people on the spectrum believed that to disclose information about their autism might make people think differently about them. For example, sometimes college professors who have autism will not disclose it because they believe their colleagues will think less of them. With the qualified deception repertoire, the idea is that if a person can pass as typical, he or she will. These people often have to actually make up stories about their lives to keep their secret. The like/as resistance repertoire group needs to be told why it is wrong to be autistic. They find it offensive that everyone is trying to fix them or cure them, and they actively speak out against the idea that autism is shameful. Those who use the education repertoire believe that it is their responsibility to educate people. They believe that people do not understand autism and that most people have stereotypes of people with autism, viewing them as either profoundly mentally retarded or brilliant in certain areas like savants, which is incorrect.

Freire (1970) has spoken out about how difficult it is for people in developing countries to take advantage of their education when they don't understand their place in this world; we take lessons from theorists who tell us that critical theory is oriented toward critiquing and changing society as a whole. It is clear from some of our interview data that the teens in our study wanted our society to change:

DANIEL: Well, I believe I disliked the amount of . . . it's a little hard to put it, let's just say, people have an idealized image of how certain people should act. And if you step outside the boundaries of what people see differently.

I: So you kind of act different. Did you act badly?

DANIEL: It's not acting badly, more just acting odd in their eyes.

The problem comes because many children with autism do not want to talk at all in class about their autism. In fact, there are a number of children who refuse to identify with the autism label.

Teachers tend to avoid topics that they see as "risky." We are often risk-adverse. It is difficult to risk pushing children into an emotional state that we, as teachers, don't know how to handle. In a pilot project with 10 children with autism, narrative therapy was shown to be effective in reducing emotional and psychological problems. Through the use of narrative therapy, the children improved their scores on posttests for hyperactivity, peer problems, and prosocial behaviors (Cashin, Browne, Bradbury, & Mulder, 2013). We do not suggest that narratives be used in the classroom as "therapy," but rather be incorporated as part of the curriculum to allow class work to be more closely tied to the children's lives.

We must make sure that we understand children with autism before we make decisions to help them reflect on their situations. We need to talk to other professionals in the school, psychologists, therapists, and other teachers, as well as the parents, and explain our methods and find out how the children might respond. Some children do not like to reflect or share their experiences (especially their feelings); however, other children do:

RAYNE: I just go on the computer and let all my feelings out on the Internet.

I: Oh, you do, you have a blog or something?

RAYNE: No, I just go on YouTube, look up videos, maybe put it in my fan fiction or fan art on Deviant Art and other stuff.

REESE: It's like a . . . it's hard to explain, but I think it's an organization for kids with autism to come and express their beliefs or their ideas and like, what they're creative thinking and like present that in short films.

ASH: Yeah, it was in eighth grade, I guess we were preparing to read for this book that had a kid with a serious case of autism, and there was a murder of a dog and him being blamed. I dunno. It's really confusing story, but the teacher wanted people to understand. But even in the book, you can tell his actions were very weird even to me, they seem kinda weird 'cuz it's a very serious case. And [my teacher] had to explain what autism was and [she told the class], "Now that you know what that is, I should say that Ash here has autism." And they just looked, and like, "What?" and "Oh," and I was like, "Yep."

I: OK, and the kids were positive about that?

ASH: Yeah.

For those who do want to talk about their autism, it is important not to avoid the topic.

Growth Mindset

According to Carol Dweck (2010), it is important for children to have a growth mindset as opposed to a set mindset. What is a growth mindset? Individuals with a growth mindset believe that they can develop their intelligence over time. Individuals with a fixed mindset believe that their intelligence is simply an inborn trait—they have a certain amount, and that's all they will ever have. Three researchers, Blackwell, Trzesniewski, and Dweck (2007) looked at more than 300 students going into seventh grade and assessed which students believed their intelligence was set and which believed their intelligence could grow. Then they looked at the students' math grades over the next 2 years. Those with the growth mindset had steadily increasing math grades over the 2 years. Those with the fixed mindset showed a decrease in their math grades. About 100 seventh graders, all doing poorly in math, were then randomly assigned to workshops on good study skills. One workshop gave lessons on how to study well. The other taught about the expanding nature of intelligence and the brain. The students in the latter group learned that the brain actually forms new connections every time something new is learned, and that over time those connections make you smarter. By the end of the semester, the group that had been taught that the brain could grow smarter had significantly better math grades than the other group.

This research was not conducted with children with high-level autism, but it is easy to see how being told that the brain can grow smarter could motivate children who have been told they have brain damage, a condition that is defined by a number of deficit symptoms.

According to Rattan, Savani, Naidu, and Dweck (2012), whether a person believes that he or she can become more intelligent is a culturally shaped belief. For example, in South Asian Indian contexts, people believe that a person can become highly intelligent, whereas in the United States people tend to believe that it is more of a fixed trait (Rattan et al., 2012). What is important about this psychosocial focus on motivation is that for children with autism these researchers would argue that it is more important to praise children for trying, no matter what the outcome. The researchers found that those children who were praised for their intelligence, for example, shied away from challenging assignments—they wanted an easy one instead—far more often than the kids applauded for their efforts. Students praised for their efforts did not lose confidence when faced with the harder questions, and their performance improved markedly on the easier problems that followed.

For children with high-level autism, we need to use strategies that we have used in the past for children with special needs, such as teaching children with autism to think socially, and also general education, such as teaching them to think about how they can have a growth mindset and praising them for effort. Allowing children to write narratives and consider their lives within a culturally responsive and socially just society will help them to move beyond a "history of discrimination" and a mindset of deficit and dysfunction.

Advice From Parents

We asked the parents we interviewed if they had advice for teachers. Everyone said something a little bit different. Many parents said it was important for teachers to get to know their children individually and build relationships. Once you get to know the children, teachers will learn to care about each child, build reciprocal trust, and believe that when a child says that he or she doesn't know or doesn't understand something it is because of the child's disability:

TAMRA: Most important thing I think is to show real interest in them as a person, and really engage them. I think that's just so important. Make sure they understand exactly what that person's all about, and how they learn. Different people learn in so many different ways, like there's a lot of kids who don't learn just by showing or by telling them, sometimes, you have to act it out.

JOAN: Hmm . . . probably to get to know them individually . . . yesterday, I did some research on . . . general . . . maybe to find out . . . challenges . . . when you think about . . . and to be flexible . . . about homework and stuff like that . . . where they sit and how they move around . . . a flexible outlook . . .

LIDIA: Everyone is different and you just have to figure out each kid, I mean it'd be so much easier, not everyone's going to fit this mold, and this is all you have to do, and it's like an infant, they change after every few weeks. It's a different kid. What worked 2 weeks ago might not work now.

Even the teenagers pointed out that it was important to get to know each child, because everyone is different. Here is a comment from one of the teenagers:

ASH: Well it kind of depends on how bad it is or how serious it is.

I: The autism?

ASH: For example, the character from that book with autism, you'd have to be very delicate with that character, he overreacts. You have to kind of figure out, like that character did not like to be touched, even if you kind of tapped him, he'd flip out and maybe punch you, something like that 'cuz he didn't like it. And it's more like a reflex. If it's like that, be very careful. But if you're told he has autism or Asperger's, but he seems normal, just try to treat him like a normal person.

One parent said that teachers needed to help their children be successful, and that meant setting up an environment that would help them be successful. Another parent said:

JAMES: But in some ways, I think it's the same as typical kids. You want kids to be challenged and learn something new, but you wanna calibrate that hurdle so that they get over it, that they succeed because I think that as much as anything that really helps kids with autism.

With schoolwork, many said that understanding that children can both be very smart in some areas and very ignorant in others was important. Knowing how to challenge children in areas where they can be challenged and being able to support them in areas where they lag behind without embarrassing them and making them seem any more different in front of their peers than they already do was also important. Parents wanted teachers to help them set up social relationships. They wanted them to be explicit in their directions, because these children often do not understand what they are told the first time:

DAWN: The kids who are going to be in a mainstream classroom, they don't have a lot of cognitive flexibility, you need to be specific in your speech and be very clear about what you say both in explaining the curriculum, and the classroom rules, in everything.

Characteristics of Good Teachers

Before talking about some of the problems that parents encountered with teachers and at schools, it is important to talk about the positive experiences these parents had with teachers. We all had good teachers when we were young who helped us through our educational experiences. The parents really liked teachers who they could tell liked their children, given their warts and all. And, the parents tied the teachers' ability to find what helped their children to the fact that they liked their children and could see them for who they were as people. This is what a few parents had to say about good teachers:

TAMRA: I would say that first of all they were friendly with him like really tried to socialize with him, and always learned about the things he cared about because Daniel likes to talk your ear off about whatever he likes. And these teachers actually went in their own personal time, they obviously went home to watch SpongeBob, and they were like I'll let you talk for about 10 minutes about SpongeBob if you give me 10 minutes of your time for reading or math or whatever else. And he would always be like, "Great!"

KIMBERLY: His freshman year, all the teachers, their comment about him consistently is, he's such a nice kid. That's what they all say, he's a very sweet kid and he asks a lot of questions. He has definite processing issues. He processes slower auditorily, and he frequently has to have things repeated. And I think he misses directives. I know he misses instructions in class, but he gets enough to do well.

EMILY: There's a PE teacher, Jack, who was never even his teacher, but took an early liking to him from early on and was just a friend even though he was a high school PE teacher. And the high school teachers, of course, he loves math. He corrects the math teacher if they make a mistake. And they laugh.

LIDIA: Mrs. Johnson during second grade had Sandy, and we really loved her. And she had seen Rayne in the playground and knew she was different. So we met with her over the summer and Sandy had a tough year that year. And, so she was prepped for Rayne and we said, "You have to be really firm with Rayne, you have to! And so she did. At one point, other parents didn't like Mrs. Johnson because she was very tough. And somebody asked Rayne in second grade about it, and she said, "Well she yells like my mom so I feel comfortable." So she was really good, and she would work with her and she understood. And she kept me posted on what the problems were.

The teenagers also had a lot of different ideas about what they liked about good teachers. They wanted teachers who understood children at a deeper, emotional level and who cared about them. They wanted them to talk to them about their personal life and be open with them and to make a connection with them. They also wanted them to be fun and interesting in class, to be funny, and to make sure they, as students, understood the content before the teachers moved on to the next assignment. And, like most children and teenagers, they wanted the teachers to be fair.

Teachers Get to Know Them, Accommodate for Them, and Make Learning Fun

DANIEL: The ones I enjoyed really understood that kids, they can be weird or cooky, they can be completely out of control and out of sync with reality, but hey, newsflash, those are kids! Yeah, and you know that they're not completely demonic because their minds haven't stopped developing yet.

CHRIS: Mrs. Jones, and uh, she was strict on us, I know that for a fact.

I: Was that good or bad?

CHRIS: Yeah, it was good. Um, and my third-grade teacher, which was my last teacher, and so far my favorite was um, a woman named Mrs. Anderson. She was technically the funniest, or most fun, whichever's proper grammar.

RAYNE: And when the teachers are fun, and like believe that homework affects the child's mental health, then you like that person, 'cuz in my opinion it does affect it. More homework means more likely to get stressed, which stress leads to self-abuse or suicide.

ASH: Back then when I was a Giants fan y'know, Ms. Wolf was a huge Giants fan, and I guess we kind of had the conversations a lot. And Ms. Garden, she's just the nicest person in the world. Like there was nothing mean about her.

Teachers Who Helped Them With Schoolwork

REESE: I think there's this one teacher in particular who I think really sticks out to me in junior high, her name was Ms. Smith. I think because, I mean it's not like there were some other teachers who also like were very helpful to me too 'cuz I have autism, but I definitely think that Ms. Smith was the most understanding and nice teacher to me and that she really helped me a lot and motivated me the most. So I really enjoyed having her throughout middle school.

GABRIELA: Sometimes regular classes are hard, that I might need help, realize. I like to talk with them sometimes, and get helped, get help with my by teachers or the aides at school.

I: Did you like the way she taught?

DANIEL: Yeah, her material was relatively easy to figure out. And as she always made sure that everyone got what she said before she moved on.

Teachers (and Other Staff) Who Spent the Time Talking and Listening toThem

JAKE: The teachers are nice and flexible for the most part, the principal is also really nice. And she's willing to hear me out. They have good counseling staff, so if I have an issue with a teacher or peer, I could talk to them.

Teachers Who Were Fair

I: Was there any teacher you liked the best, your favorite teacher?

DANIEL: I don't wanna show favoritism; however, there was one in third grade that has become a really good friend of my mother's and I got the chance to experience a lot of memorable moments with her, Mrs. Tom.

I: And what did you like about her?

DANIEL: The fact that whenever I had a problem with anything, she'd find a peaceful and socially fair way to end that dispute.

They want to learn and they know when they are learning.

I: What makes them effective teachers?

JAKE: I don't know really. I just know that they are effective because their material gets into my mind.

What Problems Did Parents Have With Teachers and Schools?

We asked the parents and the teenagers about what bad experiences they had with teachers or schools, and for the most part the families we interviewed mostly had fairly good experiences compared to some families. There were a few of lawsuits filed against the school districts, most of them were worked out and in all the cases the families did get what they needed for their children eventually.

Some of the parents did run into teachers who were not good with children, and this was difficult because children with autism do not seem to be able to handle bad teachers. They really do need expert teachers. Especially when they are young, they seem fairly vulnerable to bad teaching. Some teachers had a philosophy of teaching that did not sit well with children with autism, and they often caused more meltdowns than they prevented. Some teachers also seemed to have a philosophy about children, and how to raise children, and were inflexible with their rules. They also seemed to disregard the parents' attitudes and ideas about how the teachers might work more effectively with their children. Finally, there were teachers who just seemed uninterested in working with children with disabilities and who were easily frustrated with children who had challenges that they believed made their jobs more difficult. Many of these teachers were not convinced that the students needed all the accommodations they sometimes received.

Note, too, as you read through the following quotes that the parents are very involved in their children's schooling. Nowhere is that more clear than in the first quote where Tamra talks about how the teacher's attitude affected the entire family. It is also seen in Ana's quote, where she is suspicious that the school doesn't believe she has a college education because she is Hispanic and works as a clerk, when she actually does have a degree. In Donna's quote, she believes that the school expects that her child should be a Spanish speaker and claims that "they didn't fit." In Lydia's quote above, where she talks about her son's second-grade teacher, Mrs. Tom, she also used the word "we," as if the child is not the only person suffering, but the entire family is suffering. What teachers don't realize sometimes is that the way they are treating and talking about the children is in the parents' minds the way they are treating and talking about them.

These parents are very involved in their children's education and are working very hard to help their children achieve and live happy and productive lives, and what they want is help from the teacher in reaching these goals.

Not Good With Children

TAMRA: Daniel's first- and fourth-grade teachers both were just awful. They were so bad that—speaking of psychological problems—if they didn't cause it for him, they caused it for me. I mean seriously. The whole year was traumatizing for our whole family. I didn't know if we were going to make it. They made us come to school like every day because they couldn't handle it, or handle him.

LENA: I had watched one individual session with Ash and she was punishing him, she was setting limits and penalties, and giving him time outs in a therapy session because, he wasn't doing what she wanted him to do, and this is really not good.

Inflexible/Not Respectful of Parents

MARIA: They weren't understanding because it was like night and day, one second, he's doing great and thriving and just doing the work. That's all they seemed to care about was he did the work; he got the grades. And then when he was failing, it was, "OK, well, now he's just being a slacker." And you would think after how well he did for so long, it's like 12 years, he's been a good student, and you can't give him one accommodation for one year. Get over yourself, god.

ANA: And the other thing is, sometimes they think that you are just making excuses for your child, depending on the teacher, more so in Catholic school than public school. They just come on at some point she has to get organized on her own. I'm a registered nurse, but since I worked as a clerk they assumed I don't have a college education. And I don't tell them, but I think they think things will go over my head. And I do know more than they expect me to.

EMILY: But you really have to give him a reason why certain things are the way they are. It really bothered him that in junior high, they didn't have assigned seating, whereas all the other years, there was assigned seating and now suddenly he has to choose a seat, and someone might be in the seat he's choosing, and that person won't get out. He wants them to leave. So he's learning, he's supposed to move around. So once we got some stupid junior high teacher who decides to have assigned seating, and he couldn't get it. But I think he's over that, it took 3 years, but he figured it out.

Not Accepting of Differences

JAMES: His worst year in terms of getting along with kids was his fourth-grade year where he also had the teacher that didn't understand him as well because the teacher didn't help. The truth is, I think Reese annoyed the teacher a little bit, so she didn't really push the other kids to be accepting of him either, because she wasn't particularly accepting.

DONNA: He went into first grade; he had a teacher that was very old, ready to retire, set in her ways. Philosophically, she believed you needed to speak Spanish at home to succeed in the program. So already, we don't fit with what she thinks, and she had no patience for any differences.

The idea that having children with autism makes a teacher's job more difficult is not always true. Many children without disabilities have behavior problems, and are not motivated to do their work, and have trouble with schoolwork. It is obvious that the parents in our study were very involved in their children's school lives, but the reason is because they want their children to be happy, it is not for the parent's sake, it is for the sake of the children.

Conclusion

According to the parents we interviewed, there are a few qualities that are important for teachers to have who work with children with autism to be successful with this population. These include:

1. Develop relationships with the children, get to know them, and accept them for who they are; each child is unique.
2. Be flexible. Allow children to leave the room if they are getting overwhelmed or provide a chair that rocks if that will keep a child in his seat and provide the sensory stimulation the child needs to be successful.
3. Believe in the disability; do not question children or their parents. If the accommodations they seek help the child to improve, that is what is important.
4. Understand the disability and how to mediate some of its affects through accommodations.
5. Use the best strategies from general education and special education. Children with high-level autism are a different population that needs different types of interventions and supports; this group has a dual orientation, constantly living in between general education and special education.

References

Blackwell, K. H., Trzesniewski, K. H., & Dweck, C. S. (2007). Implicit theories of intelligence predict achievement across an adolescent transition: A longitudinal study and an intervention. *Child Development, 78*(1), 246–263.

Cashin, A., Browne, G., Bradbury, J., & Mulder, A. (2013). The effectiveness of narrative therapy with young people with autism. *Journal of Child and Adolescent Psychiatric Nursing, 26,* 32–41.

Davidson, J., & Henderson, V. L. (2010). "Coming out" on the spectrum: Autism, identity, and disclosure. *Social & Cultural Geography, 11*(2),155–170.

Dweck, C. S. (2010). Even geniuses work hard. *Educational Leadership, 68*(1), 16–20.

Freire, P. (1970). *Pedagogy of the oppressed.* New York: Continuum.

Rattan, A., Savani, K., Naidu, N.V.R., & Dweck, C. S. (2012). Can everyone become highly intelligent? Cultural differences in and societal consequences of beliefs about the universal potential for intelligence. *Journal of Personality and Social Psychology, 103*(5), 787–803.

Chapter Fourteen
Behavior and Classroom Management

Classroom management lies at the very foundation of creating a classroom environment that enables children and young adults to learn and even thrive at school. In this chapter, we put forth ideas about how to design a classroom to be an organized, consistent, and integrated setting where instructors, school leaders, students, and parents are all active participants, rather than a collection of disconnected parts. The goal of classroom management is to make sure that quality time is available for teaching and other important classroom activities, such as play for younger students and socialization activities for older students. When a teacher provides a safe, comfortable, focused, and disciplined classroom, students can focus on learning. Like all safe, functional, well-built structures, be it a home or even a relationship, a well-planned and solid foundation must be at the core of the structure.

Classroom management includes both the management of the physical environment and the behaviors of the students in the class, and this is true across all grades and age levels. If teachers believe that students come to school wanting to engage in interesting activities, discussion, and learning, as opposed to wanting to disrupt the class, they are better able to view behavior as a form of communication. Part of the effective classroom management foundation is building an effective communication system. For individuals with autism, behavior may be the only means by which they have to communicate a need or a frustration. A child's inappropriate response to the physical environment or to classroom expectations usually indicates something is not right. Mirenda (2005) has stated that individuals with autism will communicate using the most effective and efficient means possible.

Teachers are more likely to develop an effective behavior and classroom management plan if they build a strong foundation and keep six key classroom management principles in mind (see Table 14.1). After developing a strong foundation, to specifically help children with autism, the teacher must implement the

Table 14.1 Six Key Principles of Classroom and Behavior Management

Comprehensive Behavior Management: Six Key Principles	
Invest time at the front end	Teachers should spend time before school starts developing a behavior management plan. The more time a teacher spends addressing prevention before school starts, the fewer behavior problems he or she will face during the school year.
Teach well with quality instruction	Teachers should create lessons that are interesting, relevant, and within the instructional range for all students. Teachers can avoid or minimize a number of classroom disruptions by providing evidence-based supports and accommodations to students who are frustrated by challenging academic content. Note: This is the simplest, most-powerful way a teacher can prevent many problem behaviors.
Focus on positive behaviors	Teachers should recognize students who are doing the right thing. Otherwise, students may seek attention in less-than-desirable ways.
Provide supports	Teachers should be prepared to provide additional supports and strategies for students with academic and behavioral challenges.
Don't take bad behavior personally	Teachers should not take students' actions and comments personally. They should remember that the goal is to help students learn to manage their own behavior, not to get back at kids. It is important to remain professional. Remember that children with autism have problems with their brain.
Be persistent/consistent	Teachers should understand that there are no quick fixes. Consistent hard work leads to gradual yet significant changes.

Adapted from The IRIS Center for Training Enhancements. (2012). Taken from http://iris.peabody.vanderbilt.edu/beh1/beh1_04.html.

following best practices: (a) establish a specialized environment, (b) establish a good communication system, (c) use an ASD-specific approach to teaching and learning, (d) use ASD-specific strategies and interventions, and (e) individualize instruction and behavioral management techniques (Miller, 2010).

We will now look in more detail at some of these key principles and best practices.

Developing a Strong Foundation for Classroom Management

Providing Quality Instruction

It is also important to provide quality instruction. Most behavior problems arise when children are bored or unhappy with their education. If children and teenagers are interested in what they are learning and engaged, teachers do not have as many behavior problems. Children with autism are less tolerant of material that is presented in a way they find unappealing. These students already know that it is hard for them to concentrate and to pay attention, and it is even harder for them to pay attention to material that is boring. When teachers are having behavior problems the first thing they should look at is their curriculum and pedagogy. Is the content challenging? Are the teaching strategies engaging? Are the children interested in what they are learning?

I: Have you ever gotten in trouble at school that you can remember?

JAKE: Many times. I'm not exactly a model student.

I: What have you gotten in trouble for?

JAKE: Primarily just being silly in class. Acting out.

I: Why did you do that, just to joke around?

JAKE: I'm bored.

I: What would be some suggestions that you would give to teachers for the best way to teach?

JAKE: Depends on the teacher really. The best way to teach for me in general is make it interesting. Biology is automatically fascinating to me and the teacher also delivers it well, so he does a fairly good job, but some teachers just deliver in a really bland way. And that makes it hard for me to focus and my attention span gets shorter. Then I get sort of destructively bored. I definitely sort of just joke around in class or go off on a magical world of the Internet, things like that.

Investing Time at the Beginning of the Year

When working with children with autism, it is important to adhere to the foundational principles that help all children stay on track when it comes to classroom management and behavioral supports. Specifically, it is important to invest time at the beginning of the year to organize the classroom and to develop expectations for how children are to behave. Children with autism like to know what is expected and how to accomplish what is expected of them.

Sometimes teachers tell children what is expected and then assume they know what that means. It is important to remember that children with autism don't understand our social systems, so telling them, for example, "not to be bad," "to act right," or "to shape up" are confusing commands. What does it mean to not be bad, to act right, or to shape up? We are so used to children at certain ages knowing certain things that adults forget that children with autism are different. If, for example, a girl is asked to share her pencil and the child with autism grabs the pencil from her hand before she has a chance to offer it to him, the teacher may go over to the autistic child and say, "Give that back to her, and do it right." We would assume this child knows both that he should not have grabbed the pencil and that he knows how to "do it right." However, this might not be the case. So, be explicit, especially with young children. Older children learn as they grow how to understand social cues, just as a person from another culture learns the language and the culture, which is why sometimes they seem to understand and sometimes they don't.

Developing a Welcoming and Functional Physical Environment

Classroom management always begins with designing an appropriate classroom environment. School is an important and extraordinary place for children as they play, learn, and explore to develop communication and independence. A child should feel at ease in a classroom and not be in a constant struggle with visual, auditory, tactile, proprioceptive, gustatory, and olfactory stimuli (McAllister & Maguire, 2012). In response to a child's need for a classroom to be a "learning environment for life, a place of preparation for the challenges and negotiations we all face in our everyday life" (McAllister & Maguire, 2012, p. 104), we have developed recommendations for an ASD-friendly classroom (see Figure 14.1).

In Figure 14.1, the classroom is set up to scale according to an average size elementary classroom in the United States; secondary classrooms are larger. The classroom in the figure is an example of how teachers might want to set up their classrooms. It has a small, contained quiet area for calming. The classroom is

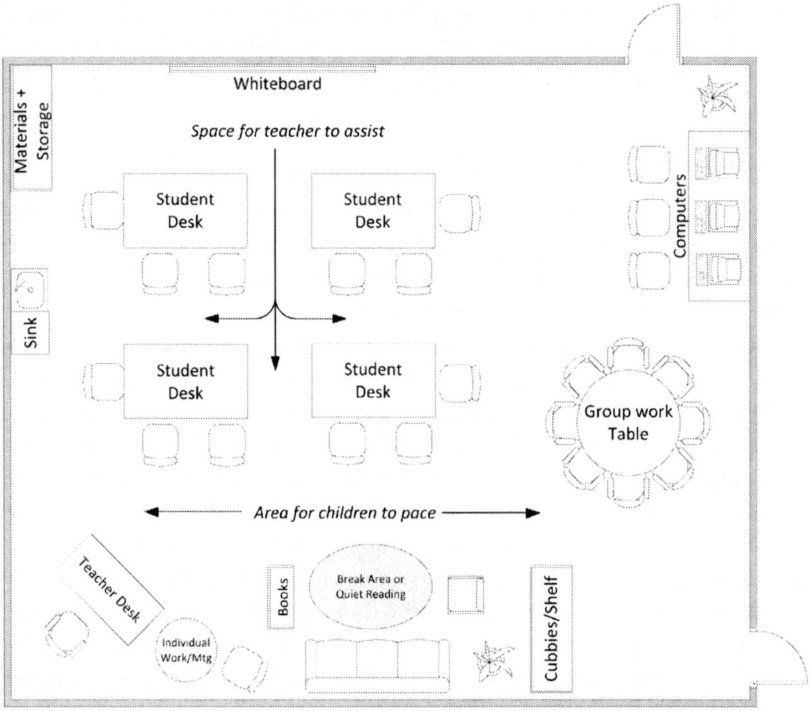

Figure 14.1 An autism-friendly classroom.

equipped with computers facing the wall away from the other students that can be used for independent work. The room has a table for group instruction, peer-assisted learning, or a place for children who might have to leave early for speech or another pull-out activity. These tables, computers, and quiet area are located in the back of the room or to the side of children's desks close to a door so an aide can move around in the back without disturbing the group instruction in the front of the room. The aide can take the children in and out of the room easily, perhaps for a walk or out into the hall for a quiet talk, without disturbing the rest of the class. The calming area in the back is not completely shut off from the rest of the class, so the student who is taking a break can still listen and watch as the rest of the class carries on with instruction. There are chairs behind a couple of tables that sit out into the open space in the pacing area where teachers might put a rocking chair or large ball to allow children with autism to sit on for those who have trouble sitting still or who need more sensory input. The children's desks are close to a material closet so children can easily get their own materials and not disturb children in the back of the room or on the computers. The teacher has plenty of room in between desks to work with children and monitor their work. The desks/tables are set up so the children can easily work together collaboratively. In the back of the room, there is also a place where a child can work independently, get one-on-one help, or talk quietly with a teacher right next to the teacher's desk. From the teacher's desk, you can see the entire class. The calming area can be used as a reading area or a rug area for younger children. There are cubbies for children to put their stuff in when they first come in the door. This is the type of room that would help keep a teacher organized and children focused on their work.

For children with autism, it is helpful to minimize distractions (Kerner, 2012). Visual displays allow teachers to post pictures, schedules, and other items that aid in learning. Although children's work should be hung up on walls, teachers should discriminate and make sure, for example, that writing projects, where children who have dysgraphia may be embarrassed of their writing, are kept in a folder, and artwork, where everyone is successful, is displayed. Don't hang things from the ceiling. Some visual aids and children's work is good, but too much stuff cluttering the room can be a distraction.

Classroom designers should use soothing, neutral colors throughout the space for floors, walls, ceilings, and furniture. White may be too bright for some students with ASD. The use of patterns and bright colors should be limited so that the classroom is less distracting. Because fluorescent lights tend to flicker and annoy students, classroom designers may want to replace fluorescent and direct lighting with more natural lighting. Noise in the classroom should be minimized by having carpet on the floor so that when children move their chairs in and out from behind desks they don't make a screeching sound. There should be seals around the doors. Cabinets should be located near instruction where children are learning, and students should learn to get out their own materials and then put them back. If students feel comfortable, safe, and relaxed, the teacher is better able to prepare them for the hustle and bustle of the mainstream school environment (McAllister & Maguire, 2012).

The parents in our study had the following comments about the classroom environment:

DAWN: Set them up with success in your classroom, whatever that takes, visual prompts, um, give them a sympathetic peer. Let them copy from their peers. Um, let them have access to movement inside the classroom, whether they sit on a cushion that bounces, or they have a squeeze ball, so that they could process their energy. Don't think because they're not looking at you, they're not listening.

JANINE: Obviously, we can't control Jake's environment for his entire life. But in these early years, it's so clear to me that his environment can make him look fabulous or it can make him look like a complete wreck. When he's in a good environment, he looks pretty typical. But if the environment stresses him in some way, he can fall apart. And this is what one of the psychiatrists that we worked with told the school district. He said Jake can absolutely succeed, but it is very easy to make him fail.

Teachers who work with children with autism often use visual supports in their classroom, and not just with young, severely challenged children. We all rely on visual supports to navigate our way through life. Have you ever been to another country where no one speaks your language and all the signs are in another language?

Many children with ASD view the world with varying degrees of language and understanding. Some researchers argue that 95% of children with ASD need visual guides to assist them with auditory processing (Plaisted, Saksida, Alcántara, & Weisblatt, 2003; Quill, 1997). Students with autism have great difficulty comprehending auditory signals when any other noise is present, because they hear more than their typical peers without being able to filter unimportant sounds. By utilizing visual strategies and environmental supports, the auditory information is combined with a visual picture, making it easier for the student to understand. In addition, environmental supports such as labeling the environment, creating boundary settings, and using color-coding help organize the classroom and create roadmaps for students. Like all classroom procedures, teachers must teach the child how to use them by modeling, supporting practice with using them, and reteaching when necessary. In Figure 14.2 we provide a simple visual support a teacher can use to tell the children in her class what the level of talk should be when children are working in different situations.

Sensory Issues for Children With Autism

Attending to a child's sensory needs will help a teacher cut down on behavior problems. For example, at home children on the spectrum often have

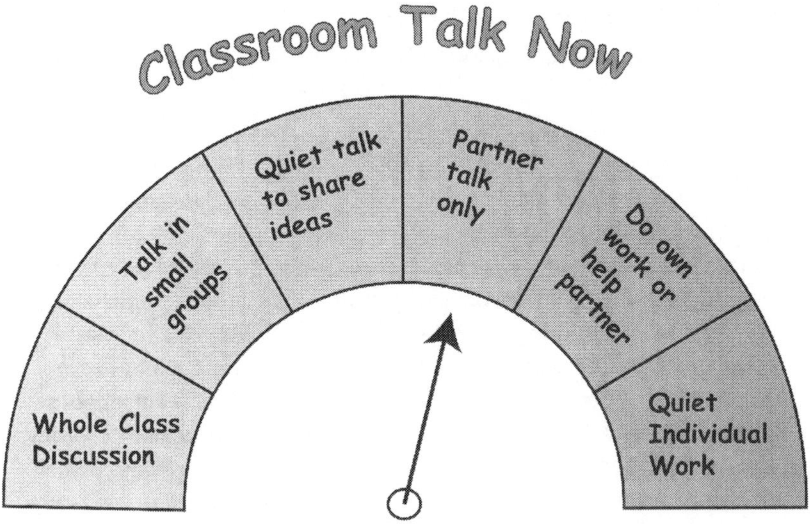

Figure 14.2 A visual support for describing the level of talk in a classroom.

meltdowns over food. Many parents of children with ASD agree that it is not worth engaging in food battles even though most children who are picky eaters are not very health conscious. In time, most children improve their eating habits and develop a more nutritional diet, but until that happens parents often avoid the battles and invest in vitamins:

SAMATHA: The things that I think he could work on is that he's got a very narrow palate of foods that he'll eat, much more so than even a lot of kids we know on the spectrum. That has not changed; the one new food he has learned to eat literally over the last 5 years is Hot Pockets.

We suggest the same course of action with teachers, rather than battling with children over trying to help a child adapt to sensory stimulation, we suggest that teachers work with the children by accommodating for their needs. By the time these children are teens, many have learned to sit in loud movie theaters or deal with the strong smells at coffee shops. And, many have even learned to like the taste of a few foods besides pizza and hamburgers. However, sensory sensitivity is something for teachers to watch out for when children with autism are both younger and older. Before problems occur, the teacher should make sure that there is nothing in the room that might trigger a sensory problem (e.g., strong smells, buzzers to bring children together, walls brightly painted in different colors, or flickering lights). When the children are younger, they are usually unable to articulate the cause of a sensory disturbance. A meltdown might occur because they can't communicate their sensory discomfort.

Establishing a Good Communication System

A college student once told us:

> When I was volunteering, a boy was playing in the kitchen area. He tried to grab some toys away from the girl who played next to him. The girl held the toys very firm and didn't give it to him. The boy got upset and ran away and knocked his head against a wall. I was really frightened that he would hurt himself. The head teacher came and used a soft voice and talked to the boy, and she said, "I know you are upset that you cannot have these toys. It looks like Kelly is using those toys right now. I will be glad to show you some other toys. Let's go over to the table together and I will show you." The boy took the teacher's hand and walked to the table. I had an opportunity to talk about this with the head teacher after lunchtime. I learned from that conversation that it is important to understand the reasons behind the boy's inappropriate behavior. The inappropriate behavior was a way for that child to communicate, to tell you something is wrong. The head teacher told me that we have to "read" the situations while we are working with children with ASD. The head teacher said, "reading" the situation is just like reading a book to understand the plot and the characters. You need to read the situation and understand what is going on. Is the child trying to tell you something? Is there too much going on? Is the classroom distracting or confusing? Was the child simply trying to get your attention? When you read the situation, you need to acknowledge what is happening. For example, "It looks like you are really upset." Your words become the words that the child wishes he could say, and that often defuses the tantrum.

Communication that is safe, good, and effective, is communication that works like two people hitting a ball back and forth on the tennis court. They simply want to hit the ball *to* each other and not "make a shot." Effective communication always includes spoken language, but it also includes behavior, body language, facial expression, gestures, and more.

With children with high-level autism, it is important that teachers and other professionals be able to sit down and talk with them about specific issues that arise that the teachers may not be used to talking about:

I: What are some things that teachers did that you found helpful?
JUAN: My advisors tell me is to raise my hand and go like this to show that I am stressed out.
I: So that was a helpful strategy when you do that. Do they let you go out in the hall?
JUAN: Well he told me he's gonna talk to me about my stress.
I: OK, so that will help with communication with the teachers, is that right?

Most children naturally learn how to interact socially, so adults are not used to explaining what might seem like obvious social rules and expectations. It surprises us when we realize that some smart children don't understand basic social rules, and sometimes we don't believe it. But children with autism frequently have social misunderstandings and teachers need to look for holes in the children's understanding. This happened a few times to the families who interviewed for this book. The following are comments from two parents:

RHONDA: I guess one important thing would be not to impute negative intentions to the behavior, and to pull them aside, just the things that we have in the dear professor letter. If they behave in a way that is not acceptable, it's not because they're intending to. And pull them aside and tell them, and this is assuming they have language. To explicitly state, what you expect, don't leave anything to chance in terms of communication. Tell them exactly, do this, don't do that. Don't just say, "Well, I don't like that," or it just has to be clear. Otherwise it's like playing hide the ball with them. They're not gonna get it. So I think that's really important.

JANINE: One teacher had a question about something, I forget exactly what it was, "Where did that come from?" And Jake understood that as, "Well it was from behind," as opposed to, "What caused that?" Just be aware that sometimes these misunderstandings will occur. And when you're giving your instructions, try to do so in an unambiguous way. And it's really hard to kind of appreciate that until you've witnessed the misunderstandings yourself.

Learning to communicate, however, includes more than just understanding social cues using straightforward language and writing out directions. Communication starts out sometimes (even for higher-level children) by finding a way for a child to express him- or herself. Some young children can't talk at all. These children might have to use alternative communication techniques before they learn to talk. Children at the higher end of the spectrum will probably have decent speech as they get older, but it may be delayed when they are younger. Children who can't read may use picture symbol systems to communicate. Two systems that people are using right now are PECS and the Mayer-Johnson system.

The Picture Exchange Communication System (PECS) has been used to help children and youth with ASD develop a system for communicating with teachers, parents, and peers. PECS was initially developed at the Delaware Autistic Program by Andrew Bondy and Lori Frost (Bondy & Frost, 2011) as an alternative communication system. There are six phases of PECS instruction, and each phase building on the last: (a) teaching the physically assisted exchange, (b) expanding spontaneity, (c) simultaneous discrimination of pictures,

(d) building sentence structure, (e) responding to "What do you want?" and (f) commenting in response to a question. One of the interesting aspects of PECS is that children are expected to pull their pictures off their boards or books (often using Velcro) and give them to another person, indicating a communication act. According to the National Professional Development Center, PECS is an evidence-based practice and has been used with younger and older children (Ganz, Davis, Lund, Goodwyn, & Simpson, 2012; Wilczynski & Pollack, 2009). Figure 14.3 is a picture of a PECS image within the PECS Phase III app for the iPad. It looks just like a child's communication notebook.

With the Mayer-Johnson system, symbols are often laid out on color-coded boards. The color in the boards denotes different parts of speech, such as nouns and verbs. The words are put together so that a child can make a sentence. With the Mayer-Johnson system, it is possible to make communication boards with the computer using an application called "Board Maker." Symbol systems can also be used with communication devices. The user puts a word or a picture over a button on the device, presses the button, and then the device speaks the word. Figure 14.4 shows an example of a Mayer-Johnson communication board.

We don't talk a lot about augmentative and alternative communication in this book because most children high on the spectrum don't need this type of accommodation, only children with high-level autism who might have speech

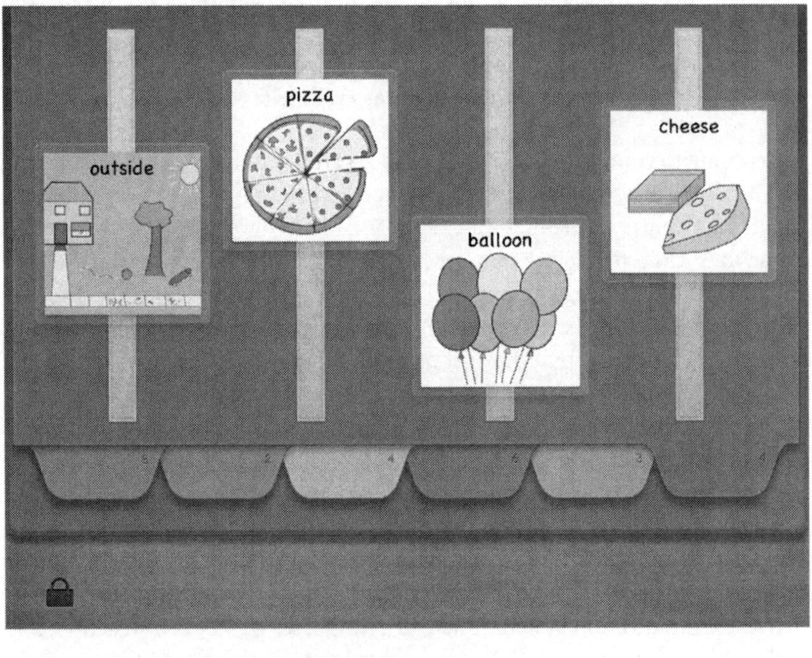

Figure 14.3 PECS Phase III app for the iPad.

Image used with permission from Pyramid Educational Consultants, Inc. (www.pecs.com)

Figure 14.4 Mayer Johnson communication board.

delays when they are young or for some reason can't speak when they are older. We offer two important points. First, using augmentative and alternative communication (AAC) when children are young does not delay the development of speech. In fact, it helps children develop speech (Mirenda, 2003). Second, children need to be able to communicate, or they will express themselves in disruptive ways.

Sometimes children with high-level autism will also engage in echolalia. The two broad categories of echolalia are immediate and delayed. With immediate echolalia, the student repeats verbatim what he hears from the teacher or another student. For example, the teacher might ask the student, "Do you want chocolate milk?" and the student repeats back to the teacher, "Do you want chocolate milk?" With delayed echolalia, the child repeats verbatim something that he or she has heard hours or days ago. Echolalia is a natural stage of language development for all children, and it should not be extinguished. More important, echolalia is often functional communication for students with ASD and is not a sign of low intelligence. Even some children high on the spectrum will display echolalia when they are young; often they will borrow phrases from TV programs and plunk them down into their sentences as they speak. They often use the phrases in the right way and in the right context, but it may sound a bit odd. For example, we know of a child who used to say, "I can't take it anymore, I am losing my mind" every time his mother asked him to do something or eat something that he was not happy about. The parents didn't know where that expression came from until they heard it on a *Winnie the Pooh* episode. It was an expression that the rabbit on the show used when he was expressing his frustration with Winnie. Although the child was about 4 years old, he repeated the phrase with the same tone, same voice, same pitch, and exactly the same words as this grumpy white rabbit on this animated cartoon show.

High-functioning children on the spectrum and those with Asperger's are often very verbal but they may still use their behavior to communicate. Despite high-level verbal skills, some children may not have the ability to understand an incoming communication from the teacher or another student. In turn, this student will use behavior until an incoming message is understood.

Comment from a Parent

JANINE: We had to negotiate with him, but, it's been like that with Jake since day one. You have to, he's got very strong views about things and it's like you have to be prepared going into a discussion to be ready to—you have to think ahead about where are the boundaries. What sort of choices are you willing to give him? And where are you really gonna pull the plug, literally, when it comes to the Internet, (or figuratively).

Comments from Teenagers

CHRIS: Probably it's best not to raise your tone with the students because they'll definitely be a lot more ignorant if you do that, but if you talk to them in a calm, meaningful manner, and like explain it to them what they should and shouldn't do, then they'll definitely understand you. But if they're still stubborn, then you may have to uh, you know, do something.

LANE: The one thing that a lot of people don't understand about autism, is that it is an actual cognitive thing. I've found that if I am under stress, then the symptoms start to appear, and I have trouble . . . When I am under stress, my brain goes out problem seeking. Whenever I used to have a bad day, I would make myself trip and fall and everyone thought it was attention seeking, but it wasn't. It wasn't attention-seeking behavior, it was introverted; I felt bad and my brain couldn't let me feel anything but bad, and my brain would actively seek out ways to feel bad.

Table 14.2 offers a list of common communication difficulties for children.

A Data-Driven Behavior Management Plan

Behavioral Foundations of Classroom Management

The behavioral theories that lay the foundation for classroom management come from the same theories underlying ABA, including Pavlov's classical conditioning, Thorndike's connectionism, and Skinner's operant conditioning. All teachers use some form of behaviorism in their classrooms. For example, in a situation where a teacher asks a group of children a question and they randomly

Table 14.2 Communication Tips

Behavior	*Tip*
Delayed response to a question	It may take a child with ASD more time to compose a response to a question because the child has to stop what he or she is thinking, put that somewhere, come up with an answer, and then say it aloud. If the teacher or peer does not wait for the answer, and repeats the question again, the child has to go through the whole process again.
No eye contact	Don't assume that a child who is not making eye contact is not listening. Forcing eye contact can actually break a student's concentration. A student may hear and understand better if not forced to make eye contact.
Professor talk	Although a student's vocabulary and use of language seems high, he or she may not know the meaning of what he or she is saying, even though the child is saying it correctly.
Monologue on a favorite subject	Students need specific direction regarding when and how they may appropriately talk about their high-interest topic in the classroom or in the playground, (can be a part of an ongoing social skills program) to learn about turn-talking and following topic-shifts in conversation.
Overly focused on favorite topic	Use student's favorite subject to actively engage him or her in the classroom, keeping high interest and motivation across all curriculum areas. To encourage students to focus on other subjects, draw similarities, or point out differences. For example, say to a student interested in trains, "unlike trains that can travel ..., a car can travel ....
Inferences, sarcasm, and humor	Understanding and using nonliteral and counterfactual language, like sarcasm, is difficult for students with ASD. Introduce the use of inference and drawing conclusions gradually through the curriculum. Sarcasm and humor, if necessary, must be carefully explained.

shout out the answer, a teacher might praise a student who is raising her hand by saying, "Thank you Amanda, I liked that you raised your hand when you wanted to answer the question. I cannot hear the right answer when everybody shouts at the same time." In this example, the teacher is praising Amanda, not only to reward her for good behavior and following classroom procedures, but also to encourage her classmates to model this behavior. No matter what people think about behaviorism in its many forms, all teachers use positive reinforcement, so everyone uses behaviorism at some point in their teaching.

Would you faithfully go to work every day if you did not receive a paycheck at some point? Much of what we do in everyday life is driven by reinforcement. What is reinforcement? Reinforcement is anything that increases a behavior. Reinforcement may be positive or negative. In special education, we emphasize positive behavior supports and the interview dialogue below illustrates why. Juan, who is a very good student, and a motivated student, was once reinforced for his good behavior, and he remembers it as one of his best memories. In another situation, he was making noise and the teacher asked him to leave the classroom. He probably couldn't help making noise at the time, and it embarrassed him in front of his peers. This was a punishment and was not appropriate:

I: What was one of your best memories of school so far?

JUAN: They said I was a good student 'cuz they always tell when they good to be the best students of every grade. There's only one from every grade, so one time it was me (ninth grade).

I: Right, that's excellent. What do you think was one of the worst things about school that you remember? Did you say you got sent out of the classroom one time?

JUAN: Yes, I said that.

I: Why, why did they send you out of the classroom?

JUAN: I was making noises.

I: Did you realize that you were making noises when you got sent out of the room?

JUAN: Yeah, there were some students hearing it.

I: Why did you make those noises?

JUAN: Because I don't know.

I: It sounds like you were embarrassed.

JUAN: I was.

Positive reinforcement can be divided into two categories: primary and secondary. Primary reinforcement is considered to fulfill a basic biological need. Examples of this include food and sleep. Secondary reinforcements include social praise, engaging in preferred activities, or receiving a token or tangible item.

Don't assume that you know what a child with ASD likes. It is important to ask a child, observe a child, talk to the child's parents, or perform a preference assessment. A reinforcement should be considered highly reinforcing to the child, and children with autism can be counterintuitive. Some common reinforcements for children on the spectrum include doing activities they enjoy, such as playing or working on a computer or reading; taking a walk outside with a favorite adult; talking about his or her latest obsession to the teacher;

being chosen to play an important role in the class, such as errand runner or time keeper; leaving 5 minutes early to lunch so he or she doesn't have to wait in the lunch line; or leaving 5 minutes early to PE so the child doesn't have to rush when changing clothes.

What is important to remember about children with autism is that many of them are eager to please the teacher, even if they don't act like it. Many have trouble making children their own age happy, but adults understand them better and accept them for who they are, so in elementary school many will focus on the teachers. After teachers develop trust with these children, it is important for the teachers to help them recognize what is special and important about their own work so that good behavior is not just about pleasing the teacher, but occurs because of intrinsic motivation.

Measuring Goals and Objectives

How do you know if a child is progressing? How do you know when you need to make changes to a child's program? How do you know when a goal has been met? Most teachers can tell when children are progressing. But how can a teacher *show* that a child is progressing? How can the teacher present evidence that the child's behaviors are improving? How can the teacher determine whether what he or she is doing is influencing these positive changes? Data can answer all of these questions. The word "data" evokes many different emotions for teachers and parents. Unfortunately, data are a necessary component of effective programming. Data collection provides a concrete objective means of assessing progress.

A teacher first collects data to find out what is causing the behavior. It might seem adequate to use one's intuition to make a guess at a cause, but, as intuitive as teachers are, intuition often fails, and we end up making wrong-headed assumptions about people's motivations. It is important to collect data systematically to test one's assumptions. We should always start collecting data by actually talking to children. Children with autism should be taught to be metacognitive about their learning and their behavior. For them to understand and regulate odd behaviors, they need to be able to recognize their challenges and discuss them openly. It is important to determine first how much they know about their behaviors.

Functional behavioral assessment (FBA) is a systematic way of determining the underlying function or purpose of a behavior that a teacher, parent, or child might not understand. An FBA provides detailed information about a behavior so that an effective intervention plan can be developed. FBA consists of describing the interfering or problem behavior, identifying antecedent or ensuing events that control the behavior, developing a hypothesis of the behavior, and testing the hypothesis. Data collection is an important part of the FBA process and allows for objective analysis of why this behavior might be occurring, when, and how often.

Conducting an FBA is important because it will help teachers to anticipate situations in which students are more likely to exhibit disruptive or inappropriate behavior, such as during transitions or unstructured time. Experienced teachers know that children are more likely to be disruptive after recess or lunch, at the end of the day, or on Fridays. Procedures are taught, modeled, practiced, and then changed as necessary to meet the unique needs of children in each classroom based on their individual profiles.

Collecting Behavioral Data

It is necessary to identify what to collect data on. It is not necessary to collect data on everything. A rule of thumb is to collect data on one objective per goal. Make it easy. If the data collection system is cumbersome, you won't use it. Most data can be permanent product or event recording. Permanent product is exactly what it says. It is permanent documentation. It could be a handwriting sample or it could be a video clip of a child interacting at recess.

Event recording is the number of times the behavior occurs. Counting behavior can be as easy as making a tally mark on a data sheet. One method for using event recording is doing something simple like switching marbles from one pocket to the other. When a behavior occurs, you can take one marble out of your left pocket and put it in your right pocket. At the end of the observation time, you simply count the number of marbles in your right pocket and record the number on the data sheet.

Many other types of data can be collected to show the progress that a child is making. The value of data collection will become obvious as it is used to make effective program decisions and to show to parents as evidence of how their children act in certain situations. Slowly build time for data collection into the daily schedule and it will become second nature. Remember, data collection holds the key to evaluating whether a child is making progress and achieving goals!

Self-Management and Choice

Self-management is a method by which learners are taught to monitor and collect data on their own behavior. This method is typically used with older, high-level children who are capable of reflecting on their actions. Children can be taught to self-monitor a variety of things, such as alertness, activity level, concentration, and problematic behaviors. Self-management helps children learn how to regulate their own behavior because it allows them to reflect on how they come across to other people and to keep data on specific behaviors. Allowing children to keep their own data can help a teacher avoid control battles with children on the spectrum. Here, a parent in our study gives an example of letting her son make his own decisions:

JANINE: The same thing happened when I picked Jake up after school on Wednesday. Jake gets in the car after school and said, "I'm not going to art!" and I said, "You know I actually talked with Carol about that and we both agreed that if you feel up for it great, but if you don't we'll leave that to you," and then suddenly he wanted to go. And so learning how to work with that kind of energy and that rigidity is really important and that's I think one of the things in terms of what works and what doesn't work, not getting confrontational with him. And being able, being comfortable with letting him feel like he has power.

I: Not getting into a control battle.

JANINE: Exactly, absolutely, we've seen that happen with a number of teachers and it's gotten really, really ugly.

To make a management plan especially effective, sit down with children on the spectrum and talk to them about what they want to change about themselves. As mentioned above, teachers need to get a sense for what children know about their own behavior and start helping children to understand what other people see and experience as typically developing children and adults get to know them. Allowing children to first think about what behaviors they have that they might want to change about themselves (being metacognitive about their behavior) allows them to ultimately decide who they want to be, and it gives them control over how they want to act, who they are, and who they want to become. By allowing children to choose the behaviors they want to change and then allowing them to self-monitor their own progress, it allows them to feel in control of their own destiny.

To systematically develop a comprehensive behavior management plan, a teacher should first create an *action plan,* a set of procedures that can support the implementation of the behavior plan. In general, an action plan will include items to be accomplished (i.e., objectives), the tasks or steps to be completed in order, and a completion date. Table 14.3 is a sample action plan.

Developing Community

From Rules to Citizenship

In contemporary classrooms, there are a number of reasons why teachers must look beyond behaviorism. First, an emphasis on controlling behavior often leads to resistance rather than buy-in (Frieberg & Lamb, 2009; Lewis, 2001), and thus a failure to develop self-maintained positive behavior in the long run. Second, researchers have found evidence that the overuse of extrinsic rewards and sanctions can undermine intrinsic motivation and eventually affect moral development because it fails to help children develop self-responsibility and an internal moral compass (e.g., Kohn, 1996; Ryan & Deci, 2000). Third, teachers need more than behaviorism to manage a classroom effectively; misbehavior can be the result of poorly planned activities, inadequate scaffolding and

Table 14.3 Sample Action Plan

	Action Plan		
Area	*Objective*	*How it will be accomplished*	*Completion date*
Develop a Toolkit	Make posters for rules and procedures.	• Enlarge rules sheet to poster size. • Select key procedures for first day of school, enlarge them, and post.	Before school year begins
	Create postcards for positive parent contacts.	• Print out or copy postcards so that only student name and positive behavior need to be added.	Before school year begins
	Prepare "Student-of-the-Week" program.	• Design certificate. • Set up "Student-of-the- Week" desk.	Before school year begins
	Design referral form.	• Review school office referral form to make sure hierarchy of negative consequences can be noted.	Before school year begins
	Create substitute teacher folder.	• Create a folder with all necessary information to implement behavior plan.	Before school year begins
Teach the Plan	Generate brochure to present key components of the plan.	• Use word processing or publishing software.	Before school year begins
	Teach relevant aspects of plan.	• Develop and implement a lesson plan.	First week of school
	Devise role play.	• Have groups of students select a rule and model what it looks like.	Second week of school
	Develop practice activities for rules.	• Create practice activities that use storybooks, songs, and creative arts.	Second week of school and as needed throughout school year

Share the Plan	Discuss with school leaders.	• Meet with school leaders to review plan.	Before school year begins and before printing brochures
	Disseminate to parents.	• Make extra copies of brochures. • Present plan during back-to-school night. • Ask parents to sign plan. • Contact parents who were not able to attend back-to-school night.	Third week of school
Review the Plan	Schedule booster sessions.	• In lesson plan book, at predetermined intervals, note need to review essential components.	Before school year begins
	Deliver booster sessions.	• Prior to scheduled booster session, select component of management plan to be highlighted.	Throughout school year
	Conduct mini lesson.	• Conduct mini lessons on areas of the behavior plan that students are struggling with.	As needed
	Follow up with parents.	• Contact parents to remind them of the plan and to provide updates.	Beginning of the second semester

modeling (so children don't know what to do), or insufficient attention to developing norms and participation routines in the classroom (LePage, Darling-Hammond, & Akar, 2005). For example if it takes 10 minutes for the class to transition between each activity, it is likely some children are going to get bored and get into mischief during this transition time. Making sure that materials are laid out and prepared and that transitions between classroom activities are seamless will reduce behavior problems.

Teachers must plan and establish an effective management plan that contains the following core components (IRIS Center for Training Enhancements, 2012; Simonsen, Fairbanks, Briesch, Myers, & Sugai, 2008):

1. **A statement of purpose:** A brief, positive statement that conveys to educational professionals, parents, and students the reasons why various aspects of the management plan are necessary.
2. **Rules:** Explicit statements of how the teacher expects students to behave in the classroom.
3. **Procedures:** A description of the steps required for students to successfully or correctly complete daily routines (e.g., going to the restroom, turning in homework) and less-frequent activities (e.g., responding to fire drills). See Table 14.4 for sample rules and procedures.
4. **Consequences:** Actions teachers take to respond to both appropriate and inappropriate student behavior.
5. **An action plan:** A method to support the implementation of a comprehensive behavior management plan.

In all classrooms, teachers should decide consequences for problematic behaviors before those behaviors occur. By developing consequences ahead of time, the teacher will be prepared to respond to the behaviors, and the students will know what to expect. Consequences work best when they are (a) clear and specific, (b) relate directly to the rules and procedures, (c) have a range of intensity or hierarchy of alternatives, and (d) are natural and logical in the school environment. More specifically, positive consequences serve to increase students' adherence to classroom rules and procedures; negative consequences usually serve to decrease rule breaking and disruptive behavior. When teachers are supportive and develop clear rules and procedures, students feel confident about their ability to do well academically (Akey, 2006).

For children with autism, it is important to use the idea of consequences sparingly, however. First, when talking about behavior problems with children with autism, we are not always talking about behaviors that make a child "bad." Often we are talking about behaviors that make a child, "odd," such as flapping his arms or walking around in circles. These types of behaviors are more like bad habits that can be regulated by children with autism, but this is usually done slowly over time. Teachers need to address these unusual behaviors carefully, because children with autism sometimes feel criticized when they are

Table 14.4 School-wide Behavior Expectations

Rules/Values	*School Setting*						
	Classroom	*Restroom*	*Hallways*	*Cubby/Closet*	*Library*	*Cafeteria*	*Yard/Playground/ Gym*
Respect	Look at the speaker. Listen to the speaker. Follow directions. Raise your hand/ wait to be called on. Use appropriate language.	Privacy, knock, eyes on you. Clean and flush. Wash hands.	Walk, don't run. Quiet. Follow hallway procedures. Go directly to class/ location.	Enter by rows. Touch only your belongings. All materials in cubby. Coats on hooks.	Quiet. Treat books with care. Put books where they belong. Ask for help when looking for books and materials.	Talk quietly. Eat your own lunch. Be kind to lunch staff. Use table manners.	Listen to playground/gym monitor. Follow procedures and rules. Include everyone.
Effort/ determination	Work is neat and complete. Do your best work.	Keep facility clean. Paper in trash.	Move carefully and purposefully. Listen to hallway monitors.	Keep cubby/ closet neat and tidy.	Work quietly at tables. Write on paper only.	Eat first, talk later. Sit in seat at table.	Play fairly.
Responsibility	Follow directions. Be on time. Follow classroom procedures.	Flush. Clean seat. Wash hands. Report mess/ damage.	See something, say something.	Organize materials. Hats on hooks.	Return materials on time. Treat materials with care.	Throw away your trash. Pick up trash on floor.	Follow game rules. Report accidents and problems to monitor.
Safety/well-being	Keep hands, feet, and objects to yourself. No bullying. See something, say something.	Use soap to wash hands. Be timely and polite. Report problems.	Walk in your line or with an adult. Keep hands to self. Keep materials in backpack.	Enter on left, exit on right. Keep path clear.	Leave with permission. Ask for help in retrieving reference materials on high shelves.	Keep floor clean. All lunch items stay in front of you. Ask for help with spills.	Report bullies. See something, say something. Use equipment properly. Take turns.
Care of environment	Reuse and recycle. Careful use of materials.	Keep clean.	Pick up trash. No food in the halls. No signs on wall without office approval.	No food out of lunch box. Keep space clean and tidy.	Put used books on return table. Throw trash away.	Recycle. Separate trash. Return unused items to lunchbox.	Run on grass. Avoid mud puddles. Use trash cans.

constantly being told to stop flapping, to stop talking to themselves, or to stop hugging other people. It is important to tell children that what they are doing isn't wrong or bad, it is just not what other people in our society do or expect, so it makes them seem odd to those who don't know them. Children need these types of behavioral issues explained to them. They need to be told over and over that these behaviors are not wrong or bad, they are just different, and they make other people have strange thoughts about them (it is a type of on-the-spot natural social-thinking training). In some things, children should have the choice whether they want to stop or not. Do children want to stop flapping? Most kids want to stop, because they don't like looking odd to their friends. In other words, there are some behaviors they must stop (touching) and other behaviors they should stop (flapping) in order to better fit into our society.

The second reason children face consequences is because they break the rules. One issue to consider here is that most children don't break rules on purpose. When children break rules, usually they either (a) simply made a mistake, (b) get into a situation where they didn't know how to respond, or (c) forgot the rule or didn't understand it in the first place. Very few children are premeditated rule breakers:

JANINE: What happens is that people start to conceptualize kids like this as being willful and intentionally disruptive. And I think it almost takes kind of a humbleness in working with kids like Jake and probably all kids, like recognizing that you don't have all the answers, you do have to approach it with an open mind and be willing to change and modify your own approach (I'm gonna see it through—that point of view).

For children with autism who have trouble with language, memory, and social understanding, most try to follow rules but can't avoid making mistakes. In settings where teachers decide that consequences are given out equally to all students, not only as punishments for premeditated rule-breaking but also as reminders for those who forget rules, or as a slap on the wrist for those who make mistakes or as the result of getting into a situations they can't handle, to some children it seems as though there is no way to avoid getting into trouble, so why try? Children with autism like rules, but they also want adults to recognize when it is important to enforce the rules and when they should be flexible.

A teenager from our study made this comment:

I: I know you went to a school up in Marin, too.

JAKE: Yeah, I went there for one year.

I: You didn't like that at all, right?

JAKE: No, that's a horrible place.

I: What was the problem?

JAKE: It was for children with severe mental disabilities, not high functioning like I am. You can just tell by the population. It felt like an insane asylum. The teachers, they were just, at first they were really too relaxed with the rules and they pretty much had no system of punishment and then a sort of a dictator came in who was obsessively punishing.

And, his mother said:

JANINE: I think previewing things is important, previewing changes in routines. Jake doesn't need a really strict routine, but it's helpful for him to know when things are going to be different. And I think the way that works well for him is this scaffolding or boundaries that are far enough apart to where there's room for flexibility within them.

We have seen a number of classrooms where a teacher will have a poster up on a wall that provides a list of virtues as part of his or her vision statement or rules (responsibility, care, honesty, helpfulness, and so on), but when we ask the teacher if he or she teaches character development or works with children on their moral development, the teacher will say, "No." For some reason, the teacher is not connecting the development of virtues and a moral vision with character development. Here is an example of a statement of purpose for a classroom:

> Our classroom will provide a safe and caring environment where all students are valued and can succeed academically. Students will be responsible for their own learning and behavior and they will appreciate other students' contributions and cultural differences. Parents will be regarded as partners in the education of all children. (IRIS Center for Training Enhancements, 2012)

In this statement it is clear that these children are expected to act in ways that are clearly "moral." They are expected not only to be respectful, but also caring. Character education has been criticized in the past for emphasizing morality in conjunction with virtues (care, responsibility, etc.) exclusively to get compliance from children instead of teaching them (for example) how to speak out against social injustice. It is important for children with autism to do both.

Although sometimes we think rules are difficult to craft and explain, rules provide a way for students to monitor their own behavior, and teachers can use them to remind and motivate students to display expected behaviors. In cases where there is a school-wide behavior management system in place, teachers should create classroom rules that align with the school's existing rules. In this way, all the rules and expectations are the same from class to class and teachers can use the same language to describe and explain concepts like consequences. The teachers should set up the school-wide behavior plan together so they all have a voice in deciding how their classes will be managed. In addition, teachers should limit the number of their classroom rules to five or fewer and make certain that those rules adhere to the following four guidelines: (a) state positively;

(b) use simple, specific terms; (c) make them measurable and observable; and (d) ensure that they convey expected behavior (IRIS Center for Training Enhancements, 2012). In Table 14.4, we provide a table that establishes rules, not only in classrooms, but in all areas of the school, so as to be clear to children with autism.

Rules are especially important for children when they are young, but when children are older, if they have absorbed the values of the school, they shouldn't need rules spelled out for them, they should be able to decide for themselves what is wrong or right based on an intrinsic understanding of right and wrong. This is especially important for children with autism. Because they don't always understand social rules or language, they often look to social rules to guide them, instead of developing their own opinions and making their own decisions. Teaching children how to make their own decisions helps them build executive functioning all the way through their childhood, preparing them for adulthood. It is important to explain to children with autism why rules are set up and enforced and how they help them and other students learn and work together. Otherwise rules to them can seem arbitrary and controlling.

Developing Friends and Interacting With Peers

In some schools that are specifically designed for children with autism, students are taught how to welcome new students. Peer buddies are assigned and new kids are immediately placed into various social groups.

If children with autism are having behavior problems, some of the first questions a teacher should ask are, "Does this child have friends?" "Are children picking on him in some ways?" and "Are children in the class making him feel like an outsider?" Teachers, and sometimes parents, forget how important other children are to kids at school. If children at school don't have friends, don't have people to eat lunch with, and are lonely and unhappy, they are going to communicate their unhappiness to the school staff in some way. And, many of them are embarrassed of their inability to make friends. Deep down they believe it is their fault, and so it is difficult for them to talk about. Some deny it and will say they have lots of friends, when their parents know they have none. Some get depressed and quiet. Some may get anxious and not want to go to school, and some may start acting badly and disrupting the class. If a child with autism has no friends, and the school is having trouble helping him develop friends at his school, the teachers should refer the child to an out-of-school socialization program where he or she might be able to make friends. These programs are few, but some are starting to take root. Some of these programs provide karate; an arts-based curriculum, such as filmmaking; or an equestrian program for children who like horses. In these programs, children with autism can sometimes find other children with autism and/or typically developing peers who share their interests, which provides a basis for them to start a relationship.

Finally, it is important in junior high and high schools for children with autism to have a place, an area, or a special program where they can get together to eat lunch (if necessary). Many children in the upper grades need a home base where they get to know a few teachers intimately and the teachers can follow their development over time and make sure they are progressing. In the home base, children feel comfortable being themselves and can ask for help when needed.

Communicating With Parents

In the university, every time we tell preservice teachers to make sure and talk about all the good things about a child when first meeting with parents, before they talk about the problems, they roll their eyes at us as if to tell us "Do you really think we need to be told something so obvious?" However, as parents, when meeting with teachers about our own children, every time we met the first thing we would hear about were all of our children's problems, and then in the last few minutes of the meeting the teacher might say, "But we love your children, they are great!"

The problem comes when teachers get a bit anxious about talking to the parents about problems so they quickly throw everything out on the table to get a difficult conversation over with quickly. Good communication is key to good teamwork and good programming. Communication needs to flow between team members. Maintaining regular and frequent communication will serve to help teachers develop trust. What is regular and frequent? That needs to be defined by the teachers and the parents they work with. For some it could be once a week or every other week. For others it can mean every day. Why communication? Because autism spectrum disorders are communication-based disorders, and parents have to rely on communication from other individuals who support their child to gain information about the child's day. You need to remember that what happens at home could affect school and what happens at school could affect home. Likewise, this can be a useful way of sharing strategies that work—what is used at home could work at school, and what is used at school could work at home.

Whatever works to pass information back and forth regarding the child's school day, evening routine, sleeping patterns, or weekend activities will do. We take for granted talking to our children after school over a snack about their school day: "What did you learn?" "Who did you eat lunch with?" "Did you see your friends today?" or "How did your test go?" Children with autism might have trouble answering these types of questions. Therefore, their parents have no way of chatting with them about their day. Consider the following quote from a parent:

ELIZABETH: I always feel like I never know enough about what is going on. I think it goes to the fact that Pete can't tell me what is going on. You know? I can't ask him what he did today. What I mean is that I can

> ask him but he is not going to tell me . . . at least not specifically. That's the frustrating part.

Communication can be established and maintained in several ways. One of the most common forms of communication is the communication notebook or the home–school journal. Oftentimes, this is just a basic small, spiral-bound notebook that is sent back and forth for communication. Parents may tell the teacher if the child had a good morning or what the child did over the weekend. A teacher may write the words that the child used to communicate with or tell the parents that the child played on the playground with another child. Some parents may prefer an e-mail or a phone call with the same type of information.

It is important to always communicate openly with families using a positive outlook and in layman's terms. The most important concept to get across is that you care about this child and are dedicated to finding ways to help this child succeed. The parent needs to know that you are just as invested in their child's welfare (that year) as they are, hoping to move him or her forward in the best possible way. Even if your strategies don't work, most parents will know (and appreciate) when you have tried your best.

References

Akey, T. M. (2006, January). *School context, student attitudes and behavior, and academic achievement: An exploratory analysis.* New York: MDRC. Retrieved from http://www.mdrc.org/publications/419/full.pdf

Bondy, A., & Frost, L. (2011). *A Picture's worth: PECS and other visual communication strategies in autism* (2nd ed.). Bethesda, MD: Woodbine House Inc.

Frieberg, J. H., & Lamb, S. M. (2009). Dimensions of person-centered classroom management. *Theory Into Practice, 48*(2), 99–105.

Ganz, J. B., Davis, J. L., Lund, E. M., Goodwyn, F. D., & Simpson, R. L. (2012). Meta-analysis of PECS with individuals with ASD: Investigation of targeted versus non-targeted outcomes, participant characteristics, and implementation phase. *Research in Developmental Disabilities, 33*(2), 406–418.

IRIS Center for Training Enhancements. (2012). Classroom management (Part 1): Learning the components of a comprehensive behavior management plan. Retrieved from http://iris.peabody.vanderbilt.edu/beh1/chalcycle.htm

Kerner, B. (2012). Classroom design for students with autism. *Dewberry Blog*. Retrieved from http://www.dewberry.com/news/blog/12–12–06/

Kohn, A. (1996). *Beyond discipline: From compliance to community.* Alexandria, VA: Association for Supervision and Curriculum Development.

LePage, P., Darling-Hammond, L., & Akar, H. (2005). Classroom management. In L. Darling-Hammond, J. Bransford, P. LePage, K. Hammerness, & H. Duffy (Eds.), *Preparing teachers for a changing world: What teachers should learn and be able to do.* San Francisco, CA: Jossey-Bass.

Lewis, R. (2001). Classroom discipline and student responsibility: The students' view. *Teaching and Teacher Education, 17,* 307–319.

McAllister, K., & Maguire, B. (2012). A design model: The autism spectrum disorder classroom design kit. *British Journal of Special Education, 39*(4), 201–208.

Miller, L. (2010). *Practical behavior management solutions for children and teens with autism.* London: Jessica Kingsley Publisher.

Mirenda, P. (2003). Toward functional augmentative and alternative communication for students with autism: Manual signs, graphic symbols, and voice output communication aids. *Language, Speech, and Hearing Services in Schools, 34,* 203–216.

Mirenda, P. (2005). Augmentative and alternative communication. In M. Hersen, J. Rosqvist, A. Gross, R. Drabman G. Sugai & R. Horner (Eds.), *Encyclopedia of behavior modification and therapy: Educational applications* (Vol. 3). Thousand Oaks, CA: Sage Publications.

Plaisted, K., Saksida, L., Alcántara, J., & Weisblatt, E. (2003). Towards an understanding of the mechanisms of weak central coherence effects: Experiments in visual configural learning and auditory perception. *Philosophical Transactions of the Royal Society Biological Sciences, 358*(1430), 375–386.

Quill, K., (1997). Instructional considerations for young children with autism: The rationale for visually cued instruction. *Journal of Autism and Developmental Disorders, 27*(6), 697–714.

Ryan, R. M., & Deci, E. L. (2000). Self-determination theory and the facilitation of intrinsic motivation, social development, and well-being. *American Psychologist, 55,* 68–78.

Simonsen, B., Fairbanks, S., Briesch, A., Myers, D., & Sugai, G. (2008). Evidence-based practices in classroom management: Considerations for research to practice. *Education and Treatment of Children, 31*(3), 351–380.

Wilczynski, S. M., & Pollack, E. G. (2009). *Autism-based practice and autism in the school.* Randolph, MA: National Autism Center.

Chapter Fifteen
Working With Parents

Do Parents of Children With Autism Feel Supported?

When talking with parents, the first thing we noticed was that all of the parents we interviewed said they were willing to give up almost anything to help their children. Many of them had already given up a lot to help their children. After their children were diagnosed with autism, most parents had to make changes in the way their families functioned in order to give their children (those with and without autism) what they needed. One parent commented:

RHONDA: I wouldn't call it giving up my career because I don't think I was in a career that had longevity for me. It's hard just suffering along with your children because all the bumps they feel, you feel; parents are only as happy as their un-happiest child. So the older boy really did suffer and we suffered along with him.

Did most of the parents feel supported over the years as their children grew up with autism? A majority of them said they felt more supported by other parents than by professionals, and most of them didn't get to know other parents until some years after their children were diagnosed:

JANA: I had more stress before I was able to hook up with other parents. And that did not happen early for me. That did not happen until like third or fourth grade. I was just hooking up with professionals and that was really hard frankly. It's a lot easier talking to parents.

It was clear that some of our parent participants did not have as much support as they would have wanted over the years. Some had family members who would help them if they asked. Some were involved in parent groups that were very helpful at various times in their lives. Most of the parents felt that they were forced to be advocates for their children. Most felt for quite some time that they were the only people who really understood their children and cared whether they would grow up and be able to live happy and productive lives as adults. Many of them saw themselves as the person who had to fight for their children's rights, hunt for services, and keep an eye out to make sure their children were getting the education they needed and deserved:

MARIA: I decide to switch my insurance company, cuz after doing research, it seemed like the evaluation was very expensive, and all this time I wondered if Kaiser was gonna do it for me, but they didn't. And I even tried calling Parents Helping Parents, the Children's Health Council and no one really got back to me over there, either. And I've tried the Regional Center, no one got back to me there. I mean, just to get a lead on where to go next. And then finally, I found a psychiatrist who was just starting up her practice after leaving the Children's Health Center.

In a recent study, Glazzard and Overall (2012) explored parents' experiences of raising a child with autism using a mixed-method approach consisting of questionnaires and semistructured interviews. Questionnaires were sent to parents of children with ASD in two special schools (50 were sent out and 20 returned). They found that the majority of the parents experienced a low level of support from agencies and professionals. The general conclusion was that parents experienced poor communication and a lack of understanding of their needs after their children were formally diagnosed.

In our study, many parents referred to their responsibilities as all-consuming as far as their time. Some parents expressed a sense of exhaustion, with little break. Three parents referred specifically to the difficulty finding a babysitter to look after their children when they were young. Many just didn't feel comfortable leaving their children alone with strangers, knowing that their children presented particular challenges that babysitters were not trained to deal with:

TAMRA: Daniel's early childhood in many ways was a blur because I was always so tired 'cuz I'd be working graveyards and then sleep a little bit when he was at school. I'm up all the time. We were running around to therapists, he started with play therapy when he was around 3 or 4 and he graduated to behavioral therapy. We tried everything. We even tried psychiatrists, tried medications—that was not good.

In another study, 20 participants were interviewed (Ludlow, Skelly, & Rohleder, 2011). We were interested in this particular study because the researchers interviewed parents of younger children. The children in this study ranged in age from 4 to 14. The themes that surfaced are common concerns of parents of children in elementary through middle school and crossed over to the themes in our study. Ludlow et al. (2011) developed five themes from their study: (a) challenging behaviors, (b) dealing with judgments from others, (c) lack of support, (d) impact on the family, and (e) coping and support. With regard to challenging behaviors and judgments from others, in the Ludlow study, most parents identified public tantrums and the reaction from others as being a difficult challenge for them to manage. Eleven parents commented on how perceived judgments from others were the most grueling part, rather than the behavior per se. A common perception from the parents was that others tended to judge their children as being "bad" children, and beyond that they were bad parents. Most didn't know how to deal with the situations and usually just ignored other people and left the place if the behavior got too out of control. In that same study, twelve parents spoke about the emotional impact that having a child diagnosed with autism had on them as parents, and the family. Parents were careful to state love for their child, but it was clear that in many cases there had been an emotional impact on the family. This was suggested by some mothers who reported having struggled with depression in the past and one who had felt suicidal during a particularly difficult period in her life as a single mother. One couple spoke of significant health problems they attributed to stress.

Differences Between Mothers and Fathers

In the current study, we spoke mostly to mothers (only two fathers); all the parents agreed that the mothers seemed more concerned about their children's possible future dependency needs than the fathers, and that the fathers expressed more hope that the child would "grow out" of his or her difficulties.

The mothers and fathers that we talked to suggested that fathers reacted differently to the child's challenges and to the diagnoses. Many of the mothers reported that they felt that their husbands or the children's fathers had difficulty coming to terms with the child's diagnoses, that initially the fathers were more in denial than they were, thinking that their child was "fine" or needed to "grow up." For example, one mother reported that her husband at first "ignored it to a great degree." Another mother reported that she felt her husband "certainly went through denial." There was some suggestion of this in terms of differences between the fathers and mothers who were interviewed with regards to acceptance of the severity of their child's difficulties, with the men believing the children were not as bad off as the mothers believed.

Parents' Experiences Seeking Interventions

In another qualitative study completed in 2012, parents were asked about their experiences seeking and using various interventions for their children on the spectrum (Mackintosh, Goin-Kochel, & Myers, 2012). Parents were asked what they liked or disliked about the treatments they were getting for their children.

Five themes emerged from that study: (a) no access to desired treatments, (b) no funding for treatments, (c) no time to do treatments (e.g., ABA and gluten-free diet), (d) concerns about medication, and (e) stress.

In other studies, many participants reported difficulties in their relationships with professionals (Altiere & Von Kluge, 2009; Glazzard & Overall, 2012; Mackintosh, Goin-Kochel, & Myers, 2012). They spoke of having to argue with doctors, teachers, and other service providers. These disagreements with service providers were likely to be a significant source of stress for the families

Parents in our study clearly expressed frustrations in accessing services, in dealing with professionals, and in paying for services themselves. Parents in our study expressed strong opinions about what they felt was best for their children and found it emotionally draining when professionals disagreed with them.

Parents' Depression

Parents of children with autism are more likely to be stressed than parents of typically developing parents or parents of children with other disabilities, including developmental disabilities (van Tongerloo, Bor, & Lagro-Janssen, 2012; Silva & Schalock, 2012; Lajiness-O'Neill & Menard, 2008). The research suggests that depression is more prevalent among parents of children with autism, even after taking into account parents' concerns for having children with autism or the extra work that comes with having to care for children with autism (van Tongerloo et al., 2012). In fact, depression is just as prevalent for parents of children with high-level autism and Asperger's as it is for parents of children with more severe classic autism, which seems counterintuitive (Mungno, Ruta, Genitori D'Arrigo, & Mazzone, 2007).

It was originally thought that parents were depressed because of the care needed to raise an autistic child, but the research indicates that the level of depression found in parents of children with autism suggests undiagnosed autism in parents or at least some link between hereditary depression in parents and autism in children. One study found that 19% of fathers of children with ASD had depression, whereas only 2.9% of fathers of typically developing children had depression, and 35% of mothers with ASD had depression, and only 11.8% of mothers of typically developing children had depression (Bölte, Knecht, & Poustka, 2007). The same results have been upheld in other studies as well. One study found that 16 out of 45 (35%) mothers of children with autism were depressed, but only 9 out of 76 (11%) of the mothers of typically developing children were depressed (van Tongerloo et al., 2012). In the United States, about 9% of adults are depressed at least occasionally, so 35% is also a much higher number than the average number of depressed people in the U.S. population (CDC, 2010).

Hodge, Hoffman, and Sweeney (2011) took the question a little further to determine whether depression was the only psychological issue that came up among parents of children with autism and whether any differences were due to the fact that parents had to care for a special needs child or reflected a possible genetic predisposition. They compared rates of psychopathology in mothers and fathers of children on the spectrum to rates of psychopathology in parents of typically developing children. Their study included 269 parents of children with ASD and 446 parents of typically developing children. Mothers and fathers of children with ASD reported significantly more depression, interpersonal sensitivity, paranoid ideation, and obsessive-compulsive behaviors.

Hodge and colleagues (2011) also looked at the psychopathology of biological caregivers of children with autism as opposed to those caregivers who were not biologically related to the children, including step-parents, adoptive parents, and foster parents. They found that it was the biological parents who suffered from the psychological problems. They concluded that genetic factors, as opposed to caregiving demands, contributed more to the risk of psychopathology in parents of children with ASD. They also found that parents of children with ASD might also struggle with psychosomatic disorder (feeling sick when a person is not sick) more than others as well.

Quality of life is another topic that has been covered in autism research. In one study, researchers compared parents of typically developing children to parents of children diagnosed with autism spectrum disorders (ASD), intellectual disabilities (ID), and cerebral palsy (CP) (Mungno et al., 2007). All together they studied 212 parents with ASD, ID or CP and 77 parents of children without disabilities. Parents of children diagnosed with ASD reported impairments in physical activity and social relationships and worse overall perception of their health. Scores in the physical, psychological, and social relationships domains for parents of the children with ASD were lower compared to the families with children with intellectual disabilities and cerebral palsy. However, few differences were observed between families who had children with intellectual disabilities, cerebral palsy, and typically developing children. Levels of impairment of physical and psychological well-being were higher in mothers than in fathers in the ASD and cerebral palsy groups, respectively. There were no statistically significant differences in the scores between the classic autism, high-function autism and PDD-NOS subgroups, but according to these researchers, the parents in the high-functioning autism and Asperger's subgroup seemed to display a lower quality of life and more stress as compared to the classic autism subgroup.

It is much more difficult for people to become advocates for themselves than to become advocates for others. It is a lot easier for a wealthy person to be an advocate for the poor than for a poor person to ask for money. It is easier for people with healthy children to say that children who need health services should get help. Because of the changes in our society, the individualistic focus, parents have had to take care of their own children with special needs. It is likely that parents have not felt that their children with autism have been understood or supported and they have been alone or working mostly with other parents to provide for their children.

The problem with the individualistic ideal is that people in the United States do not compete on equal footing. On average, mothers of children with ASD earn 35% less ($7,189) than mothers of children with other health limitations and 56% less ($14,755) than mothers of children with no health limitations (Cidav, Marcus, & Mandell, 2012). They are 6% less likely to be employed, and work 7 hours less per week, on average, than mothers of children with no health limitations (Cidav et al., 2012). There were no statistically significant differences in fathers' labor market outcomes across these groups. On average, children with ASD are 9% less likely to have both parents working. Family earnings of children with ASD are 21% less ($10,416) than those of children with another health limitation and 28% less ($17,763) than those of children with no health limitations (Cidav et al., 2012). Family weekly hours of work are an average 5 hours less than those of children with no health limitations. The cost of a child on the spectrum is about $3.2 million dollars over a lifetime, which is, in large part, paid for by those families (Ganz, 2006, 2007).

This is not true for children with other disabilities. Funding for services for children with autism has been scarce because no agency wants to take responsibility for paying for the costs of autism, including the insurance companies; the state, federal, or city governments; or the schools. Money from charities has been funneled into paying for research to try to find causes or a cure rather than to provide services.

Over the last 25 to 30 years, politicians have allowed the autism funding issue to drift, waiting for the economy to get back into shape so some entity could take on the increasing burden of services that need to be paid for as the autism community continues to grow. Unfortunately, because of this oversight, the expenses will likely be huge as the first large wave of autistic children graduate from high school and the state and federal governments find themselves paying for adult services for the next 60 years for adults with high-level autism who could have been working but are now unable to work or live independently because as children they didn't get the services they needed.

Issues of Marriage

Most of the parents in our study were married. We interviewed one single parent, and one parent was in a second marriage. Most of the parents interviewed for this book stated emphatically that having a supportive spouse was important for them and their children and found it difficult to see how anyone could raise a child with autism on his or her own.

When looking at research on marital status and autism, we found a longitudinal study with a fairly large sample of families involving 406 families of children who were at least 10 years of age (Hartley, Barker, Baker, Seltzer, & Greenberg, 2012). The women who participated were in mid to late life and had remained married to the father of their grown child with autism. The researchers analyzed the mothers' satisfaction with the marriage and how their satisfaction affected their child.

The results indicated that mothers' marital satisfaction changed across time as the child's behavior problems changed. Marital satisfaction was not related to the child's health, autism symptoms, or the parent–child relationship. The mothers' initial level of marital satisfaction was positively related to the closeness in the mother–child relationship and household income, even after controlling for maternal education level. No significant changes in marital satisfaction occurred following the departure of the son or daughter on the spectrum out of the family home. The child's age, gender, and intellectual disability level were not related to the mothers' initial level of marital satisfaction.

The researchers found that the parents' marital relationship, in addition to their emotional well-being, was intimately linked to the life of their grown child with autism. Thus, there continues to be a need for services for parents during the later parenting years. Unfortunately, family services are almost exclusively focused on parents of young children (Howlin, 2005). Services designed for parents of adolescent and adults with ASD should include education regarding the associations between parents' marital satisfaction and their son's or daughter's behavior problems. Interventions aimed at supporting parents with regard to managing their son's or daughter's behavior problems, and encouraging coping strategies in the face of such challenges, may help strengthen the parents' marital relationship. Health providers should also be aware that in families with poor marital quality there is also likely to be poor parent–child relationship quality. Finally, policies geared toward providing financial aid to families of children with autism who have low income may help reduce stress on marriages. This added financial support may not only ease general family stress, but also increase access to services for the adolescent or adult on the spectrum, which may reduce parenting stress and contribute to positive marital interactions.

EMILY: We didn't have the money to go to Michelle Garcia Winner's Program in San Jose, or to go to these things or to do these organized playgroups. And then I find they really don't work. And then I was like, "Oh, thank God!" Now I don't have to feel guilty.

Reactions to Children's Diagnoses

Parents will have different reactions to a child's diagnosis. Some will read books, others will get information online. Many will spend a lot of time speaking to professionals and other parents. Given their motivation and interest, it doesn't take long for them to learn as much as some "experts" in the field. Some parents are in denial about their children's challenges and are unwilling to learn about autism. Others don't know where to go for information or might not have a computer or speak English. Some parents may simply give up on their child, thinking there is nothing they can do for their "autistic child." And then some parents will lose their objectivity and try anything to help their child:

EMILY: I did stupid stuff. I researched hyperbaric chamber therapy. I actually went to UC San Diego; I called the Marine Biology Department and asked about their hyperbaric chamber. I had a friend, who did wound care, and I called her and she's at University of Texas, Galveston. I was like, "Can you tell me anything, is anybody doing anything with autism?" This was like 10 years ago too. I would've paid any amount of money. I would've done anything.

What we have found is that many parents don't always understand how children change over time. It is hard for parents to see beyond a child's current age. This is especially true for parents of children who are very young. By the time a child is a teenager, parents do realize that their child will one day be an adult and that the years go by fast. But, when a child is 3 years old it is not quite the same. Some want their children to be cured in preschool. This is partially because of all the hype about early intervention. Early intervention is, of course, about helping children later in life by taking advantage of their quickly developing brains; it is not about curing them, but parents don't always understand that. But children do change, and the way they change is something that parents need to learn as the children grow older.

Another aspect of raising a child with autism is that parents might not understand their own strengths and weaknesses when it comes to giving their children what they need. It is hard to admit when it is difficult to provide for your child what "a parent should be able to provide for them." For example, many parents of children with autism might not be terribly social themselves, which makes it difficult for them to help their children become social.

What should a teacher do? First, the teacher should ask the parents about their comfort with social interactions. Do they feel comfortable setting up play dates for their child with other children with autism or typical peers? Has the child had any type of social skills training or naturalistic socialization outside of the school? Have they gotten together with parents in various settings? Has it gone well? Why or why not (without judgment)? Parents of children with autism usually have had experiences where parents of typically developing children tell them that their children do not want to play with their child. These parents are often apologetic, and frustrated with their own children, who are not as accepting as they would hope they would be; not all families roll out the welcome wagon for an autistic child. Most of them don't want to force their children to play with children they don't like.

Second, a teacher should come up with a plan to help the child make a friend at school. If a child with autism does not have one friend at school, this can be psychologically damaging to a child. A child's social life at school is very important, especially as the child gets older. No child can survive school completely isolated and alone, and children with autism feel especially vulnerable because they already seem odd. Many have dealt with sneers and jeers and feel out of place. They need friends.

Third, the teacher can work with the parents to get the child into some type of social group where the child can meet other children with autism (the same level of autism) or typically developing children who are open to friendships outside of school at the same time the teacher works on helping the child make friends at school. Children need to make friends for two reasons, for their psychosocial health and to develop their social skills. It is impossible to learn how to make friends and keep friends until you know what it means to have friends.

The Problem With Blame

It is also common for parents and teachers to regularly communicate around negative issues, rather than positive ones. Because children with autism often struggle at school, teachers sometimes have to call parents about problems that children are having at school. During IEP meetings, teachers have to go over test scores and achievement gaps. This often causes guilt among parents and/or teachers, and teachers or parents may blame themselves or each other:

EMILY: My stresses are always that I'm not doing enough. I talk to other people who are doing more and they make me feel insecure. And you talk to anybody else who has an autistic child, you hear what they're doing and you're like, "Oh my God, I didn't do that, and I haven't done that!" Again, like I said, I put my head in the sand. I let somebody else handle it for a while, and I feel guilty. And so the stresses would be, of course, I yell at my kids. We all do, right? But just having that, and I've had a lot of support, nonautistic parents, autistic parents, the school where I am.

It is normal for teachers to think the parents should be doing more and for the parents to think the teachers should be doing more. This is where parents and teachers often get into problematic relationships.

Parents' Choices

Disclosing Information About Autism

Most children like being told they have autism. Most are happy to be told there is a reason they have trouble getting along with other children. They like to know there is a reason that other children at school have lots of friends and they have few or none. Some struggle in school, and they like to know there is a reason why they struggle in school and other children seem to breeze through their schoolwork (which is their impression). Here are some comments from the teens in our study:

I: And how did you feel about that when you found out?

MASON: I didn't necessarily know what it was at first, but really deep in my subconscious, it was a clicking moment like I knew I never fit in.

I: Did it make you happy that you finally had an idea there was something there?

MASON Well, yes and no. Yes because there was an excuse to why I always was awkward, but no because let's face it, you're always different from everyone, you really want it to be like, I dunno, like a superman finding out he is from another planet or something. I guess, like every kid diagnosed with Asperger's really wishes that it'd be something more spectacular than just something that's, I dunno, just makes you seem a little different.

I: Were you happy or were you sad when you found out you had autism?

REESE: To be honest, I really wasn't very happy but I guess it was kind of helpful. I wouldn't have wanted to go around the school not knowing.

Based on our interviews, we found that the children's responses to the news were mixed. One of the teens said that when he heard the news that it was both good and bad! Every child in our study knew they were different, and it was good that they knew why, but it was bad in that they wished they were like the other children.

One mother from our study said that she told her child in a very nonchalant way and he seemed unaffected by the news. When her son was asked how he felt about it, he said that when he found out he had autism it didn't bother him because by then he had met other kids, his friends who also had autism, and so he realized it didn't matter.

Another child said he was happy to find out he had autism because it helped him to understand why other children had so many friends and he did not. He thought perhaps he was a bad person and that was why people didn't like him. When he found out that he had autism, he realized that wasn't true.

One challenge that teachers face is what to do when parents don't want to tell their children they have autism and the children don't know or don't want to talk about it themselves. This is usually only a problem with very high-level children who can hide their autism because most children, even those with higher-level autism, usually cannot hide their autism. Some of these very high-level children might not even be diagnosable, so the parents wonder if it would be better to skip the label and simply help the child work through his or her challenges. They worry whether it would be worse to burden the child with a label that might make life more difficult as the child gets older. Most teachers believe that it is better to be open with a child. Parents, however, are mixed about this topic. The following comments demonstrate four ways that parents handle disclosure:

JAMES: We told him when he was about 8 after he came home from a summer camp crying. He had been hassled by other kids. And, he was upset and he asked us why do other kids hate me? Why do other kids have so many friends and I have none? What's wrong with me? And, we knew it was time, so we sat down with him and told him there is nothing wrong with you, you are just different than other kids, you think differently, you talk differently and you play differently and they don't understand you and you don't understand them. And, it is because you have this condition called autism. And we explained it and he knew it was true.

SAMATHA: I don't think we ever made that big a deal about it; we always used the words around him. We always answered whatever questions he had. So I don't know if I would say that there was a big sit down and "Honey, we have something to tell you." He actually very recently, like literally in the last couple of weeks asked me, "So, Mom, how did you know that I had autism?" And I just very matter of factly explained what I just explained to you that, "They had a screening at preschool, and they said that you had some delays so we took you." And it was kind of like, "How did you know I had red hair? How did you know I didn't like broccoli?"

KIMBERLY: I feel like I don't think his journey in the public school system or in school has ever felt to me, and this might be my issue more than a reality, but I have, I'm guarded and I know that parents that saw him when he was young in elementary school, and saw him losing it, saw him losing it on the playground and saw him losing it in the classroom, have this memory and see how much he's changed, but that memory is still with them. And they look at him in a different way. So I see the wisdom in keeping things private, but I've always been honest with people that have been a part of my life. I don't talk with people I have casual relationships with. But people knew and I think it will be good for him when he enters the bigger world and he can establish relationships that there's no history.

EMILY: When he was first diagnosed, my husband and I were at each other. I mean, just differing opinions. My husband was under the impression that we should keep this a secret. And I was under the impression that I feel like the reason that God gave me an autistic child was because I am an open book, and I will tell anybody at any time. I will meet someone at a park, and I've been at parks and I've talked about my son, and they said, "Wow, my sister's son is like that. I wonder if I should say something." And I've said, "Look, if my friend hadn't come to me, I might not know." I would've figured it out, but I feel

> like my job is to just tell the world. And I did that at an early age, and people weren't talking about it back then.

We believe the best way to deal with disclosure is for parents to be open, but we also understand why some parents choose to hide their children's autism. Some children don't want others to know they have autism, and parents want to respect their children's wishes. Others believe it might change people's opinions of their child. And, sometimes people do treat these children differently once they know they are autistic. Sometimes peers do not want to be around them if they know a friend has autism. Sometimes parents of typically developing children don't want their child to be around another child who has autism. Unfortunately, it happens.

Ultimately, teachers can talk about their beliefs and teaching philosophies with parents, but ultimately, the teacher has to respect the parents' wishes. Teachers do, however, have the right to talk openly about disability in their classrooms and/or to allow other children to talk openly in the classroom about their disabilities. As a teacher, you can tell parents that you have a policy of openness in your classroom and that their child doesn't need to be open about his or her diagnosis, and you don't have to talk about the child's disability, but other children can talk about their diagnoses, and you will encourage others to be open. Don't let one child who doesn't want to talk about his or her autism discourage everyone else from discussing the topic.

Should Kids With Autism Be Together as Friends?

Should kids with autism or Asperger's be around other kids with autism or Asperger's? Many parents of younger children like for their children to be with typically developing children so they can model peer culture. However, this approach is limited. If peer modeling worked really well, then children with ASD in general education would change, and they do without intervention. In the integrated program where we volunteered, it took the staff years before they realized that most of the teenagers thought everyone in the group was autistic. And, when they found out that many of the kids in the program were typically developing, they were surprised. It is unlikely any changes seen by researchers in integrated settings can be attributed to "typically developing children modeling peer culture."

However, when children with autism are very young, typically developing children are more flexible and accepting, so it is actually easier sometimes for children with autism to get along with these children. Children with ASD are sometimes annoyed by other children with autism.

When children get older, however, and can discuss their disability, they start to understand other children's disabilities. So, children with autism and Asperger's, especially those at about the same level can sometimes become friends. Children at any age want friends who they enjoy and share something in common, and often they find this with others who are like themselves. So, we encourage parents to introduce their children to both children with and without autism when they get older.

Teachers' and Parents' Assessment of Abilities

With children with autism, nobody understands the relationship between the parents and their children, because children with autism act so differently when they are around their parents. When children are with their parents, they are not socially anxious. They know the routines. In contrast, at school or in the classroom, they may act socially awkward and seem much more intellectually disabled. When they go home, they might spend hours doing intellectual work on the computer, and they can have an interesting and sophisticated conversation with their parents, but at school they have trouble talking. This is when a big disconnect happens between parents and teachers.

Parents want teachers to bring out the amazing abilities they witness in their children at home. Below Alonzo and Juanita talk about their experiences trying to get their son Juan proper school placement:

ALONZO: Since the beginning, he was very good in learning. He learned to count very early. He was very smart boy, he was so smart, he could memorize everything, date, time, everything. And that's why, OK, if he can learn, why . . .

JUANITA: We say, "What do you offer him, what do you offer him for a high school?" What they said was, "OK, he can go to a special education school in Alameda." We noticed the student population there. They let everybody to do whatever they want. So what's our concern? He will go backwards. Yeah, and he needed to be challenged because he's smart.

The interviewer asked Juan their son:

I: Right, you wanna work hard.

JUAN: Yes, I do.

ALONZO: Even though we know this sometimes is hard for him, he's been doing very well.

However, they don't always act the same at home as at school. Just because children can do things at home does not mean they can do the same things in other contexts. However, teachers need to realize that if the environment is set up for these children to succeed, they might be able to achieve at a higher level.

Homework Hell

Significant homework starts in middle school, correct? Well, not exactly. A lot of children are expected to do homework in elementary school, and often this is where the battle starts. There are a number of things that teachers need to consider when it comes to homework. First, homework should be something the children can do without being taught by their parents. It should be something they can practice, not something they do not know how to do. This does not mean that parents are always ignorant; it is just that parents don't always know how to work with children in the same way teachers work with children. For example, most math teachers want children to "show their work," and most adults don't show work on math problems; in fact, they use calculators. Most adults know how to do long division, but for many adults it has been a long time since they've done long division by hand. Also, most parents do not know how to teach. Teachers are skilled at what they do, and they take teaching jobs because they are patient and interested in teaching children. By asking parents to teach their children at the end of the day when they get home from work, teachers are putting autistic children through homework hell and they are undermining their own work because they are saying that anyone can do their job and they can't.

Finally, parents of children with autism already have different types of homework they have to deal with every week. Most of them need to teach their children how to socialize. They need to find ways to get their children to exercise because most of them are not involved in team sports. They must attend IEP meetings and take their children to therapists and socialization programs on the weekends. They need to teach their children to button their clothes and tie their shoes and wash their clothes and do the dishes. All these chores and heavy work take longer to teach than they do for typically developing children. And, all this training helps children do better at school.

The last thing parents need to do every night is fight with their child about homework. There are generally two types of children with autism when it comes to homework—those who are perfectionists and those who refuse to do it. Both types generate a lot of work for the parents. The following are some comments from teens about homework:

RAYNE: And you should also have less homework because sometimes, it was tempting just to point a pencil at my face and be like, but then I decided to take it out on paper.

I usually have to get help from my mom or dad, but it usually breaks down to an argument with me and my dad because we work very differently.

I: OK, what about homework, do you have any feelings about homework?

MASON: I really despise it. I know we have to practice things, but really, it's just like a blank page that really is full of empty promises. I wish they can give us homework that's more specialized with our environment. Like for social studies, they say, "What do you think the future will look like?" Or math like you write your own problem based on this you'd like to have. Like one complaint when I was taking algebra was when we were learning really complicated equations, most of the students asked when were you gonna use this in life. And that's when the teacher was kind of a little stopped. She didn't know what to say because you don't really use it in life unless you're gonna become a mathematician.

REESE: I hate homework; they give us way too much homework.

I: Does your mom and dad help you with homework?

REESE Yes, my mom is okay, but my dad isn't very patient. He helps me with math.

JUANITA: He gets too much homework. When he comes back home, he's overwhelmed. He brings that up in a way that he wants to hit things.

I: Do you have a lot homework?

JUAN: Yes.

I: And do you get it all done?

JUAN: Sometimes I don't.

I: Are you tired when you're trying to finish your homework?

JUAN: Yes, I'm tired.

I: Do you find it difficult to concentrate on your homework?

JUAN: Yes, I find it difficult.

I: Have you ever asked your teacher if you could have less homework? And what do they say?

JUAN: I really don't do it.

Placing Children

It is not uncommon for teachers and parents to sometimes disagree on where a child should be placed. There is no "right or wrong" answer to this question, so our advice is not to get too invested (and argue about) where a child should go to school. This can be the most contentious issue that comes up between parents and teachers, and ultimately no placement is perfect. Each has its drawbacks. A more sheltered environment allows children to be less anxious; it gives them more access to teachers; it helps them make more friends; and they sometimes do better in school. For the more inclusive setting, the child is often more challenged; they are working with all children, including the types of personalities that they may someday work with when they leave school; the social atmosphere is more typical; and the children might feel more confident and proud to be in general education.

No placement is perfect.

The most common problem is when a teacher thinks a child with a behavior problem should be placed in a more restrictive environment and the parent wants the child to stay in general education. Some parents want their child fully included, and the teacher may think that the child would be better off with more support in special education. Sometimes it is the other way around.

Children with autism can be fragile, and one bad year can set these children back academically and socially. They are especially vulnerable during times of transition.

A number of parents in our study had to go through courts to get funding to send their children to alternative placements when they did not think their children were being properly supported by their home school districts. At least five families had some interaction with the legal system when they were trying to get their children placed. One family had to home school their child for a year because the school district did not have an appropriate placement for their child. Another family took the school district all the way to the federal courts to try to get money from the district for an alternative placement:

TERESA: The judge admitted he knew nothing about special education. The judge never even looked at any of the evidence, nobody even scratched the service.

TERESA: Our attorney said, "The good news is there is 10,000 pages of evidence." It's a joke! So, when we got the results, our attorney couldn't even speak. So, she told us to send it to the federal court.

TERESA: With the federal court, they just looked at the hearing officer's results and they turned us down.

TERESA: Our attorney said we could take it further. But, if this judge wouldn't look at it (appointed by Obama) there was no use—we lost $60,000 dollars.

I: And, you had to pay for the private school as well.

TERESA: Yes.

By learning how to support children with autism, public school districts will have less trouble dealing with lawsuits from parents trying to get their children placed in specialized schools where teachers are trained in special ways to work with children with autism.

Providing Support

Teachers often decide to become teachers believing they will be working mostly with children, when in reality teachers work with children about 60% of the time and with adults the other 40%. The adults that teachers work with are parents, teachers, principals, therapists, psychologists, and coaches, who are all doing their best to help children; none of them have easy jobs. Even if you are a new 23-year-old teacher and the parents you are working with are 45-year-old doctors, as the trained professional, it is your responsibility to be the psychologist, the family therapist, and the caregiver. You are the one providing the caring, and the children and the parents are the ones being cared for (Noddings, 1984). That is part of your job.

It is difficult to find articles about how to work with parents of children with high-level autism. Not because there are no articles about working with parents, but because most articles on this topic are focused on children with more severe autism, in part, because that is what people have mostly worked with over the last 50 years (e.g., Konstantareas & Homatidis, 1992). Also, people often assume that parents of children with classic autism will have more problems, more stress, and more frustrations than parents of those children with high-functioning autism, when in fact this is not true (Mungno et al., 2007). It seems that parents of children with higher-level autism have just as much stress, and are just as depressed, as parents of children with severe autism. Although this is counterintuitive, it makes sense based on the research we have read here for a number of reasons. First, it is likely that parents of children with autism, whether high level or severe, are genetically predisposed to having some psychological problems, especially depression. Second, children with high-level autism have more trouble with diagnosis, services, and funding than parents of children with other types of disabilities. They also may experience less support than other parents from teachers and other service personnel who do not yet believe that autism truly exists in the higher-level form. Some people believe that children with high-level autism are the same as typically developing children, especially if they do not "look" autistic.

So, how might a teacher work with a parent of a child with autism? People who provide support want to train parents to be advocates for their children (Foster, Rude, & Grannan, 2013). This is a worthy goal, but teachers also have to remember that they need to find ways to not only train parents, but to also support parents. The research in this chapter points out that not only do children need support, but the parents of children with autism also need support, and the children who have parents who receive support do better in school.

Teachers should help families develop support networks. In a recent study, experts examined the characteristics of the support networks of 106 mothers of children with ASD and their relationship to perceived social support, depressed mood, and subjective well-being. Results supported the idea that perceived social support predicted decreased depressed mood and increased well-being (Benson, 2012). But, what does it mean to develop a support network? Helping a parent develop a support network is very complex. It takes a lot of work to develop a network of professionals and friends who can support a person.

Some strategies might include talking to the parents openly about how they plan to communicate with their child, the school, and friends and family about their child's autism. If the parent comes across as aggressive and angry, perhaps you need to sit down with them and let them tell you why they are angry. It is likely they have a good reason. Help the parents understand what barriers they have had to deal with and what barriers they might face in the future. Are they shy and socially anxious themselves? Is it possible to start parent support groups at your school or help the parents find these groups? Such groups should match the parents' needs—age, level of autism, school, and interests—and the time should be convenient. Find a mentor/friend who is a parent who could introduce your parent around in the community. Help your parent talk with other teachers and professionals who can advocate for them. The following quotes describe how one parent found her support network:

RHONDA: When the kids got their diagnosis, the best thing my developmental pediatrician said was go get in touch with these parents at this location because I'm fortunate to live in an area where there are a couple schools oriented specifically towards kids on the spectrum. And those parents have set up a lot of support groups and there's a lot of opportunities to network with those people and get a lot of support. And, they understand what it's like. You can say all the things you want to say and be understood, and not have people be horrified or mortified or judgmental about things your kids do, or your frustrations. That's hard, that's very hard. So that's really been helpful. And the other thing that's been helpful is having an understanding spouse. He's not as hands on with reading up on autism, but he is wonderful. And he's wonderful with the boys and that's been very, very, very helpful. I can't take that for granted at all 'cuz I know it's hard on a lot of marriages. And the other thing, which has been helpful, and I'm not gonna lie, it's been helpful that we've had financial resources because I know I have plenty of friends and arguing with the school districts is so stressful. It's more stressful than having a kid with a disability. So that's the hardest part, is just argue to try to get the kid what they need. And that's something out there that we haven't had to deal with.

Research on parent-support networks shows that it is the close interpersonal relationships within the person's networks that are the most supportive and also the relationships that cause the most stress (Benson, 2012). Some of these relationships can increase maternal depression and stress. So, make sure your parents are aware of any close relationships that are bringing them down.

Have an understanding of what parents are going through by listening to the parents describe their experiences. Listen to them and respond to them in the same way you would respond to a child, kindly! Recognize that not all parents are going to be perfect.

One of the most important parts of being a teacher is recognizing that parents make mistakes. In one article, a mother who is part of a parent advocacy group is giving advice to parents when she says:

> "Parents must rein in their anger and calm down. You have to almost be a therapist, a doctor, and a lawyer. You have to do this and get on with your life. You have to do this without burning bridges." Franklin fully understands that while parents sometimes understandably want to write angry six-page letters (and she recently found one she wrote herself when her child was three), what parents really have to do is get schools and teachers on their side. (Foster, Rude, & Grannan, 2013, p. 18)

This is good advice for parents, but in a perfect world the parent shouldn't have to be a therapist, a doctor, and a lawyer. First, parents shouldn't feel like they have to be "nice to the teachers" in order for teachers to be nice to their children. Second, if people are stressed out and depressed, it seems that, as professionals, teachers should be able to move past a nasty letter or a snappy remark. Let's face it, most people write well-deserved nasty letters to their bosses sometime in their lives, and those were not written to stand up for their child with autism (most of the time). Teachers need to just move past a nasty letter or try to understand, by doing so they will most likely win over the parents.

Finally, it is important to give parents a central voice in discussing their child's needs. Most parents do not believe that teachers understand their children with autism. It is important for agencies and schools to listen to parents as they talk about what they believe their children need. Parents have intuition about what their children need, and they can see when children change for the better. Professionals often don't know enough about children with autism to decide what each child needs. For example, to assume that parents of children with autism are deluded when they tell you that their children are brilliant is to deny that a lot of children with autism have savant-like splinter capabilities and that maybe those parents have seen some of those abilities that the teacher has not. And for an agency to deny a parent funding for what looks like a needed social program because it is not "research based" is just a way to make excuses not to fund important services.

Coping Strategies

In a recent study, researchers explored the experiences of parents raising a child with ASD and looked to provide strategies for working with parents (Glazzard & Overall, 2012). In this mixed-method study consisting of questionnaires and semistructured interviews, parents were asked to provide some coping strategies that teachers might like to share with other parents. The parents presented a range of coping strategies, from relying on family and friends for support to ignoring behavior and avoiding certain social situations. One family used an ABA technique to manage their child's behavior. Others worked at being organized and sticking to a routine. Table 15.1

Table 15.1 Parent Coping Strategies

1. Advance warnings always work for us so that he has time to understand what will be happening. Avoidance, redirection, distraction, rewarding good behavior, removal including removing ourselves from the situation!
2. Using ABA techniques (we have a part-time home program, which is beneficial).
3. A sense of humor.
4. My son is very loving, funny, and charismatic and in many ways I find him no more difficult than his sister who is 13 and presents her own difficulties!
5. When she gets over excited I tell her to look at me in the eyes that seems to help her calm down.
6. Calling on family for support, separating everyone, using distraction strategies.
7. Provide a safe zone, access support groups, and use social stories.
8. Pick your battles carefully. Stick to routines wherever possible. Lots of deep breathing and patience are required.
9. Keeping calm is important. If possible, trying to calmly talk to her and calm her down as well as being firm and consistent.
10. Ignoring comments/outbursts, allowing own way. Routines and preparing for events are important.
11. Talking to other parents in same situation and being aware of helpful support groups.
12. Talking with partner, long walks, taking time out.
13. We try to remember that things will change over time. I tend to ignore her tantrums as this seems to work best. It calms her down quicker.
14. I have read on the Internet and developed my own coping strategies for challenging behavior etc. (e.g., having strict routines, discussing change in advance). No behavioral help given from professionals, this is an area of need in general.
15. Using favorite TV programs and favorite things as bargaining tools.
16. Try to stay calm. Don't argue, but remain firm and fair.

Adapted from a Qualitative Study by Glazzard and Overall, 2012, pp. 42–43.

presents a list of coping strategies from the parents from Glazzard and Overall's (2012) study.

Parents will do well to have good communication with the teachers and other professionals, to build a network of friends and family who are supportive. It is very helpful to build relationships with other parents of children with autism. Not only is it helpful for the parents, it can help parents help children develop friendships. It is also important for teachers to listen to parents and to understand that parents do know a lot about autism and have some ideas about what their children need in regard to services and that parents of children with autism suffer more than others with depression and other psychological problems. This doesn't mean they are crazy. Most parents are very good at hiding their own depression and focusing on their child, but parents also need support, and teachers need to recognize that it is part of their jobs to support the families and the children. Finally, teachers should get to know the children so the parents know that they understand their children and know what they need to succeed and care about them succeeding.

References

Altiere, M. J., & Von Kluge, S. (2009). Family functioning and coping behaviours in parents of children with autism. *Journal of Child and Family Studies, 18,* 83–92.

Benson, P. R. (2012). Network characteristics, perceived social support, and psychological adjustment in mothers of children with autism spectrum disorder. *Journal of Autism and Developmental Disorders, 42*(12), 2597–2610.

Bölte, S., Knecht, S., & Poustka, P. (2007). A case-control study of personality style and psychopathology in parents of subjects with autism. *Journal of Autism and Developmental Disorders, 37,* 243–250.

Center for Disease Control (CDC). (2010). *Current depression among adults—United States, 2006 and 2008 Report.* Washington DC. Retrieved from http://www.cdc.gov/features/dsdepression/

Cidav, Z., Marcus, S. C., & Mandell, D. S. (2012). Implications of childhood autism for parental employment and earnings. *Pediatrics, 129,* 617–623.

Foster, A., Rude, D., & Grannan, C. (2013). Preparing parents to advocate for a child with autism. *Phi Delta Kappan, 94*(4), 16–20.

Ganz, M. L. (2006). The costs of autism. In S. O. Moldin & J.L.R. Rubenstein (Eds.), *Understanding autism: From basic neuroscience to treatment.* 475–502 Boca Raton, FL: Taylor and Francis.

Ganz, M. L. (2007). The lifetime distribution of the incremental societal costs of autism. *Archives of Pediatric Adolescent Medicine, 161(4),* 343–349.

Glazzard, J., & Overall, K. (2012). Living with autistic spectrum disorder: Parental experiences of raising a child with autistic spectrum disorder (ASD). *Support for Learning, 27*(1), 37–45.

Hodge, D., Hoffman, C. D., & Sweeney, D. P. (2011). Increased psychopathology in parents of children with autism: Genetic liability or burden of caregiving? *Journal of Developmental and Physical Disabilities, 23,* 227–239.

Howlin, P. (2005) Outcomes in autism spectrum disorders. In F. Volkmar, A. Klin, R. Paul, & D. Cohen (Eds.), *Handbook of autism and pervasive developmental disorders* (3rd ed., pp. 201–222). Hoboken, NJ: Wiley.

Konstantareas, M. M., & Homatidis, S. (1992). Mothers' and fathers' self-report of involvement with autistic, mentally delayed, and normal children. *Journal of Marriage and Family, 54*(1), 53–164.

Lajiness-O'Neill, R., & Menard, P. (2008). Brief report: An autistic spectrum subtype revealed through familial psychopathology coupled with cognition in ASD. *Journal of Autism and Development Disorders, 38,* 982–987.

Ludlow, A., Skelly, C., & Rohleder, P. (2011). Challenges faced by parents of children diagnosed with autism spectrum disorder. *Journal of Health Psychology, 17,* 702.

Mackintosh, V. H., Goin-Kochel, R. P., & Myers, B. J. (2012). "What do you like/dislike about the treatments you're currently using?": A qualitative study of parents of children with autism spectrum disorders. *Focus on Autism and Other Developmental Disabilities, 27,* 51.

Mungno, D., Ruta, L., Genitori D'Arrigo, V., & Mazzone, L. (2007). Impairment of quality of life in parents of children and adolescents with pervasive developmental disorder. *Health and Quality of Life Outcomes, 5*(22), 1–9.

Noddings, N. (1984). *Caring: A feminine approach to ethics and moral education.* Berkeley: University of California Press.

Sigan, L., Hartley, E. T., Barker, J. K., Baker, M., Mailick, S., & Marital, J. S. (2012). Satisfaction and life circumstances of grown children with autism across 7 years. *Journal of Family Psychology, 26*(5), 688–697.

Silva, T., & Schalock, M. (2012). Autism parenting stress index: Initial psychometric evidence. *Journal of Autism and Development Disorders, 42,* 566–574.

Van Tongerloo, M.M.A.M., Bor H.H.J., Antoine L.M., & Lagro-Janssen, L. M. (2012). Detecting autism spectrum disorders in the general practitioner's practice. *Journal of Autism and Developmental Disorders, 42,* 1531–1538.

Chapter Sixteen
Conclusion

What does it mean to teach? Just as diagnosing and solving problems is at the heart of medicine and finding evidence to support a position is at the heart of law, we believe that moral decision making is at the heart of teaching. That does not mean that teachers have to decide whether schools should hand out condoms to teenagers or whether kids should be kicked out for smoking pot, it means that every day teachers make hundreds of decisions, and those decisions are moral decisions. Why are they moral decisions? Even though each decision is small, when added up together those decisions can affect a child's life.

For example, teachers decide every day whether children should be placed in homogeneous or heterogeneous reading groups. That is, they decide whether they should be put in groups where everyone reads at the same level or at different levels. According to Oakes (2005), whether a child is placed in a mixed group or at the same level can have an effect on the child's self-confidence years later because children remember whether they are put in low-, medium-, or high-level reading groups in school, even if teachers try to disguise them as the red, blue, or yellow reading groups, children still know that the "yellow" group was the "dumb" group. Even a simple decision such as choosing a reading group is just one of the many moral decisions that a teacher makes on a daily basis. Think of all the other decisions a teacher makes on a daily basis. A teacher decides how to arrange the desks in the classroom, what textbooks to use, what books to read, what stories to write, who to call on, who not to call on, what to do when someone acts out, or what to say when someone does well. Special education teachers help make big decisions such as whether a child will be placed in special or general education and what supports the child will have access to during his or her school career. Special education teachers make hundreds of decisions every day that make up their teaching practice, and they make a few big decisions that can have a huge impact on children's lives. That is why teaching is a moral occupation and decision-making is at the heart of teaching (Sockett, 1993; Sockett, DeMulder, LePage, & Wood, 2002; LePage & Sockett, 2002).

Our job as authors is not to tell teachers what to do, but to give you information that will help you make those difficult decisions. In the next section, we summarize some of the outcomes that we believe are important for you to remember. As mentioned in Chapter 1, this book was broken into four parts; the first part presented the basics of autism, providing information about autism and its prevalence in the United States. In the next part, we discussed some of the characteristics of autism, which is very important to know if teachers are to work appropriately with these children. In the third section, we talked about children's development and what constituted evidence-based practices. In the final parts, we talked about teaching strategies and provided suggestions on how best to teach children with autism.

Supports Children With High-Level Autism Need to Succeed

Learning about the characteristics of children with autism may seem old fashioned and simplistic, but it is neither. Children with autism do have some overlapping characteristics, but no child has all of the characteristics common to children with autism, and very few of the characteristics manifest themselves in exactly the same way. Understanding the characteristics of children with autism is the first step to understanding how to provide supports, strategies, and services for children and teenagers. Many teachers use intuition to teach children, and sometimes this is problematic, because teaching is often counterintuitive (Shulman, 1987). Teaching children with autism is even more counterintuitive than teaching typically developing children. An example of a strategy that may be counterintuitive is for a teacher to allow children to embrace their obsessions rather than to continually tell them to stop obsessing. This allows them to engage in something they love and it sometimes helps them to stop obsessing.

As we look at strategies for working with children with autism, we can break them down into more refined categories. Teachers need strategies for instruction, for changing behaviors, and for providing supports so children can function well in public school settings.

Socialization is the most important skill professionals will be teaching children with autism because it is the area where their atypical behavior can provide the biggest hurdles, precluding them from having friends, achieving academically, getting and maintaining jobs, or living a happy life.

In this book, we discussed the importance of academic supports. Some educators believe that high-level children with autism do not need academic supports. But even those who do well in school are often anxious about continuing to do well and they consequently work very hard. Some take hours to complete homework or to learn concepts that are not that difficult for typically developing children. Some parents are teaching or reteaching academic content at home, believing they are the only ones who can help their children succeed in school.

In our interviews the parents were very involved in their children's education, which might have been in part due to the limitation placed on this research; our families were allowed to volunteer, making them more interested in the research process and the results of this research.

It is important for teachers to work with parents, because although teachers can make a significant impact at school, they will make a much greater impact if parents are working with their children provide them with extra therapies. Parents also have to answer question, discuss social issues, and constantly be working with children to understand the social world in a way that other parents don't with their children. They need to work with teachers to help children regulate behaviors so they are regulating in and out of school. Teachers also need to work with parents to help them develop a social network and support system outside of school.

Finally, it is important the teachers realize they do not have to teach a child with autism all alone, or even just with the parents' help. There are many out-of-school programs and therapy options for children with autism such as naturalistic socialization programs for teenagers or ABA programs for young children, or speech and language and occupational therapy options for children as they grow older. When children are growing up, if they are more obviously autistic, once they move past their obsessions and repetitive movements, it is usually some type of speech difference (impediment, stutter, voice modulation or sound) that is a bit different than other children. If the child and parents choose, they can work on speech differences with a speech therapist, or they can work with fine motor delays (e.g., bad handwriting) with an occupational therapist. Below, we have spelled out some of these supports that we talked about earlier in the book set out in a four-pronged approach:

A Four-Pronged Approach

A four-pronged approach to education and support services that are meant to work closely together include, (a) school supports, (b) social supports, (c) out-of-school supports, and (d) parent supports. It is impossible for one institution to provide everything a child with autism needs to reach his or her full potential. These children need supports both in and out of school. Many high-level children with autism are smart and able to get accommodations that enable them to succeed academically. However, socially they have trouble, and their social issues are often so pronounced that parents who are financially able place them in expensive private schools to protect them from social ostracism and neglect so they can focus on academics and get the education they need.

Children with autism need a four-pronged approach with serious social supports and education built into their IEPs. Outside the school, supports could include added therapies, including speech, occupational therapy, and psychological services, as well as respite and childcare for their parents.

Social Supports Organized Around a Developmental Process

In the past, socialization and social supports have not been taken seriously enough. People have looked at social supports for children with autism as if they are synonymous with recreation. These children have social disabilities; therefore socialization needs to be emphasized. Children and adults will need some type of focus on social supports throughout their lives, starting with play dates (prekindergarten); then moving to social skills training (early elementary); then moving to fun, natural socialization programs with friends (late elementary through early high school); then on to cognitive programs (high school); and finally having teenagers work on identity development as they get older (late high school and adult). According to our interviews the children's social development followed a fairly consistent pathway from preschool through adult: (a) social isolation and play (prekindergarten), (b) intense self-focus and repetition (early elementary, ages 5 to 8), (c) rejection and setback (late elementary and middle school, third through seventh grades), (d) self-awareness and regulation, and (e) fragile friendships and identity (high school and early college).

This book has focused specifically on how teachers can support and educate children with high-level autism. The supports we mentioned in this book need to exist not only in special education, but also in general education, especially for children with high-level autism. Below we have listed some important aspects of our four-pronged approach:

1. Social supports
   a. Social skills need to be more naturalistic, allowing children to make friends and enjoy being social, rather than telling children what is wrong with them and forcing them to change themselves. Children and teen-agers will naturally change as they make friends.
   b. Society needs to allow being autistic to be acceptable so children can be honest and open about who they are so they can become self-advocates.
   c. Social skills training needs to include more identity development from when children are young to help them build confidence.
   d. Teachers need to learn (and remember) to explain social situations to children on the spectrum directly, because children with autism do not understand some social concepts that most other children already understand.

e. We suggest that typically developing peers be taught to be social coaches in schools to help children with autism learn social cues and to be included. At least they need to be taught how to be inclusive and accepting.
f. Parents and children and adults with autism and Asperger's need to be accepted.

2. Academic supports
   a. Teachers need to remember that children with autism have extra burdens that come from dealing with social deficits that other children do not have. Teachers need to be flexible in their assignments and homework and remember what these children need to succeed in school, college, and work.
   b. We need to do more research on the cognition of children with autism so that we can better understand their thinking and use these differences/strengths to help children with autism achieve. This includes doing practical education research, not just abstract psychological or medical research or behavioral research.
   c. We need to introduce more personal/narrative work into the curriculum for children with autism so they have more time to reflect on themselves and their behaviors.

3. Parent supports
   a. Research indicates that parents of children with autism, specifically mothers, are depressed more often than parents of typically developing children and parents of children with other types of disabilities. If this is true, we need to take into account that these parents may need more support.
   b. Part of the problem with parents of children with autism is not just the burden of caring for their children, but the fact that there are few supports for these children and these children are often unhappy due to their social problems. Parents are unhappy if their children are unhappy.
   c. Parent supports need to be individualized based on their children's supports.
   d. Parents are often isolated because their children are isolated. It is hard for them to socialize, just as it is hard for their children to socialize. Both parents and children need support to socialize. Parents need this support to help their children.
   e. Child and respite care are important for parents who need to have time away from children to attend to other children in the house as well as to the marriage.

4. Out of school supports for behavior, language and social communication (therapy and social programs, etc.)
   a. Out-of-school supports need to be tailored to the child and organized around a developmental process.

b. Pragmatic speech, fine and gross motor skills, sensory integration, and play-based interventions can be organized around clubs and social programs where children make friends, not necessarily around formal therapy programs all the time.
c. Staff at after school programs need to be trained to address the needs of children with ASD.
d. Appropriate ABA programs need to be identified for children who need them and not overused.

Parents' Pride in Their Children

With supports, children with autism can do very well. We will end this book with quotes from some of the parents who interviewed for this book talking about how proud they are of their children and looking at the reasons why. All of the parents we interviewed believe their children have great potential and will live up to that potential. In each of the statements below, it is possible to see the many ways the parents are proud of their children:

Believing Their Child Will Succeed: Seeing No Limits

KIMBERLY: That's [i.e., Chinese] just something that he's interested in that he just has taken upon himself and he'll do without any kind of prompting. I think the sky's the limit in terms of what he might be capable of in his life, and so we want him to do to the best of his abilities, and so we keep raising the bar on him.

SAMANTHA: I think he'll be able to live on his own and have a job, and hopefully, get married. I am not sure, what that's going to look like and feel like, I have no idea, but the general shape of it, I think will be pretty good, just great . . .

Ability to Talk About Feelings

LENA: I'm really proud of the strides that he's made and his ability to talk about his feelings, I think his willingness to confide in me is also very meaningful that I can support him in social situations in schools like helping him talk through it. And that he can express, that he is perceptive enough to notice when situations are awkward when he doesn't know what to do, he can describe pretty well what his issues are in a way that I can help him. I really enjoy our relationship.

Being a Good Citizen

TAMRA: So his volunteer hours, that's the one thing he's not by the book about because technically you're only supposed to do 100 hours volunteer work a year to graduate from that school because that's a requirement for them, and he's obviously doing more than that because this summer he's accumulating a lot of hours. And he hasn't mentioned to me, "I'm gonna be over my limit of 100 hours," but I was trying to tell him, that if you graduate with over 400 hours, they'll sometimes give you a special ribbon. You'll accomplish so much if you just do it. I said just do it, go for that extra, hours. It's gonna help you in your future to have more. It's good because he has some incentive. He's helping with the surf instructing and he did so awesome. He was in charge with a group of kids and one of the kids got caught in a current and no one else saw it. So Daniel got a save because he was the only person who saw this kid and saved him in this situation. So he was really inspired by that and the person who owns the camp gave him a pay of $60 last year for the week's work. So it made Daniel feel like this was more than just a volunteer assignment, it's like a job.

ELIZABETH: I found that my kids are very sweet. Actually a lot nicer than a lot of teenagers that I do know.

I: That's really good to hear. It sounds like you enjoy your sons.

ELIZABETH: I do.

Doing Well in Spite of Challenges

JAMES: I am very proud of my son, I think he's done very well in a typical education environment, even though he's had a lot of challenges to face, and he's a jock too.

Being Competent and Impressive/Role Models

EMILY: He and this one friend entered the Tech Challenge at the Tech Museum and they actually won an honorable mention. It was "Most Risk Takers." You had to be able to create a machine that would remove water plastic bottles and caps from the ocean floor without disturbing the marine life. So my son and his friend came up with this robotic light censored machine that would go out and calibrate based on the size of the bottle. It calibrated and it closed the claw and came out and so, we went to the San Jose Tech Museum and they called them up on stage and gave them this award for "Biggest Risk Takers." They had to go alone together, explain what they did, how they came up with the project. They had to interview, and afterward, the interviewer came, found us in the stands and said, I am so inspired, I have a 6-year-old who was just diagnosed with autism and I didn't know what life was gonna be like. But now that I've met your son, and your son, I have hope. So he seems to be better with adults of course, because we're impressed by them; kids are not impressed.

SAMANTHA: Working with Chris?
I think it's absolutely been a joy.
I mean, in some ways, I wonder if he shares stuff with me in a way that is higher than typical, and so I get pleasure out of that, even though I realize that, in some cases, it's not appropriate. But y'know, I enjoy his company, it's a pleasure and it's been so rewarding to me that he's made great progress, and I see potential for even more great progress. I read some place recently something like if you have multiple children, and they all are very different, the one who is the most successful in conventional terms is not necessarily the one who's going to give you, personally the most pleasure. And it's like I totally relate to that.

I: Because you feel like the one you've helped move along is the one that you connect with most?

SAMANTHA: Or, you enjoy their company and you don't care that they're not a rocket scientist.

There is a common theme among these quotes; these parents are not only proud that their children are successful, but that their children have impressed even them with their openess, their care for others, and their work ethic. They plan to support them as far as they are willing (and able) to go. They are proud that their children have faced challenges and have overcome those challenges, and they are proud of the young men and women these children are becoming.

This new generation of high-level children with autism is different because there is more awareness and openness due, in part, to the growing numbers of children with autism and Asperger's. There are more services available, although not nearly enough, and as more services become available, more children will be able to impress us with their abilities.

In this book, we have provided up-to-date information about how teachers can help children with autism and Asperger's reach their full potential. According to the experiences and the advice of the families we have interviewed for this book, and current research and anecdotal evidence and the experiences of college faculty, teachers, and students in the autism community, we believe it is important for children with autism to learn how to fit into our society, but also for our society to understand and accept people who are different. One aspect of teaching children with autism is to teach them how to interact better with others, but another aspect is to think critically about how our society functions and to figure out when and where we all need to change.

References

LePage, P., & Sockett, H. (2002). *Educational controversies: Toward a discourse of reconciliation.* London: Routledge.

Oakes, J. (2005). *Keeping track: How schools structure inequality.* New Haven, CT: Yale University Press.

Shulman, L. (1987). Knowledge and Teaching: Foundations of the New Reform. Harvard Educational Review, 57(1). 1–23.

Sockett, H. (1993). *The moral base for teacher professionalism.* New York: Teachers College Press.

Sockett, H., DeMulder, E., LePage, P., & Wood, D. (2002). *Transforming teacher education: Lessons in professional development.* Westport, CT: Bergin and Garvey.

Index

Italic formatting indicates references to tables and figures.